Praise for
Lynsey Addario's *It's What I Do*

"Beautifully written and vividly illustrated with her images—which are stunningly cinematic, often strange, always evocative—the book helps us understand not only what would lead a young woman to pursue such a dangerous and difficult profession, but why she is so good at it. Lens to her eye, Addario is an artist of empathy, a witness not to grand ideas about human sacrifice and suffering, but to human beings, simply being."   —*The Boston Globe*

"[An] unflinching memoir. [Addario's] book, woven through with images from her travels, offers insight into international events and the challenges faced by the journalists who capture them."
                              —*The Washington Post*

"The opening scene of Lynsey Addario's memoir sucker punches you like a cold hard fist. She illuminates the daily frustrations of working within the confines of what the host culture expects from a member of her sex and her constant fight for respect from her male journalist peers and American soldiers. Always she leads with her chin, whether she's on the ground in hostile territory or discussing politics."
                              —*Entertainment Weekly*

"[A] richly illustrated memoir. [Addario] conveys well her unstated mission to stir the emotions of people like herself, born into relative security and prosperity, nudging them out of their comfort zones with visual evidence of horrors they might do something about. It is a diary of an empathetic young woman who makes understanding the wider world around her a professional calling."   —*Los Angeles Times*

"Addario's narrative about growing up as one of four daughters born to hairdressers in Los Angeles and working her way up to being one of the world's most accomplished photojournalists, male or female, is riveting. [She] thoughtfully shows how exhilarating and demanding it is to cover the most difficult assignments in the world. Addario is a shining example of someone who has been able to 'have it all,' but she has worked hard and absolutely suffered to get where she is. My hope is that she continues to live the life less traveled with her family, as I will be waiting for her next book with great anticipation."

—*San Francisco Chronicle*

"A rare gift: an intimate look into the personal and professional life of a war correspondent . . . a powerful read . . . This memoir packs a punch because of Addario's personal risks. But some of the power in this book comes from the humanity she holds on to despite the horrors she witnesses. [*It's What I Do*] should be read, processed, and mulled over in its entirety. . . . In [Addario's] words and photos, readers will see that war isn't simply a matter of black and white, of who's right and who's wrong. There are as many shades of gray as there are sides to every story."

—*The Dallas Morning News*

"[Addario's] ability to capture . . . vulnerability in her subjects, often in extreme circumstances, has propelled Addario to the top of her competitive field."

—Associated Press

"A remarkable journalistic achievement from a Pulitzer Prize and MacArthur Fellowship winner that crystalizes the last ten years of global war and strife while candidly portraying the intimate life of a female photojournalist. Told with unflinching candor, the award-winning photographer brings an incredible sense of humanity to all the battlefields of her life. Especially affecting is the way in which Addario conveys the role of gender and how being a woman has impacted every aspect of her personal and professional lives. Whether dealing with ultrareligious zealots or overly demanding editors, being a woman with a camera has never been an easy task. A brutally real and unrelentingly raw memoir that is as inspiring as it is horrific."

—*Kirkus Reviews* (starred review)

"A highly readable and thoroughly engaging memoir . . . Addario's memoir brilliantly succeeds not only as a personal and professional narrative but also as an illuminating homage to photojournalism's role in documenting suffering and injustice, and its potential to influence public opinion and official policy." —*Publishers Weekly*

"Addario has written a page-turner of a memoir describing her war coverage and why and how she fell into—and stayed in—such a dangerous job. This 'extraordinary profession'—though exhilarating and frightening, it 'feels more like a commitment, a responsibility, a calling'—is what she does, and the many photographs scattered throughout this riveting book prove that she does it magnificently."

—*Booklist*

"*It's What I Do* is as brilliant as Addario's pictures—and she's the greatest photographer of our war-torn time. She's been kidnapped, nearly killed, while capturing truth and beauty in the world's worst places. She's a miracle. So is this book."

—Tim Weiner, author of *Legacy of Ashes* and *Enemies*

"Lynsey Addario's book is like her life: big, beautiful, and utterly singular. With the whole world as her backdrop, Addario embarks on an extraordinary adventure whose overriding effect is to remind us of what unites us all." —Dexter Filkins, author of *The Forever War*

"A gifted chronicler of her life and times, Lynsey Addario stands at the forefront of her generation of photojournalists, young men and women who have come of age during the brutal years of endless war since 9/11. A uniquely driven and courageous woman, Addario is also possessed of great quantities of humor and humanity. *It's What I Do* is the riveting, unforgettable account of an extraordinary life lived at the very edge."

—Jon Lee Anderson, staff writer for *The New Yorker* and author of *The Fall of Baghdad*

"A life as a war photographer has few parallels in terms of risk and reward, fear and courage, pain and promise. Lynsey Addario has seen, experienced, and photographed things that most of us cannot imagine. The brain and heart behind her extraordinary photographic eye pulls us inexorably closer to the center of each story she pursues, no matter what the cost or danger."

—John Prendergast, founding director of the Enough Project

PENGUIN BOOKS

IT'S WHAT I DO

LYNSEY ADDARIO is an American photojournalist whose work appears regularly in the *New York Times*, *National Geographic*, and *Time* magazine. She has covered conflicts in Afghanistan, Iraq, Lebanon, Darfur, and the Congo, and has received numerous awards, including the MacArthur Genius Grant. In 2009, she was awarded the Pulitzer Prize as part of the *New York Times* team for International Reporting.

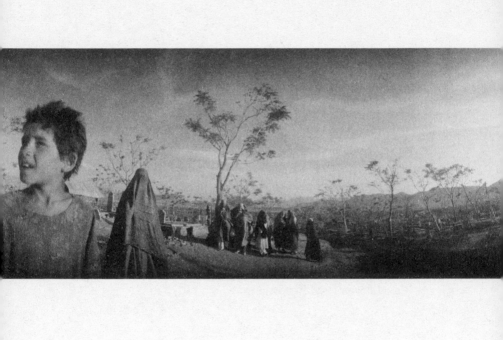

It's What I Do

A Photographer's Life of Love and War

L Y N S E Y   A D D A R I O

P E N G U I N   B O O K S

PENGUIN BOOKS
An imprint of Penguin Random House LLC
375 Hudson Street
New York, New York 10014
penguin.com

Photograph credits
All images, unless credited below, are by Lynsey Addario. Insert 1, pages 4–5: © Bryan Denton; Insert 1, pages 6–7: Courtesy of the author; Insert 3, page 2: Photo by Chang W. Lee / *The New York Times* / Redux; Insert 3, page 14 (top): © Bruce Chapman; Insert 3, pages 22–23: © Landon Nordeman; Insert 3, page 27 (bottom): Publicly distributed handout, courtesy of Associated Press

THE LIBRARY OF CONGRESS HAS CATALOGED THE HARDCOVER EDITION AS FOLLOWS:
Addario, Lynsey.
It's what I do : a photographer's life of love and war / Lynsey Addario.
pages cm
Includes index.
ISBN 9781594205378 (hc.)
ISBN 9780143128410 (pbk.)
Special Markets ISBN 9780525504030
1. Addario, Lynsey. 2. War photographers—United States—Biography. 3. Women photographers—United States—Biography. 4. War photography—20th century. I. Title.
TR140.A265A3 2015
779.092—dc23
[B]   2014036653

Printed in the United States of America
1 3 5 7 9 10 8 6 4 2

BOOK DESIGN BY CLAIRE NAYLON VACCARO

This is a work of nonfiction. Nonetheless, some of the names and personal characteristics of the individuals involved have been changed. Any resulting resemblance to persons living or dead is entirely coincidental and unintentional.

Penguin is committed to publishing works of quality and integrity. In that spirit, we are proud to offer this book to our readers; however, the story, the experiences, and the words are the author's alone.

For Paul and Lukas, my two loves

Contents

It's What I Do

Prelude

In the perfect light of a crystal-clear morning, I stood outside a putty-colored cement hospital near Ajdabiya, a small city on Libya's northern coast, more than five hundred miles east of Tripoli. Several other journalists and I were looking at a car that had been hit during a morning air strike. Its back window had been blown out, and human remains were splattered all over the backseat. There was part of a brain on the passenger seat; shards of skull were embedded in the rear parcel shelf. Hospital employees in white medical uniforms carefully picked up the pieces and placed them in a bag. I picked up my camera to shoot what I had shot so many times before, then put it back down, stepping aside to let the other photographers have their turn. I couldn't do it that day.

It was March 2011, the beginning of the Arab Spring. After Tunisia and Egypt erupted into unexpectedly euphoric and triumphant revolutions against their longtime dictators—millions of ordinary people shouting and dancing in the streets in celebration of their newfound freedom—Libyans revolted against their own homegrown tyrant, Muammar el-Qaddafi. He had been in power for more than forty years, funding terrorist groups across the world while he tortured, killed, and disappeared his fellow Libyans. Qaddafi was a maniac.

I hadn't covered Tunisia and Egypt, because I was on assignment in Afghanistan, and it had pained me to miss such important moments in history. I wasn't going to miss Libya. This revolution, however, had quickly become a war. Qaddafi's famously thuggish foot soldiers invaded rebel cities, and his air force pounded fighters in skeletal trucks. We journalists had come without flak jackets. We hadn't expected to need our helmets.

My husband, Paul, called. We tried to talk once a day while I was away, but my Libyan cell phone rarely had a signal, and it had been a few days since we'd spoken.

"Hi, my love. How are you doing?" He was calling from New Delhi.

"I'm tired," I said. "I spoke with David Furst"—my editor at the *New York Times*—"and asked if I could start rotating out in about a week. I'll head back to the hotel in Benghazi this afternoon and try to stick around there until I pull out. I'm ready to come home." I tried to steady my voice. "I'm exhausted. I have a bad feeling that something is going to happen."

I didn't tell him that the last few mornings I had woken up reluctant to get out of bed, lingered too long over my instant coffee as my colleagues and I prepared our cameras and loaded our bags into our cars. While covering war, there were days when I had boundless courage and there were days, like these in Libya, when I was terrified from the moment I woke up. Two days earlier I had given a hard drive of images to another photographer to give to my photo agency in case I didn't survive. If nothing else, at least my work could be salvaged.

"You should go back to Benghazi," Paul said. "You always listen to your instincts."

When I arrived in Benghazi two weeks earlier, it was a newly liberated city, a familiar scene to me, like Kirkuk after Saddam or Kandahar after the Taliban. Buildings had been torched, prisons emptied, a parallel government installed. The mood was happy. One day I visited some men who had gathered in town for a military training exercise. It resembled a Monty Python skit: Libyans stood at attention in strict configurations or practiced walking like soldiers or gaped at a pile of weapons in bewilderment. The rebels were just ordinary men—doctors, engineers, electricians—who had thrown on whatever green clothes or leather jackets or Converse sneakers they had in their closets and jumped in the backs of trucks loaded with Katyusha rocket launchers and rocket-propelled grenades. Some men lugged rusty Kalashnikovs; others gripped hunting knives. Some had no weapons at all. When they took off down the coastal road toward Tripoli, the capital city, still ruled by Qaddafi, journalists jumped into their boxy four-door sedans and followed them to what would become the front line.

We traveled alongside them, watched them load ammunition, and waited. Then one morning, one of the first days on that lonely strip of highway, a helicopter gunship suddenly swooped down low over our heads and unleashed a barrage of bullets, spitting at us indiscriminately. The gaggle of fighters shot up the air with Kalashnikovs. One boy threw a rock; another, his eyes wild with terror, ran for a sand berm. I ducked beside the front of a tin-can car and took a picture of him and knew this would be a different kind of war.

The front line moved along a barren road surrounded by sand that stretched flat to the blue horizon. Unlike in the wars in Iraq and Afghanistan, there were no bunkers to jump into, no buildings to hide behind, no armored Humvees in which to crouch down on the floor. In Libya, when we heard the hum of a warplane, we went through the motions: We stopped, looked up, and cowered in anticipation of rounds of ammunition or bombs and tried to guess where they would land. Some people lay on their backs; some people covered their heads; some people prayed; and some people ran, just to run, even if it was to nowhere. We were always exposed to the massive Mediterranean sky.

I had been a conflict photographer for more than ten years and had covered war in Afghanistan, Iraq, Sudan, the Democratic Republic of the

Congo, and Lebanon. I had never seen anything as scary as Libya. The photographer Robert Capa once said, "If your pictures aren't good enough, you're not close enough." In Libya, if you weren't close enough, there was nothing to photograph. And once you got close enough, you were in the line of fire. That week I watched some of the best photojournalists in the business, veterans of Chechnya and Afghanistan and Bosnia, leave almost immediately after those first bombs fell. "It's not worth it," they said. There were several moments when I, too, thought to myself, *This is insane. What am I doing?* But there were other days when I felt that familiar exhilaration, when I thought, *I am actually watching an uprising unfold. I am watching these people fighting to the death for their freedom. I am documenting the fate of a society that has been oppressed for decades.* Until you get injured or shot or kidnapped, you believe you are invincible. And it had been a few years since anything had happened to me.

The other journalists were leaving the scene at the hospital. I knew it was time to return to the front line. The sounds of war echoed in the distance—shelling, antiaircraft fire, ambulance sirens. I didn't want Paul to hear the noise. "Baby, I have to go. I'll see you soon, my love. Love you."

Long ago I learned that it is cruel to make loved ones worry about you. I tell them only what they need to know: where I am, where I am going, and when I am coming home.

I WAS THERE on assignment for the *New York Times* with three other award-winning journalists: Tyler Hicks, a photographer and a friend whom, oddly enough, I had grown up with in Connecticut; Anthony Shadid, arguably the best reporter working in the Middle East; and Stephen Farrell, a British-Irish journalist who had worked in war zones for years. Between us, we had about fifty years of experience working in awful places. We had entered the country illegally from Egypt, along with hordes of other journalists.

We left the suburban hospital together and headed toward the center of Ajdabiya to look for the front line. Anthony and Steve were in one car, and Tyler and I were in another with our driver, Mohammed. It had been difficult to find a good driver in Libya. Mohammed, a soft-spoken university student with a fresh face and a gap between his front teeth, drove us around long after most other drivers had quit. To him, the job was a contribution to the revolution. A driver like Mohammed, who was tapped into a network of other drivers and rebels, helped us decide where we could go and how long we could stay. His directions often determined our fate. His contribution was invaluable.

As we edged down an empty road in the center of town, artillery shells pierced the pavement nearby, sending shards of shrapnel in every direction. Anthony and Steve's driver suddenly stopped his car and began off-loading their belongings onto the pavement. He was quitting. His brother had been shot at the front line. Without pausing, Mohammed pulled up our car and put their gear in our trunk, and Anthony and Steve piled into our car. I felt uneasy. In war zones journalists often travel in convoys of two vehicles, in case one vehicle fails. Two vehicles also ensure that if one is hit or attacked, fewer people will suffer the consequences.

Four journalists in one car also meant too many chefs in the kitchen: We each had a different idea of what we wanted to do. As we drove on, Anthony, Tyler, Steve, and I debated the level of danger. It is often this way in war zones for journalists and photographers: an endless negotiation of who needs what, who wants to stay, who wants to go. When do we have enough reporting and photographs to depict the story accurately? We want to see more fighting, to get the freshest, latest news, to keep reporting until that unknowable last second before injury, capture, death. We are greedy by nature: We always want more than what we have. The consensus in the car at that point was to keep working.

Ajdabiya was a prosperous, low-slung North African city of peach, yellow, and tan cement buildings with thick-walled balconies and vibrant storefront signs in painted Arabic. The few civilians on the streets were fleeing. They ran with conviction, carrying their belongings atop their heads. An endless stream of cars sped past us in the opposite direction. Families had crammed into every inch of pickup trucks and four-door sedans; blankets and clothes packed haphazardly into rear windows spilled out the back. Some families crouched under tarps. It was the first time I actually saw women and children in the town of Ajdabiya. In a conservative society like Libya's, women often stayed indoors. I was seeing them outside their homes now only because they were leaving, heading east as the fighting pushed into the city from the west.

I feared that it was our time to leave, too. The steady exodus of civilians out of the city meant the locals anticipated that Ajdabiya would fall into the hands of Qaddafi's troops. Had they already arrived? We knew what might happen to us if Qaddafi's men discovered four illegal Western journalists in rebel territory. He had declared in public speeches that all journalists in eastern Libya were spies and terrorists and that, if found, they would be killed or detained.

We returned to the hospital to check in with other journalists and gauge the casualties from the encroaching battle. Anthony, Steve, and Tyler went inside to get the phone numbers of a Libyan doctor so they could call him later that night from Benghazi and report the final casualty toll for the day. For reporters it was necessary to have sources inside the city in case power changed hands and we couldn't get back in. I stayed on the side of the road across the street from the hospital to photograph fleeing Libyans.

On the sidewalk where I stood a French photographer I knew from Iraq and Afghanistan deliberated his next move with several French journalists. They spoke in low, serious voices tinged with the sarcasm journalists use to temper their nerves. French journalists, in general, are known for being fearless and crazy. The joke was that if the French left a combat zone before you, you were screwed. Laurent Van der

Stockt, a notoriously gutsy conflict photographer, who had covered most of the major wars of the past two decades—he had been shot twice and hit once by shrapnel from a mortar round on the front line—was staring at the long line of cars draining out of the city.

He turned to me. "We're leaving," he said. "It's time to go back to Benghazi." This meant they had made the decision to retreat from the action to a city that was as much as one hundred miles, and two hours, away. They were calling it a day. Laurent had decided the pictures weren't worth the risk. They thought the situation too dangerous.

I watched in horror as they scrambled into their cars, but I said nothing. I didn't want to be the cowardly photographer or the terrified girl who prevented the men from doing their work. Tyler, Anthony, and Steve had each spent more than a decade working in war zones; they knew what they were doing. Maybe my judgment was off that day. As we continued the drive into Ajdabiya, I looked out the window and tried to retreat to a comforting place in my mind. The mosques around the city blasted the call to prayer.

Cars streamed past us. We were the only car going the other way.

"Guys, it's time to go," Steve said, and I sensed I had an ally in my fear.

"Yeah, I think so, too," I said.

I was grateful for Steve's voice of reason, but our suggestion went unanswered by Tyler and Anthony.

WHEN WE REACHED A ROUNDABOUT, Tyler and Anthony got out and walked off to interview some rebels. Some were watching the approaching action with nonchalance; others were scurrying around, shooting their weapons into the air. I was directionless. I didn't want to be here or there, and could barely lift my camera to my eyes. Even the most experienced photographers have days like this: You can't frame a shot, catch the moment. My fear was debilitating, like a physical handicap. Tyler, meanwhile, was in his element, focused and relentless. I imagined the images he was capturing while I was clumsy, scared, missing the scenes, clicking the shutter too late.

As I ran forward to follow him, I heard the familiar *whoosh* of a bullet. I looked up at the rooftops: Qaddafi snipers were in the city. I assumed that everyone realized the gravity of the situation, but back near the car Anthony was drinking tea with a handful of men beside an ammunition truck, chatting happily in Arabic. He looked older than his forty-something years, with his gray beard and soft stomach. His eyes sparkled, warm and friendly, as he listened to the Libyans, calmly smoking his cigarette and throwing his hands around as he spoke, as if hanging out with friends by a pool.

But Steve, who had been kidnapped twice—once in Iraq, once in Afghanistan—looked spooked. He stood by our car with Mohammed, as if this might inspire the others to finish their work. The locals around us were screaming, "Qanas! Qanas!" (Sniper! Sniper!)

Mohammed was getting frantic. "We have to go to Benghazi," he pleaded. His brother had been calling, warning that Qaddafi's men had entered the city from the west. He called us all back to the car, and we took off for the eastern gate of town.

On the road toward the exit Tyler asked Mohammed to stop the car one last time to check out a team of rebel fighters setting up rocket-propelled grenades. He reluctantly pulled off to the side of the road, and Tyler leapt out to shoot, buoyed by a rush of adrenaline I knew well—that feeling of satisfaction when doing reporting that few others would dare do. Mohammed immediately called his brother again to check in. I knew we were pushing the boundaries, lingering after we had been warned to leave, but my desire to pull back to safety felt like a terrible weakness. My colleagues would never have accused me of being wimpy or unprofessional; I was the one who was all too aware of being the only woman in the car.

A car pulled up alongside us: "They're in the city! They're in the city!"

"Tyler!" Mohammed shouted, his face wrecked with fear.

"Let's *go!*" Steve screamed. Tyler clambered into the car and we took off.

The night before, my editor, David, and I agreed that I would call him at 9 a.m. in New York. I checked my watch and dialed his number. I couldn't get a line out. I dialed again. Nothing. I kept redialing his extension, over and over and over, punching at the phone. When I looked up and squinted into the distance, I saw something I hadn't seen in weeks: traffic.

"I think it's Qaddafi's men," I said.

Tyler and Anthony shook their heads. "No way," Tyler said.

Within seconds, the fuzzy horizon distilled into little olive figurines. I had been right.

Tyler realized it, too. "Don't stop!" he screamed.

You have two options when you approach a hostile checkpoint, and both are a gamble. The first option is to stop and identify yourselves as journalists and hope that you are respected as neutral professionals. The second option is to blow past them and hope they don't open fire on you.

"Don't stop! Don't stop!" Tyler was yelling.

But Mohammed was slowing down, sticking his head out of the window.

"Sahafi! Media!" he yelled to the soldiers. He opened the car door to get out, and Qaddafi's soldiers swarmed around him. "Sahafi!"

In one fluid movement the doors flew open and Tyler, Steve, and Anthony were ripped out of the car. I immediately locked my door and buried my head in my lap. Gunshots shattered the air. When I looked up, I was alone. I knew I had to get out of the car to run for cover, but I couldn't move. I spoke to myself out loud, a tactic I used when my inner voice wasn't convincing enough: "Get out of the car. Get out. Run." I crawled across the backseat with my head down and out the open car door, scrambled to my feet, and immediately felt the hands of a soldier pulling at my arms and tugging at my two cameras. The harder he pulled, the harder I pulled back. Bullets whipped by us. Dirt kicked up all around my feet. The rebels were barraging the army's checkpoint from behind us, from the place we had just fled. The soldier pulled at my camera with one hand and pointed his gun at me with the other.

We stood like that for ten interminable seconds. Out of the corner of my eye I saw Tyler running toward a one-story cement building up ahead. I trusted his instincts. We needed to get out of the line of fire before we could negotiate our fate with these soldiers.

I surrendered my waist pack and one camera and clutched the other, pulling the memory cards out as I ran after my colleagues, who, in the chaos of bullets, had also escaped their captors. My legs felt slow as my eyes stayed trained on Anthony ahead of me. "Anthony! . . . Anthony, help me!"

But Anthony had tripped and fallen to his knees. When he looked up, his normally peaceful face was wrenched with panic, oblivious to my screams. His face looked so unnatural that it terrified me more than anything else. We had to reach Tyler, who had sprinted ahead and seemed likeliest to escape.

Somehow the four of us reunited at the cinder-block building set back from the road, sheltered from the gun battle that continued to rage behind us. A Libyan woman holding an infant stood nearby, crying, while a soldier tried to console them. He didn't bother with us, because he knew we had nowhere to go.

"I'm thinking about making a run for it," Tyler said.

We looked into the distance. The open desert stretched out in every direction.

Within seconds, five government soldiers were upon us, pointing their guns and yelling in Arabic, their voices full of hate and adrenaline, their faces contorted into masks of rage. They ordered us face-down into the dirt, motioning to us with their hands. We all paused, assuming this was the moment of our execution. And then we slowly crouched down and begged for our lives.

I pressed my face into the soil, sucking in a mouthful of fine dirt as a soldier pulled my hands behind my back and kicked open my legs. The soldiers were all screaming at us, at one another, pointing their weapons at our heads as the four of us sank into silent submission, waiting to be shot.

I looked over at Anthony, Steve, and Tyler to make sure we were all still there, together and alive, and then quickly looked back down at the sand.

"Oh, God, oh, God, oh, God. Please, God. Save us."

I raised my eyes from the ground and looked up into a gun barrel and directly into the soldier's eyes. The only thing I could think to do was beg, but my mouth was so dry, as if my saliva had been replaced with dirt. I could barely utter a word.

"Please," I whispered. "Please."

I waited for the crack of the gun, for the end of my life. I thought of Paul, my parents, my sisters, and my two grandmothers, well into their nineties. Each second felt like its own space in the universe. The soldiers continued barking at one another, with their guns leveled at our heads.

"Jawaz!" one of them suddenly yelled. They wanted our passports, and we surrendered them. The soldier leaned down and started searching my body for my belongings, pulling things out of my jacket pockets: my BlackBerry, my memory cards, some loose bills. His hands moved quickly, skipping over my second passport, which was secretly tucked into a money belt inside my jeans, until they reached my breasts. He stopped. And then he squeezed them, like a child honking a rubber horn.

"Please, God. I just don't want to be raped." I curled as tightly as I could into a fetal position.

But the soldier was preoccupied with something else. He removed my gray Nikes with fluorescent yellow soles, and I heard the whipping

sound of the laces being pulled out. I felt air on my feet. He tied my
ankles together. With a piece of fabric he pulled my wrists behind my
back and tied them together so tightly they went numb. Then he pushed
my face down into the filthy earth.

*Will I see my parents again? Will I see Paul again? How could I do this
to them? Will I get my cameras back? How did I get to this place?*

The soldiers picked me up by my hands and feet and carried me away.

THAT DAY IN LIBYA I asked myself the questions that still haunt me:
Why do you do this work? Why do you risk your life for a photograph?
After ten years as a war correspondent, it remains a difficult question to
answer. The truth is that few of us are born into this work. It is something we discover accidentally, something that happens gradually. We
get a glimpse of this unusual life and this extraordinary profession, and
we want to keep doing it, no matter how exhausting, stressful, or dangerous it becomes. It is the way we make a living, but it feels more like
a responsibility, or a calling. It makes us happy, because it gives us a
sense of purpose. We bear witness to history, and influence policy. And
yet we also pay a steep price for this commitment. When a journalist
gets killed in a firefight, or steps on a land mine and loses his legs, or
tears his friends and family apart by getting kidnapped, I ask myself
why I chose this life.

I had no idea that I would become a conflict photographer. I wanted
to travel, to learn about the world beyond the United States. I found
that the camera was a comforting companion. It opened up new worlds,
and gave me access to people's most intimate moments. I discovered the
privilege of seeing life in all its complexity, the thrill of learning something new every day. When I was behind a camera, it was the only
place in the world I wanted to be.

It was in Argentina, at age twenty-two, that I discovered I could
make a living—at first, $10 a photograph—from this hobby that I

loved. Once I began to work, a career in photojournalism didn't seem like such a distant dream. The question was how to move forward in such a competitive industry. I got a job as a stringer for the Associated Press in New York, and once I had experience, I took a risk and began to travel, first to Cuba, then India, Afghanistan, Mexico City. I became comfortable in places most people found frightening, and as I saw more of the world, my courage and curiosity grew.

I was just finding my way as a reporter when the September 11 attacks changed the world. Along with hundreds of other journalists, I was there to witness the invasion of Afghanistan; it would be the first time many of us would participate in a story that involved our own troops and our own bombs. The War on Terror created a new generation of war journalists, and as the wars became more unjust, our commitment deepened. We had an obligation to show the world the truth, and our sense of mission consumed our lives. On the front lines we became a family. We've seen one another through affairs, through marriages, divorces, and deaths. Now that combat operations in Iraq and Afghanistan have mostly ceased, we meet most often at weddings and funerals.

When I was first starting out, I raced to cover the biggest stories, but over time my choices have become more personal. I see images in newspapers, magazines, on the Internet—refugee camps in Darfur, women in the Democratic Republic of the Congo, wounded veterans—and my heart leaps. I am suddenly overcome with this quiet angst—a restlessness that means I know I will go. The work takes on a rhythm all its own. I may spend two weeks photographing women dying of breast cancer in Uganda, and on the plane home I am already sketching out my next assignment, on the Maoist rebels in the jungles of India. When I return home to London—to my husband, Paul, and my son, Lukas—I'll edit some eight thousand Uganda photos, break to take Lukas to the park, and perhaps discuss with an editor a future assignment in southern Turkey. When people ask me why I go to these places, they are asking the wrong question. For me, the conundrum is never whether or not to go to Egypt or Iraq or Afghanistan; the problem is that I can't be in two of those places at once.

With my subjects—the thousands of people I have photographed— I have shared the joy of survival, the courage to resist oppression, the anguish of loss, the resilience of the oppressed, the brutality of the worst of men and the tenderness of the best. I maintain relationships with drivers and fixers, the trusted locals I relied on for setting up meetings, translating interviews, and navigating a foreign culture, for years. An interpreter I worked with thirteen years ago in Afghanistan can unexpectedly pop up in a meeting at a United Nations office today. They are as much a part of my circle of humanity as anyone else, and when a new tragedy is visited upon their country, I feel a sense of responsibility to see how it is affecting them. Often they write to me, "Are you coming, Miss Lynsey?"

Of course, there are dangers, and I have been lucky. I have been kidnapped twice. I have gotten in one serious car accident. Two of my drivers have died while working for me—two tragedies that I will always feel responsible for. I have missed the births of my sisters' children, the weddings of friends, the funerals of loved ones. I have disappeared on countless boyfriends and had just as many disappear on me. I put off, for years, marriage and children. Somehow, though, I am healthy. I have maintained warm and wonderful relationships; I even found a husband who puts up with it all. Like many women, once I started a family, I had to make tough choices. I struggle to find the imperfect balance between my role as a mother and my role as a photojournalist. But I have faith, as I've always had, that if I work hard enough, care enough, and love enough in all areas of my life, I can create and enjoy a full life. Photography has shaped the way I look at the world; it has taught me to look beyond myself and capture the world outside. It's also taught me to cherish the life I return to when I put the camera down. My work makes me better able to love my family and laugh with my friends.

Journalists can sound grandiose when they talk about their profession. Some of us are adrenaline junkies; some of us are escapists; some of us do wreck our personal lives and hurt those who love us most. This work can destroy people. I have seen so many friends and colleagues become unrecognizable from trauma: short-tempered, sleepless, and alienated from friends. But after years of witnessing so much suffering in the world, we find it hard to acknowledge that lucky, free, prosperous people like us might be suffering, too. We feel more comfortable in the darkest places than we do back home, where life seems too simple and too easy. We don't listen to that inner voice that says it is time to take a break from documenting other people's lives and start building our own.

Under it all, however, are the things that sustain us and bring us together: the privilege of witnessing things that others do not; an idealistic belief that a photograph might affect people's souls; the thrill of creating art and contributing to the world's database of knowledge. When I return home and rationally consider the risks, the choices are difficult. But when I am doing my work, I am alive and I am me. It's what I do. I am sure there are other versions of happiness, but this one is mine.

PART ONE

Discovering the World

CONNECTICUT, NEW YORK, ARGENTINA,

CUBA, INDIA, AFGHANISTAN

CHAPTER 1

No Second Chances in New York

My oldest sister, Lauren, likes to tell a story about me. One summer day our entire family was in our backyard pool. I was only a year and a half old and couldn't swim, so I was standing on my father's shoulders. My three older sisters and my mother splashed around us. Suddenly, without a word, I bent my knees and jumped into the water. My sisters were stunned. My father said he let me go because he knew I would be fine. When I emerged from the water, I was smiling.

The Addario house in Westport, Connecticut, was a kaleidoscope of transvestites and Village People look-alikes, a haven for people who weren't accepted elsewhere. My parents, Phillip and Camille, both hairdressers, ran a successful salon called Phillip Coiffures, and they often brought home their employees and clients and friends. Crazy Rose, a manic-depressive former employee, spent most days chain-smoking, spewing non sequiturs. Veto, an openly gay Mexican—rare in the late seventies—solicited show-tune requests from my sisters and banged them out on the living room piano. When my sisters and I came home from school, we were frequently greeted by Frank, known to us as Auntie Dax, dressed as a woman and wearing a feather boa. In the summer my parents brought in two DJs from Long Island to spin Donna Summer and the Bee Gees records. Hors d'oeuvres, Bloody Marys, and bottles of wine were passed around poolside, as were quaaludes, marijuana, and cocaine. Uncle Phil, a scowl on his face, sometimes appeared in a wedding gown for a mock ceremony on the lawn. No one ever seemed to leave. It never occurred to me that any of this was strange, because that was just how our house was.

We were four sisters—Lauren, Lisa, Lesley, and I—and only two to three years apart in age. I was the youngest and relied on Daphne, our beloved Jamaican nanny, to rescue me when Lisa and Lesley beat me up or stuck puffy stickers up my nose. Our house was rambling and lawless. On a typical day ten to fifteen teenage girls were running around the yard, raiding the never-ending supply of junk food in the kitchen cupboards, skinny-dipping in the pool, and leaving wet towels and underwear along the deck and in the grass. All down the street you could hear us squealing as we pulled our bathing suits up high, rubbed Johnson's baby oil on our butts, and shot down the big blue slide.

My mother and father were a sun-kissed and smiling team. I never heard them raise their voices, especially at each other. My father, towering over her at six foot one, called my mother "doll." She was always befriending someone, taking someone under her wing. On Westport's Main Street we couldn't walk five feet without one of their clients stopping us, looking me in the eye as if I had a clue who they were. "You've gotten so big. I've known you since you were this high," they'd say, gesturing to their knees. All of Westport watched me grow up through my mother's stories. Every day someone told me what a *wooooonderful* mother I had.

My father was quieter, an introvert who would speak to one person for hours—if he was forced to speak to anyone at all. He spent most of his time out in his rose garden—one hundred bushes of more than twenty-five species of roses—or in his two-story greenhouse, full of ferns, birds-of-paradise, jasmine, camellias, gardenias, and orchids. When I wanted to find him, I followed the long garden hose to the puddles of water that collected around the drains on the greenhouse's redbrick floor.

I never realized how much work his flowers required, because they made him so happy. Even before a ten-hour day of cutting hair, he spent the wee hours of dawn in his greenhouse, tending to his plants as if each one were a small child. When I watched him, I tried to understand what about these plants captivated his attention. He would lead me through the labyrinth of gigantic pots and show me the mini mandarin tree that always bore succulent fruits, or the orchids that blossomed from seedlings he had ordered from Asia and South America. He grew them off slabs of bark, as they grew in their native rain forests.

"This is a *Strelitzia reginae,* also known as a bird-of-paradise," he'd say. "And this is a *Gelsemium sempervirens,* a Carolina jasmine, and a *Paphiopedilum fairrieanum,* a lady's slipper orchid."

The names were long, an endless stream of vowels and consonants that I didn't understand. But I was in awe of his knowledge of something so foreign, curious why this exhausting work brought him such mysterious joy.

ON SEPTEMBER 27, 1982—when I was eight years old—my mother piled my three sisters and me into our station wagon, drove us to the parking lot of the hair salon, and turned off the engine. She must have chosen the parking lot of the salon because it was her second home, and neutral ground for her and my dad. "Your father went to New York with Bruce," she said. "He is not coming back."

He was coming out.

Bruce, a manager in the design department at Bloomingdale's, was one of the many men who hung around our house when I was growing up. One afternoon my mother went to Bloomingdale's in search of someone to design shades for my father's greenhouse. Bruce went home with her in her two-seater Mercedes to see the greenhouse and walked in on a typical afternoon at the Addario house: several pots of food on the stove, and family and friends lounging about, talking and laughing loudly. He felt the warmth of our house immediately. "Oh, my God!" he cried. "What a beautiful house!"

Bruce grew up in an icy family in Terre Haute, Indiana, and he was enthralled by the Italian-style camaraderie of ours. He was charismatic, talented, and very flamboyant, and he and my mother became fast friends. They ran around together, shopping and socializing, as if my father didn't exist. My parents sent Bruce to hairdressing school to become a colorist and gave him a place to stay in our house when he didn't want to commute back to his apartment in New York. For four years Bruce was part of the family.

It wasn't until 1978 that my father made a pass while he and Bruce were running an errand for my mother. The affair went on for a few years before my dad was able to admit to himself that he had fallen in love. My father had suppressed his homosexuality since his teenage years. His mother, Nina, had come to Ellis Island in 1921 along with thousands of other Italian immigrants. They brought their prejudices and conservative Catholic views with them. In the 1950s and 1960s homosexuality was considered a mental illness and was against the law. To this day my father thinks his mother would have committed him to an asylum had he come out back then. When he finally mustered the courage to tell her he was in love with Bruce, she said, "Can't you just make believe you're straight?"

I was too young to fully understand why my father was leaving. It was something we deduced on our own or learned at school. "Phillip Coiffures . . . gay . . . their dad is gay" we heard kids whispering in the halls. I don't remember the women in our family ever having a conversation about my father being homosexual. We only seemed to talk about everyone else's lives.

We visited Dad and Bruce on weekends in their new home at the end of a half-mile path by the beach in Connecticut. Lauren, the oldest of us girls, was overwhelmed by a sense of betrayal. Two years later she finished high school and left to study abroad in England. Lisa, Lesley, and I bonded together. For the next fifteen years my father seemed to vanish from our everyday life. I reached most early milestones without him.

My mother filled in the gaps: Between clients, she came to all my high school softball games, rewarded me with admiration when I brought home A's from school, and counseled me on my first love. My mother was infinitely resilient—a trait she learned from her own mother, Nonnie, who'd raised five children on her own—and she tried to stay strong and positive about my father. She kept repeating the mantra they had always told us—"Do what makes you happy, and you will be successful in life"—as if to discourage any negative feelings about him, as if nothing had changed. Perhaps it was the way my mother portrayed their separation, or perhaps it was because I'd grown up my whole life witnessing the sorrow of outcasts, but I accepted that my father had found the happiness he'd longed for. I even found solace in the idea that my dad left my mother for a man rather than a woman.

The weekend parties came to an end. My father stayed in business with my mother for moral and financial support for years after he left to be with Bruce, but the strain of remaining in business together was difficult for everyone. Six years after my father left, he and Bruce opened a new salon; most of my mother's stylists and clients followed them. She struggled to keep the shop going. Managing money was never my mother's strength, and without my father she could no longer maintain our expensive lifestyle. The first casualty was the two-seater Mercedes. She was unable to pay the bills on our house and our cars. Almost every month either the electricity or the water was cut off, or the repo man came in the middle of the night to take our car away. In middle school I often looked out the window at daybreak to see if our car was still in the driveway.

We moved out of the house with so many memories on North Ridge Road and moved into a smaller house a few miles away. There was no swimming pool and no big backyard. My three sisters had all moved on to start their lives, and my mom and I were alone.

It was around that time, when I was thirteen, on one of my rare weekend visits to his house, that my father gave me my first camera. It was a Nikon FG, which had been given to him by a client. The gift happened by chance: I saw it, I asked about it, and he casually handed it over. I was fascinated by the science of the camera, the way light and the shutter could freeze a moment in time. I taught myself the basics from an old "how to photograph in black-and-white" manual with an Ansel Adams picture of Yosemite National Park on the cover. With rolls of black-and-white film, long exposures, and no tripod, I sat on the roof and tried to shoot the moon. I was too shy to turn my camera on people, so I photographed flowers, cemeteries, peopleless land-scapes. One day a friend of my mother's, a professional photographer, invited me to her darkroom and taught me how to develop and print film. I watched with wonder as the still lifes of tulips and tombstones twinkled onto the page. It was like magic.

I photographed obsessively, continuing when I went off to the University of Wisconsin–Madison, where I majored in international relations. Still, I never dreamed of making photography a career. I thought photographers were flaky, trust-fund kids without ambition, and I didn't want to be one of those people.

Then I spent a year abroad, studying economics and political science at the University of Bologna. Free from the academic and social demands of Wisconsin, I embraced street photography. Between lectures I photographed Bologna's arches and ancient nooks with my Nikon. During holiday breaks, I teamed up with new, instantly intimate friends, the kind who typified a college year abroad, and went backpacking around Europe, photographing the ruddy cheeks of Prague and the nude thermal baths of Budapest, the coast of Spain and the crowded streets of Sicily. I soaked up the architecture and the art I had read about my entire life, went to museums and photo exhibitions. I saw a Robert Mapplethorpe retrospective, from when he first began photographing until his death, and for hours I sat and studied his composition and use of light. I was inspired to photograph more.

The more I traveled, the more I craved a life of travel. I could wake up on any given morning and go to almost any destination; the countries of Europe were accessible by train and inaccessible only because of my own inhibitions or fear. This was such an unfamiliar luxury to me, an American who grew up on an isolated continent. I imagined a life overseas—as a diplomat, maybe, or a translator.

But one day as I was leaving the darkroom with a stack of prints, an Italian man approached and asked to see them. After flipping through them for a few minutes, he offered to turn them into a line of postcards. I was so excited that I happily handed them over without signing a thing. They were sold in Rimini, an Italian resort near Bologna, but I never saw a dime. It was the first time I realized photos could be published and seen by hundreds of people, maybe more.

When I graduated from college, I moved to New York City for the summer and waited tables at night at Poppolini's restaurant in Greenwich Village. During the day I got an internship assisting a fashion photographer who shot for catalogues. I hated it. It was too predictable. So once I'd made about $4,000 from waitressing, I moved to Buenos Aires to learn Spanish and to travel around South America, as I had in Europe. Taking pictures became a way for me to travel with a purpose.

I rented a room from an arrogant Argentinean man in his late twenties who spent a good portion of his time looking in the mirror, getting ready to go out partying, or sleeping off his hangover. To support myself, I taught English at Andersen Consulting for $18 an hour. It afforded me free afternoons, when I could wander through the alleys of the city, photographing tango dancers on narrow streets or ancient men in smoke-filled cafés. I often ended up at the Plaza de Mayo, where every Thursday Las Madres de Plaza de Mayo, Argentinean mothers, marched in protest of their children's disappearances during Argentina's Dirty War.

When I started photographing the mothers, I didn't know what ingredients produced a powerful photograph. No one had taught me about composition, or how to read light. I knew that the mothers' expressions spoke to me, but I wasn't sure how to capture the scene I was experiencing. Each Thursday I went back to the plaza, unsatisfied with the images I had composed the week before. I sensed I was too removed from the women, so I got a little closer to them as they circled the plaza. I tried to frame their pain and unresolved sadness in my viewfinder. Sometimes their expressions were shielded by dark shadows on their faces, because they were in the wrong place in relation to the sunlight. Sometimes I was simply too tentative and insecure to get close enough to them. Sometimes I missed a perfect moment, unsure of my instincts. I was untrained, but I began to teach myself, studying photography in books and newspapers, to see how powerful scenes could make a tired old story new again. I kept going back to try.

A month after I arrived in Argentina, my boyfriend, Miguel, a writer ten years my senior, joined me in Buenos Aires. Miguel and I rented a room for $500 a month, and for little, we received little. The bathroom was across a cement courtyard. When a cold rain descended on the city in the winter, we had to run from the nest of our bedroom into the brisk evening air, down a set of wet stairs, and around the corner to the tiny toilet. I all but stopped drinking water during the day.

Every few weeks I traveled around Latin America to photograph. I went from seaside villages in Uruguay to Pablo Neruda's houses along the Chilean coast to Machu Picchu in Peru; I photographed volcanoes, mountains, lakes, plush green fields, towns propped on hillsides, craft fairs, fish markets; I took long bus journeys around hairpin turns marked by crosses where others had fallen and died, and searched for beautiful light at dawn and dusk. My quest was simple: to travel and photograph everything I could with what little I had.

Miguel had recently completed a master's degree in journalism. We were both curious and cared deeply about what was happening in the world; it was our bond. But Miguel was a very private man. In me he recognized an extrovert, someone who loved to meet people and ask questions. He suggested I go to the local English daily newspaper, the *Buenos Aires Herald*, to see if I could freelance for them as a photojournalist. I had no experience in newspaper photography, but I was convinced they should offer me work because of my determination. The first time I approached the two editors in the photo department—two middle-aged men who smoked cigarettes all day while pulling pictures off the AP wire—they told me to come back after learning to speak the language. I thought I was already fluent, so I went away, brushed up on my Spanish, and went back to the paper a few weeks later.

Annoyed by my persistence, they finally gave me work—assignments I was convinced were fabricated just to keep me out of their hair. They'd write down the address of some location outside Buenos Aires, and I would have to find my way there, take a photo, and return and show them. None of these ever got published.

One day they told me that Madonna was filming the movie *Evita* that night at the Casa Rosada, the president's house in the city's main square. I already knew that, because I'd read in the paper that she was staying in a hotel suite for $2,500 a night and had set up her own gym in the room. I'd thought about her personal gym all morning as I went for a jog in tired shoes and sidestepped piles of dog shit.

The photo editors made me a proposal: If I could sneak onto the set of *Evita* and get a photo of Madonna filming, they would offer me a job.

That evening I pleaded with the security guards at the perimeter of the Casa Rosada for access, explaining that my entire career and future as a photojournalist depended on their allowing me onto the set. "I will be famous someday," I told them, "if you just let me in."

I must have looked sufficiently pathetic, because the guard smiled and cracked open the gate just enough to let me sneak through. I walked over to the press riser, about three hundred yards from the balcony where Madonna was due to appear, climbed up the stairs, raised my tiny little Nikon FG with a 50mm lens that my father had given me years before, and peered through the viewfinder. The balcony was nothing more than a microscopic speck.

I lowered my camera and just stood there, looking out at the balcony in the distance, convinced my career was over before it had even begun. And then I felt a tap on my shoulder.

"Hey, kid. Give me your camera body."

I had no idea what this stranger was talking about. I stared at him blankly.

"Take your lens off your camera," he said, "and give me your camera."

I did as instructed. He latched my minuscule camera onto a heavy 500mm lens—I hadn't even known that all Nikon bodies could be used with all Nikon lenses—and said, "OK, now look."

I squealed. Madonna was right there, huge in my frame. Everyone on the riser paused to look at me and rolled their eyes.

My image of Madonna at the Casa Rosada made the front page of the newspaper that morning, and I got a job at the paper, where I was paid $10 a picture.

While I was working for the *Herald*, I went to see an exhibition of Sebastião Salgado's work: enormous images of impoverished workers around the world who toiled under harrowing conditions. The photos were an enigma to me: How had he captured his subjects' dignity?

Until I saw Salgado's exhibition, I wasn't sure whether I wanted to be a street photographer or a news photographer or whether I could make it as a photographer at all. But when I entered the exhibition space, I was so overcome by his images—the passion, the details, the texture—that I decided to devote myself to photojournalism and documentary photography. Something I had perceived until that moment as a simple means of capturing pretty scenes became something altogether different: It was a way to tell a story. It was the marriage of travel and foreign cultures and curiosity and photography. It was photojournalism.

Until that exhibit I hadn't quite known what that was or could be. I hadn't thought of photography as both art *and* a kind of journalism. I hadn't known that my hobby could be my life. I knew then that I wanted to tell people's stories through photos; to do justice to their humanity, as Salgado had done; to provoke the kind of empathy for the subjects that I was feeling in that moment. I doubted I would ever be able to capture such pain and beauty in a single frame, but I was impassioned. I walked through the exhibition and cried.

I never felt the uncertainty that typically plagues people in their twenties. I was lucky enough to discover something that made me happy and ambitious at an age when I couldn't conceive of fear or failure, when I had very little to lose. But when I began working for the *Herald*, Miguel gave me possibly the best advice I ever got in my career.

"Stay in Latin America, learn photography, and make all your professional mistakes in Argentina," he said, "because if you make one mistake in New York, no one will give you a second chance."

WHEN WE FINALLY RETURNED to the States, in 1996, I was ready. I carried my mediocre clips from the *Buenos Aires Herald* around to the *New York Post*, the *New York Daily News*, and the Associated Press (AP), marching into photo editors' offices with groundless confidence that they should hire me. I was an overzealous twenty-two-year-old, dressed in stylish jeans, a crisp button-down shirt, and black rubber-soled platform shoes. (At five foot one, I hated flat shoes.) The newspapers put me on their "stringers" list, which they consulted when they needed to call a photographer for an assignment. No photographer on that list would ever say no to an assignment, even if it meant ditching a romantic dinner, or waking up at 5 a.m. to stand outside a courthouse on a freezing New York morning for a perp walk, or taking lame photographs of a kid playing in a leaking fire hydrant on a hot summer's day. In the early days the assignments were grim, but I took them—happily.

The AP gave me steady work almost immediately. During my years there I covered protests, press conferences, city hall, accidents. I shot Monica Lewinsky making one of her first public appearances, on the *Today* show. I photographed people watching the big screens in Times Square as the Dow Jones soared past 10,000. I covered the Yankees' ticker tape parade, which seemed like an annual event, because the Yankees always won the World Series. I never came back empty-handed or without a compelling image. Wire services, like the AP or Reuters, supplied news articles and photographs to newspapers, magazines, and television. They had freelance photographers in every country around the world and didn't accept excuses.

My mentor was an AP staff photographer named Bebeto, who worked as an editor on weekends. He called me almost every Saturday morning for three years: "You ready?" he would say in his slight Jamaican lilt. Bebeto was in his midforties and towered over me. He was intensely focused, but when he was unguarded, laughter would rush out of him like a lightly rumbling drum. He decided early on that he was going to take me under his wing and school me in photography. When I returned to the fifth floor of the AP offices with film canisters in hand, he stood over the rolls of negatives with a magnifying eyepiece called a loupe and went over each image with me, frame by frame, on multiple negative strips of thirty-six images per roll. He articulated what I had been trying to intuit. He taught me how to read light. He taught me the power of the sun at a low angle in the sky just after sunrise or before sunset to illuminate the world in that golden, magical way with long, dancing shadows. He talked of how a shaft of light fell onto a street corner in between buildings. He explained how to enter a room and look for the light by a window, or from a door slightly ajar. He taught me about composition. He showed me how to fill the frame of my viewfinder with the subject and important contextual information—something that lent the image a sense of place.

More than anything, he taught me the art of patience. Cameras introduce tension. People are aware of the power of a camera, and this instinctively makes most subjects uncomfortable and stiff. But Bebeto taught me to linger in a place long enough, without photographing, so that people grew comfortable with me and the camera's presence. A perfect photograph is almost impossible; a good one is hard enough. Sometimes the light is there, but the subject is in the wrong place, and the composition doesn't work. Sometimes the light is perfect, but the subject is uncomfortable, and his awkwardness shows. I learned how difficult it is to put all the elements in place.

While I was working, all my faculties were attuned to the scene in front of me. Everything else in the world, in my life, in my mind, fell away. He taught me to stand on a street corner or in a room for an hour—or two or three—waiting for that great epiphany of a moment, the wondrous combination of subject, light, and composition. And something else: the inexplicable magic that made the image dive right into your heart.

As Bebeto reviewed my work, I learned. He looked over the negatives, image by image, drawing a giant red, waxy X over the frames he thought were below average. I worked to meet his standards.

Seven days a week I ran around New York with a pager and a cell phone and waited for the photo desk to call with an assignment. In my downtime I worked at Craig Taylor, a high-end shirt company, running errands and stuffing envelopes. I had barely $75 in the bank on a good week, scraped by for rent, and scrounged to pay the bills for the phone and pager—my two most crucial possessions, aside from my cameras.

Photography required thousands of dollars in initial investment to amass the proper equipment: two professional camera bodies, then $1,500 each (it was predigital); fast professional lenses with an aperture of 2.8, which ran from $300 to $2,500; a long zoom lens, about $2,000; a flash, $200; and a Domke camera bag, $100. I needed about $10,000 in total. I spent days walking around B&H and Adorama camera stores, dreaming of the gear I would purchase one day when I had money.

Sometime around my twenty-fifth birthday, the last of my three sisters got married, and I had an epiphany. My father and Bruce had given each of my sisters $15,000 to spend toward their wedding costs. Miguel and I had broken up when we moved back to New York, and I knew I would never get married in my twenties; in fact, I wasn't sure I would ever love anything as much as photography. So I made my father and Bruce a proposition: "If you advance me my wedding money now, I can use it to invest in my career, and I will one day have enough money to fund my own wedding." They agreed. I bought new cameras and lenses and put the rest of the money in the bank.

AFTER LESS THAN A YEAR back in New York, I was desperate to travel and looked to Latin America once again. One country intrigued me most, perhaps because it was off-limits: Cuba. In 1997, Communist Cuba was embargoed, and Americans rarely visited. Being a foreign journalist in Cuba was also risky; the government monitored foreigners they suspected would publish negative stories about the ailing Communist system. I didn't know anyone who had been there; at the time I didn't know one foreign correspondent and knew few other journalists. But I was bursting with curiosity and the daring of youth. I was fascinated by the steady rise of capitalism in such a steadfastly Communist country.

I landed in Havana in May. As I rode the minivan from the airport into the city, I looked down at my nervous hands holding a sheet of paper with fading blue lines and the address of my destination and realized I was very alone. I read the address to the bus driver in rusty Argentine Spanish and felt an instant attachment to him. I wanted to spend the rest of my trip on the bus. Through the window I saw that Havana was decrepit. Some buildings had paint peeling away from their facades; others were just a heap of exposed, rotting wood. Rooftops had lost shingles; clothes were hanging up to dry in the pouring rain; boys nonchalantly rode their bikes through twelve-inch puddles. When I got out at my stop, two women and a man looked at me as if I carried a banner that said AMERICAN CAPITAL-ISM. I was a stranger: My shoes were too new and well made for me to be Cuban. Even my hair clip would cost a month's wages there.

In a travel book I had found an agency that arranged home stays, and they placed me with a woman named Leo, whom I paid $22 a night for a small room. She greeted me as if I were an old friend. On my dresser she left two tiny bars of soap stolen from an American hotel in the mid-1970s. She left chocolates next to the soap. They were stolen from the same hotel.

Three rocking chairs awaited on the glassed-in terrace with a ninth-story view, and Leo and her mother, Graciela, took their places and motioned me to sit. We began exchanging the usual questions, small talk, one-word inferences, and waited for intonations that quickly became familiar. We rocked in our chairs, and everything I had read about the situation in Cuba—the failures of communism, the poverty, the hardships, the lines for food, the struggle for basic amenities, the disparity between those who paid in dollars and those who paid in meager pesos—was confirmed by Leo and Graciela in the span of hours. Our conversation carried on from early evening into the night, and we lingered comfortably with the Cuban breezes blowing in and out of the patio windows. I had expected Cuba to be this ominous, scary dungeon, but the people were so warm, so candid—just like anyone else.

Several days after I arrived, I finally went to Publicitur, the organization that represented Cuba's International Press Center and provided minders for foreign journalists. Minders were government-appointed guides who accompanied journalists around, wrote up reports detailing every person the journalists interviewed and every place they visited, and then passed this information on to the government. I introduced myself to the secretary at the front desk. They recognized me as "the American journalist"; they were expecting me. The secretary led me to a room where two young women who prided themselves on their textbook English and secondhand knowledge of the outside world were seated at a table. The directors of Publicitur who oversaw the minders were eager to answer a list of questions I had prepared about Cuba and its mechanisms and to arrange my requests to photograph in certain places. I could tell instinctively I would never get the information I wanted from them. They claimed they would arrange shoots for me inside government buildings and hospitals, but I knew that in a country like Cuba they would not. It was my first experience in a country that provided government minders to journalists and blatantly restricted my movements.

While all who worked at Publicitur and the International Press Center were eager to show me Cuba's touristy sights—Varadero Beach, the Tropicana, the recently restored Old Havana area—they were equally eager to keep me away from the run-down neighborhoods.

It was the rainy season, and the streets were hard to photograph. I walked the city from end to end, for hours and hours each day, in search of images, drenched from the humidity, exhausted from the heat, and sick of hearing the flirtatious *"ssssst"* from men surprised to see a foreigner. I walked so much and spent so much time looking for the right light or the right angle of a shiny old American car in front of a decaying building that even my minders got bored with me and decided I wasn't worth following around. For a few days, there wasn't enough water for bathing, and soon I smelled from my long days of walking. I thought I might collapse from the heat. But as I roamed around the Cuban villages alone, camera in hand, I also felt satiated, at peace. I felt at home.

As soon as I returned to New York after a month in Cuba, I thought only about getting back on a plane. I didn't want to lose the momentum of travel and discovery or sink into the trap of a comfortable life. But I trudged through two more years of paying my dues in New York, visiting Cuba again in 1998 and 1999 to satisfy my wanderlust.

In 1999 Bebeto came to me with an idea. In the past year there had been a series of murders in the transgender-prostitute community in New York. Rather than order an investigation into the crimes, the AP had heard that Mayor Giuliani had decided the community wasn't worth the city's resources. An AP reporter wanted to explore the idea that transgender prostitutes were society's throwaways. It was my first long-term assignment, my first opportunity for a real photo-essay.

In the beginning, the reporter and I ventured out together in the Meatpacking District to make inroads into the seemingly impenetrable world of transgender prostitutes. We traveled with a local organization that distributed condoms and information on sexually transmitted diseases on the neighborhood's busiest weekend nights. I never took out my camera. Once we made some initial contacts as a team, I decided to venture out on my own, and for weeks I went out almost every Thursday, Friday, and Saturday night—often without my cameras—and hung around the Meatpacking District like a groupie, trying to gain the women's trust. I was the only white girl among a tribe of Latinas, blacks, and Asians, and they were skeptical of my intentions. Finally a woman named Kima, who walked the then desolate streets in front of what is now the fashionable Pastis restaurant, invited me to her apartment in the Bronx projects. "Be there around midnight. You can hang out with us and then come downtown to work with us." I asked if I could bring my cameras. She agreed.

I showed up at Kima's with chocolate-chip cookies and milk. I'm not sure what I was thinking, bringing chocolate-chip cookies and milk to an apartment full of transgender prostitutes who lived on drugs, alcohol, and fast food—but I didn't want to arrive empty-handed, and I didn't think it was ethical to bring booze. (I later learned otherwise.) A handful of women were there, injecting themselves with black-market hormones, drinking, dancing, getting made up. They let me shoot whatever I wanted. For five months I spent almost every weekend with Kima, Lala, Angel, and Josie. As I gained their trust, my photographs became more intimate; time allowed me to see things I hadn't before, like when a tough guy who looked as though he had strutted out of a Snoop Dogg video would gently comb his transgender girlfriend's hair in the dim light of a street lamp while she waited for her early morning clients.

One night I went on my first date in months, with a musician who played the saxophone in a Cuban band. Around 1 a.m. he walked me home along Christopher Street to the corner of West Tenth Street. We looked down at our feet and kicked our heels around in circles as we made meaningless conversation. Finally he kissed me.

Minutes had gone by when I sensed a group of people too close to us. I opened my eyes and saw shadows dancing around our feet.

"IT'S THE PHOTO LADY!"

It was Kima and Lala and Charisse and Angel—an entire posse of the trannies. They screamed and laughed, and they got closer and closer to me and the poor musician. *"Woohoo, you go, girl!"*

The musician was confused: "What did you say you did for a living again?"

"I'm a photographer."

"And these are your friends?"

"Yes, I guess."

The kiss ended there.

WHEN IN THE BEGINNING OF 2000 I got an invitation to go to India with a family friend—a business professor who was taking his students abroad for a field study that had virtually nothing to do with any of the subjects I was interested in photographing—I considered it an opportunity to leave New York for good. I asked the Associated Press if they thought I might be able to get work in South Asia, and they responded encouragingly. At the time, I had no idea if I would really stay. But at that point in my life I didn't think that far in advance; I didn't wring my hands over seemingly enormous decisions. I just saw the door and went through it. That was the case with moving to India. It would turn out to be the last time I lived in the United States.

CHAPTER 2

How Many Children Do You Have?

My first night in New Delhi I stayed with two foreign correspondents: Marion, a reporter for the *Boston Globe*, and her boyfriend, John, a staff photographer at the AP. I could tell when I arrived late one evening that they were used to the constant traffic of guests. John answered the door sleepily, unfazed, showed me to my room, and went back to bed. I lay there, staring into the dark, suddenly overwhelmed by loneliness.

But the next morning, as I drank the coffee Marion cursorily plopped down on the counter for me, I saw the life I dreamed of right there in her kitchen. "We haven't stopped working in years," Marion said pointedly. She was trim and attractive and had no time for bullshit. "From India and Pakistan's nuclear testing to the hijacking of the Indian Airlines jet to Kashmir . . . we are exhausted." I watched her face turn serious and focused, my stomach flipping with admiration and anxiousness. Marion and John, who were roughly my age and from the United States, were covering major international news events, working hard, and establishing their careers while maintaining a comfortable home overseas. Instead of wondering whether I had made a mistake moving to India, I felt as if I had squandered my life in New York.

Everything that made India the rawest place on earth made it the most wonderful to photograph. The streets hummed with constant movement, a low-grade chaos where almost every aspect of the human condition was in public view. The vast disparity between India's wealthiest and poorest made for an incredible juxtaposition of people and street life. Few subjects or scenes were off-limits in India. The country was a photographer's ideal laboratory. The morning and evening light illuminated a rainbow of brilliant, saturated hues: I followed women draped in magentas and yellows and blues as they disappeared into dusty crowds. I spent ten days along the Ganges River in Varanasi, photographing Hindu devotion from the predawn hours until long after sunset; eight days in Calcutta, shooting men bathing on the street and children caked in dirt and begging for food. When the stimulation got overwhelming, I hid inside my viewfinder, outside of my body. Images were everywhere, and my eyes got tired. But I could endure anything for the prospect of beautiful negatives. I spent all my money on film.

I found a room in the dark, slightly depressing apartment of an easygoing thirty-something named Ed Lane. He was the bureau chief of the financial news company Dow Jones and loved his whiskey. The AP helped me get press credentials and an Indian residential visa. Ed took me to the run-down Foreign Correspondents' Club, where international journalists gathered every week to gossip about their lives as expats, like something out of a Hemingway novel. They were a worldly but friendly bunch, used to meeting new people and welcoming them to their homes. Hearing their stories made the world appear smaller and more manageable—as if going to difficult or dangerous places were just a matter of knowledge and logistics, part of the job and the life.

When I wasn't photographing, I watched Bollywood films in Hindi or went swimming at the American Club, an elite club run by the U.S.

Embassy, with Marion. Life was difficult in India, but it was also cheap. Personal space did not exist, but a little money could buy luxury. I paid rent with one assignment and paid for a maid with another.

Back home my college and high school friends embarked on a year of endless engagement parties and weddings. I was often invited to be a guest photographer. Everyone's life was moving forward while I was chasing good light and village women in India. I envisioned a nomadic life of adventure for myself, but I worried sometimes whether I was condemning myself to a spinster's future: forever single, having affairs with random men, my cameras dangling all over me.

It could have been worse.

Within months I had gotten myself into a rhythm of steady work, pairing up with Marion for the *Boston Globe* and the *Houston Chronicle* and shooting the occasional story for the *Christian Science Monitor* and the AP. I wrote to the photo desk of the *New York Times* several times, offering myself up as a stringer, and each time my e-mail went unanswered. I wrote directly to the *New York Times* correspondents based in India and asked if I could shoot anything for them. They told me they took their own pictures while on assignment. I would keep trying. I felt that if I could only shoot for the *New York Times*—to me, the newspaper that most influenced American foreign policy and that employed the world's best journalists—I would reach the pinnacle of my career.

AROUND MID-APRIL 2000 Ed returned from a reporting trip to Afghanistan. He came home with fifteen Afghan carpets and some advice: "You should go to Afghanistan to photograph women living under the Taliban."

"What do you mean?" I honestly didn't know much about Afghanistan, aside from the *Times* articles I had read while on the elliptical machine in New York.

"You're a woman, and you're interested in photographing women's issues," Ed said. "There are few female journalists doing these stories there now. You should go."

I had never been to a hostile country. Afghanistan had been destroyed by war, first when the Soviets occupied the country in the 1980s and later when Afghan factions fought each other for power. By 2000 one of these groups, the Taliban, had taken over about 90 percent of the country, promising to end the violence, thievery, and rape. It installed Sharia, Islamic law requiring strict obedience to the Koran; forced the entire female population to wear the burqa; and outlawed television, music, kite flying—any form of entertainment. Men had their hands cut off for robbery, and women were stoned to death for adultery. But everything I had read was from an outsider's perspective, from articles usually written by Westerners and non-Muslims. Were Westerners imposing their own set of values on a Muslim country? Were Afghan women miserable living under a burqa and under the Taliban? Or did we just assume they were miserable because our lives are so different?

I didn't know how I'd pull off such a trip. The only governing body was the Taliban, and almost all foreign embassies and diplomats had pulled out. I was an unmarried American woman who would want to photograph civilians. In Afghanistan women were not allowed to move around outside the home without a male guardian. Photography of any living being was illegal. According to one famous hadith, the Prophet Muhammad said: "Every image-maker will be in the Fire, and for every image that he made a soul will be created for him, which will be punished in the Fire."

But aside from a brief moment when I wondered whether I would be able to carry out my work, I wasn't scared. I believed that if my intentions were for a good cause, nothing bad would happen to me. And Ed was not a daredevil journalist. I didn't think he would recommend a trip that might end in my death.

On Ed's recommendation I immediately sent a bunch of e-mails to the Office of the United Nations High Commissioner for Refugees, and to several local nongovernmental organizations (NGOs), introducing myself as a freelance photographer interested in photographing the lives of women under the Taliban. Almost immediately I began to receive responses. I was shocked: I didn't have backing from a major publication—to them I was a nobody—but they still took the time to answer my e-mails and offer logistical support. Few journalists were covering Afghanistan under the Taliban, and they were grateful for my interest. I arranged to arrive in two weeks.

The week before I was scheduled to go, I checked my bank balance. The remnants of my wedding money had dwindled to nothing, and most of my freelancing payments hadn't come through. I couldn't possibly cancel this trip because of money. In most war zones credit cards were not accepted: The only accepted currency was a wad of dollars. And I didn't have dollars. Or rupees, for that matter. My mother couldn't lend me money; I refused to ask my father and Bruce for anything beyond the wedding money, because they had repeatedly expressed their belief that I needed to make it on my own. I called my sister Lisa and her husband, Joe, and without hesitation—and without asking why I was traveling to Afghanistan or whether that might be a bad idea—they wired a few thousand dollars into my bank account that very day.

IT WAS MAY 2000 when I arrived in Pakistan, in transit to Afghanistan for the first time, with my Nikons, one panoramic camera, one suitcase, and four worries: I was from America (a country that had recently sanctioned Afghanistan because of sheltering the Islamic fundamentalist leader Osama bin Laden); I was a photographer (and photographing any living thing was strictly prohibited under the Taliban); I was a single woman (and according to the Taliban should be kept in my father's house or travel at all times with a *mahram*, a husband or male relative who functioned as a guardian); and I was arriving at a time of extreme censorship by the Taliban.

Pakistan was the country closest to India that had a working Afghan Embassy, where I could apply for a visa. Several colleagues at the Associated Press in New Delhi recommended that I contact the AP correspondent in Pakistan, Kathy Gannon, to help facilitate the visa process and brief me on the logistics of operating as a woman in Afghanistan under the Taliban. Kathy, like very few other journalists in the world, had been working there for more than a decade. Over a drink at the UN club in Islamabad, she casually navigated me through the process of working under the Taliban, offered me a place to stay at the AP house in Kabul, and put me in touch with Amir Shah, the AP's local stringer. Her enthusiasm eased some of my fear.

The next morning I wondered what to wear to the Embassy of the Islamic Emirate of Afghanistan. I forgot to ask Kathy that most basic question. But I knew that modesty was essential. Afghan women wore burqas, but Western women in Pakistan did not. I settled on a *salwar kameez* (the traditional baggy pants and long shirt worn in the region) and a wide, draping head scarf, referred to as either a chador or *hijab*, depending on what part of the Muslim world one was traveling through. I opted for a large head scarf rather than the type of all-encompassing fabric that wrapped around both the head and the body. I prepared my papers, passport photos—ones I had shot with me wearing a heavy black head scarf—and made my way with all my paperwork to the embassy. For journalists, no matter who they are, there are few experiences filled with more terror than the infuriating, bureaucratic, often arbitrary, but necessary process of getting a visa.

Ed's advice rang in my ear: "Do not look any Afghan male directly in the eye. Keep your head, your face, and your body covered. Don't laugh or joke under any circumstance. And most important, sit each day in the visa office and drink tea with the visa clerk, Mohammed, to ensure that your application will actually get sent to Kabul and processed."

The Afghan Embassy was a rudimentary, nondescript building in the diplomatic quarter of the city, and the visa office was a small, bland room off to the side with its own entrance from the outside. The other officials inside the embassy could see what happened in the visa office through a small window. The air inside was stiff with body odor. A youngish man with puffy cheeks and a white turban piled atop his head, a dark beard hovering above his chest, and a prematurely aged face—Mohammed—sat behind a desk across from a tattered couch and a few chairs. A steady stream of UN workers and their Afghan drivers shuffled in and out of the room. They were all men. When I entered, Mohammed registered my gender with a faint flicker of surprise, directed me with his eyes to the ratty couch, and proceeded to attend to every male in the room, whether they'd come in before me or not.

He finally called me to the desk. He spoke simple English. I handed him my passport, wondering if he would eject me because I was American.

"Are you married?" he asked.

"Yes, married," I said. "With two boys back in New York."

He took my papers and told me to return in three weeks. I nodded. I returned the next day.

He didn't seem to mind. I was careful not to speak to him unless he first directed a question to me. For the first two of what would be nine mornings, we sat in silence. On the third morning I decided to break Ed's rule.

"Are you married, Mohammed?"

Without missing a beat, he replied: "No. No wife. My mother died, and there is no wife. I cannot find one. My brothers are looking, but it is taking too long."

His body language changed as he talked about himself; he lifted his chin and directed his eyes toward me. It was clear the woman issue made him fearful and sad. An Afghan man's status depended in part on having sons.

"But there must be a woman for you," I said.

"Too difficult . . . ," he explained, suddenly seeming vulnerable. "It is impossible to meet a wife in Afghanistan without the help of mother, sisters. Men and women do not mix outside. I need my family to find me a wife."

At that point another embassy worker walked in the room, and Mohammed shut down. I dropped my eyes to the floor and left.

The next morning Mohammed grinned when I entered.

"Your visa application has gone to Kabul." He spoke to me in front of a fellow Taliban member for the first time. "You can remove your *hijab* here. No need to wear this—you are not Muslim."

I had come to appreciate the respect I'd showed Mohammed and his colleagues by arriving at the embassy in proper *hijab* (which generally means being covered and wearing modest, unrevealing clothing). The notion of revealing so much of my hair and face to two male strangers made me uncomfortable. I also feared that Mohammed's comment might have been an obscene request from Taliban officials who wanted to take advantage of an American woman's openness.

"No, thank you. I will wear it."

THAT WEEKEND I WENT to the Pakistani town of Peshawar to photograph the Afghan refugee camps set up to accommodate the thousands of Afghans who fled during the wars. When I returned to the embassy that Monday, Mohammed projected a strange ease, smiling and acting as if he had been happily anticipating my visit. We shared our morning tea.

"There is no word yet from Kabul on your visa." He was busy, and there were many officials around, so I lingered until we were alone again. "How was your weekend?" he asked.

"I went to the Afghan refugee camps in Peshawar." I offered this but little else. I didn't know what might offend him.

"Where did you stay? A hotel? Where do you stay in Islamabad?"

I skirted around the answers to his questions about where I was sleeping with a demure smile. It didn't feel right to divulge such information to a young Talib.

Mohammed suddenly leaned forward, glancing through the window to the inside of the main embassy, looking for anyone who might have been listening. There was no one.

"Can I ask you a question?" he whispered.

"Sure, ask me anything, sir," I said, "as long as my answers do not inhibit my getting a visa."

He smiled nervously. "Is it true . . . ," he started. "I mean . . . I hear that men and women in America go out in public together without being married." He paused again, leaning in to look out the window until he was reassured no one was listening. "That men and women can live together without being married?"

I knew he was taking a chance with the question. The Taliban insists its members renounce sexual curiosity; his anxiety flooded the room.

"Are you sure my answers will not affect whether I get my visa?" I asked.

"I promise you they will not."

"Unmarried men and women in America spend a lot of time together," I said. "They go on something called 'dates' to movies, to the theater, to restaurants. Men and women sometimes even live together before they marry, and"—unlike in Afghanistan, where most marriages were arranged by and among relatives—"Americans marry for love."

Why was I saying this to a Talib at the Afghan Embassy? Given the cultural and language barriers between us, I felt certain that he understood no more than 10 percent of what I was saying. But he was enthralled.

"Do men and women . . . Is it true that men and women touch? And have children before they are married?"

"Yes," I replied gently. "Men and women touch before they are married."

"You are married, right?" he asked.

I smiled, finally comfortable enough to tell him the truth. I don't know why I felt comfortable enough to tell him anything. Maybe because he felt comfortable enough to ask such racy questions? To admit that his mind went to a place forbidden to an unmarried man by the Taliban's severe interpretation of the Koran? "No, Mohammed. I am not married. I lived with a man for a long time—like we were married."

He interrupted me. "What happened? Why did you leave? Why are you not married?"

Mohammed was no longer a Talib to me. We were simply two people in our twenties, getting to know each other.

"In America women work," I said. "And right now I am traveling and working."

He smiled. "America is a good place," he said.

"It is."

Five days later I picked up my visa.

DRIVING THROUGH THE KHYBER PASS, along a road as rocky as the terrain, I watched the jagged Spin Ghar mountains slice into the cobalt sky. Some male employees of the UN refugee agency, UNHCR, had agreed to drive me from the Pakistan border to Jalalabad and then Kabul. We rode in silence through the stunning, otherworldly landscape. Every few miles an old Russian tank sat, poised in its death and riddled with bullets—a stark reminder that Afghanistan's beauty could not hide its bleak, troubled history. Afghanistan was one of the poorest countries in the world. Carcasses of bombed-out buildings lined long stretches of barren road. Ghostlike women shrouded head to toe in the traditional blue burqas wove in and out of the dust. Young boys filled potholes with shovels, and drivers pelted them with coins.

I stayed at the United Nations guesthouse in the decrepit clay city of Jalalabad for $50 a night—a sum that did not pass through most Afghans' hands in a year. A laminated sheet listed the UN's rules and regulations: "Curfew at 7 p.m. No interaction with the locals. Must be escorted at all times by a United Nations driver. *This is an active war zone. In the case of shelling, the bomb shelter is located behind the house, and equipped with bottles of water, food, and supplies.*"

I removed my brown chador and my *salwar kameez* in the bathroom. My costume hadn't shielded me from the Afghans' heavy stares; few foreign women, women without burqas, traveled through the country. Only in the shower did I relax. The freedom, independence, and sexuality that I, as an American woman, held at the core of my being completely contradicted the Afghan way of life under the Taliban. I knew I had to shed my own views in order to work successfully here.

The UNHCR team passed me off to two men from the Comprehensive Disabled Afghans Program (CDAP), an organization that, among other things, rehabilitated Afghans injured by the thousands of land mines buried throughout the countryside by the Soviets. The mujahideen—Afghan factions who fought the Soviet occupiers—also took up the tactic, and as a result millions of mines continued to blow off the legs and hands of Afghans innocently walking or playing in the fields. As a journalist I was supposed to register with the Foreign Ministry in Kabul, but I decided to risk a few days in the countryside first. If the ministry knew of my presence in the country, they might forbid me from visiting certain areas or put a Taliban minder on my tail. My two CDAP escorts, my driver, Mohammed, and my guide and interpreter, Wahdat, weren't members of the Taliban and thought we could travel undetected. Wahdat, who insisted I also call him Mohammed, would serve as my *mahram* in the absence of a male relative. In order to bring my cameras into the country, I said I was photographing the physical destruction left by war, but the two Mohammeds had planned an ambitious journey through the provinces of Logar, Wardak, and Ghazni, where they could introduce me to Afghan civilians: land mine victims, widows, doctors, families.

Afghanistan was a tribal culture. Women were cloistered inside large compounds that only other women or male relatives could enter, and I knew it would be impossible to get a candid interview with a woman the moment they saw Mohammed. My guide was in his early forties, with gray-streaked dark brown hair and the long black beard customary among Pashtun men. Their tribe is the largest in Afghanistan and widely considered the most conservative. The Taliban comprised primarily Pashtun men, though some Tajiks and Hazaras were also members. Mohammed's wrinkled map of a face reflected a lifetime of war, repression, and poverty and obscured any trace of his youth. As my *mahram*, he had to accompany me, a woman alone, wherever I went. From the start of my journey, I struggled with how to skirt the Taliban photography ban: Images burned my eyes and my soul, but I was too nervous about the consequences to dare sneak a picture as I looked out the car window and watched potential frames fade into the moving countryside. This was a country where a machine gun was more prevalent than a Nikon, and I knew that every picture I took would require an intricate process of negotiation—with both my *mahram* and my subject. Without speaking Persian or Dari, I had to rely on my guide to be my voice in a delicate situation. I was stripped of my ability to work myself into a scene, to gain access into people's lives with the ritual of negotiation that photographers depend on. Over the last several years I had learned how to observe people by establishing that initial rapport through eye contact. In Afghanistan I could barely look at people. I had to constantly remind myself not to look men in the eye. There were so many rules and restrictions, especially against photographing women.

But because the Taliban had banned TV, foreign media, and newspapers—any publications aside from religious documents—most Afghans knew the images I shot would never make it back into their country. They did not have to worry about Afghans seeing their women in, say, the *Houston Chronicle*. Much to my surprise, many Afghans, male and female, were open to being photographed.

We drove for hours over the skeleton of a road, a patchwork of stones and gravel and dust, alongside herds of camels, and made our way into the provinces. Mohammed's prayers rose above the hum of the engine as he fingered his *tespih*—Muslim prayer beads, similar to a rosary. I still didn't take out my camera. On occasion I was so enraptured by the gorges and rivers and sharply sloping green hills that I allowed my scarf to slip from my forehead back to the nape of my neck, my sleeves down from my wrists to my forearm. When I refocused, I sensed Mohammed's obvious discomfort with the sight of the skin on my wrist.

Our first stop was a house in Logar Province; Mohammed wanted to show me normal family life in Afghanistan. A young child stood in the weeds in front of a clay compound built to house an entire Afghan family of forty or so. Mohammed sent for the man in charge. There were no telephones, and our visit was unannounced. Mohammed introduced me as a foreign journalist, interested in the state of Afghanistan and its people following twenty years of war, and soon the kettle for tea was lit.

The man of the house gave me permission to join him and the other men in their meal, and I was pleased to have the opportunity to partake in an experience off-limits to Afghan women. As a foreign journalist I was exempt from all the norms and rules that applied to the women here. I was androgynous, a third, undefined sex. We spent the first twenty minutes of lunch in tangible discomfort. Clearly no man in the room had ever eaten with a foreign woman present, save for the occasional four-year-old girl or elderly aunt.

I brought up the one subject everyone in Afghanistan could speak freely about: family.

"How many children do you have?" I said.

Most Afghan men prided themselves on having many children, and their faces gleamed as they rhapsodized about their eleven kids.

"How many children do you have?" they asked me, perhaps assuming that at twenty-six years of age I'd be well on my way to the double digits.

"None," I answered.

There was silence. I ate my meal quietly. The question of how many children I had would plague me throughout this trip—and for years to come. I was too shy to ask to take a photo.

After lunch, Mohammed took me to a secret school for girls. The Taliban had banned girls' schools, but some Afghans so desperately wanted to educate their daughters that they established makeshift pop-up classrooms in private basements. The father of the house greeted us at the door. Because there were young women inside, Mohammed was prohibited from entering, but the father led me through three rooms where young female teachers held classes in cavelike spaces for swarms of colorfully swaddled girls—in greens and purples and oranges—from the surrounding villages. One teacher, no more than twenty-five years old, held a baby in her arms as she conducted a lesson with one chalkboard and some handwritten posters. The children sat on a dirt floor. Only a handful had books.

The children seemed surprised by the sight of a foreigner; the teachers, I suspected, were stunned that a foreigner would take the risks I was taking. I was still afraid, too. I managed to take out the camera concealed in my bag but could barely get off a decent shot. Half of my pictures were out of focus.

We headed out again through the countryside, then up a narrow road carved into rock-spattered mountains until we reached a small plateau between two peaks. There was a pond of oddly still water and a silence that beckoned prayer. Mohammed and our driver had forgone prayer all morning and had twitched anxiously as we drove. Before Mohammed began to pray, I dredged up the courage to ask if I could photograph him. He agreed. I was happy to watch them in the open air going through the graceful motions of their devotion. Mohammed looked so serene as he stood against the backdrop of sharp mountains and a crisp sky and began his prayer, raising his thumbs to his ears. We were far from the Taliban's grip here. From then on, I knew to search for moments like that—more intimate, more private, when Afghans were so enveloped in thought that they forgot to worry about whether the Taliban might be lingering nearby. We drove again, and I watched the sandy brown mountains fold like rumpled bedsheets into layers of vegetation, and clay houses fade into the land.

On our fourth day we arrived at Mohammed's home late in the afternoon, when the light was a velvety gold and the sun cast long shadows along the snaking road. I had been curious about his family. We entered his sparsely furnished home, and no one greeted me. The women lowered their eyes, and out of respect the men barely acknowledged my presence, except for the common polite greeting of placing the right hand on one's chest with a slight bow forward. Mohammed walked me across the outdoor courtyard and up three stairs to my room, then disappeared. I knew it would have been improper for me to go out into his home and try to communicate with his family. Earlier he had made it clear that he didn't feel comfortable with me photographing "his" women. It was as if he were scared to take me on a tour of the house, as if I would sneak photos anyway.

Yet his nieces and nephews, sons and daughters, and eventually even his wife peered into my bedroom window from the courtyard and stared at me. I motioned to them to enter, thinking it was a futile effort; nothing could break a barrier constructed by years of humility and privacy. Finally a girl in her early teens with big-boned, dirty hands barged in to greet me and extended her hand. Without a shared language, the conversation ended with the handshake. I felt like a terminally ill patient, quarantined to a room where people just come and stare through the glass and pity me.

It had been a mere four days since I'd arrived, and I wondered what the world had been doing since I'd left it. Afghanistan hid in a time capsule of war. Many Afghans had no idea how the rest of the world had advanced technologically. There were no foreign newspapers; there was no television news, and very little electricity, for that matter. I felt claustrophobic. Anxious. I hadn't bathed once, and the stench of my sweat—a layer of filth—seeped through my clothes. I missed my dawn runs through Lodhi Gardens in New Delhi, passing the rotund Indians fixed in yoga poses. I missed my swims at the American Club and a frothy, cold beer at the end of the day at the Foreign Correspondents' Club. I missed all the things I hadn't realized I had grown to love. The things I hadn't even been aware of before. Like my freedom.

But as I stretched out on the thin mattress, I also considered the benefits of being a female guest in Afghanistan. I would always have my own room—this one was a big, carpeted, empty space with a huge bay window—separate from the men. I did not think about my appearance, or looking sexy, or male-female attraction. In America I expended an incredible amount of energy on things that in Afghanistan seemed vain if not pointless, and it was refreshing to submerge myself in an unfamiliar perspective and ideology, to assimilate in both mind and dress.

In fact, during the last few days, as I walked through the streets and into people's homes, I had started to welcome the cover and anonymity of the thick cloth I wore draped over my head and around my shoulders. I understood the urgency of wanting to be covered at all times. As I awoke the next morning and prepared for my day, I realized that I had even grown to appreciate the constant presence of my *mahram*, the unfamiliar peace I found when I surrendered control to Mohammed, to our driver, to a man.

KABUL WAS GRAY and lonely in June 2000. Its monolithic, graceless buildings, as well as its aura of paranoia, betrayed Afghanistan's heavy

Soviet influence. Parts of the city looked as if they'd been half-buried beneath a giant dust storm: Hills of dirt faded into rusting cars, which faded into the broken clay buildings. The mood starkly contrasted with the lively, sun-dappled countryside villages that had been relatively free from the Taliban's watch. In Kabul everyone was cautious of where he stepped and with whom he spoke. The United Nations workers— typically Afghans, Pakistanis, or people from other Muslim countries— were welcoming inside the UN compound, but I rarely saw them outside on the streets of Kabul. Locals avoided conversation with foreigners entirely in public.

I finally had to face the Taliban at the Foreign Ministry, where foreign journalists were required to check in upon entering the country. This was the Afghanistan I had been warned about. Everything I wanted to do had to be approved with a letter handwritten in Dari, stamped by the government ministry responsible for the issue I was covering, and signed by a man named Mr. Faiz.

In the ministry compound prepubescent boys with layered turbans stacked on their heads sashayed in and out of the high-ceilinged building. I waited for two hours, drinking sugary tea and improving my chances of developing diabetes. Once nervous about the prospect of meeting a Talib, I now knew the rules. By the time Mr. Faiz called me in, my nervousness had disappeared.

He was a burly press minister no more than twenty-eight years old, wearing the customary turban and beard. He welcomed me to his country. Our words ricocheted off the twenty-foot-high ceiling. Intricate patterns danced on the tattered carpet beneath our feet. I thought of the men and women who were shot and stoned to death for adultery and murder in the soccer stadiums across Afghanistan on Fridays.

"Thank you," I said, eyes lowered. "It is an honor to have the opportunity to come here. To see Afghanistan with my own eyes. I am doing a story on the effect of twenty years of war on Afghanistan."

I did not mention that I had already spent almost a week in the provinces of Ghazni, Logar, and Wardak and that I had spent several nights in the homes of warm, generous Afghans who all reinforced my belief that Afghanistan was much more than a terrorist state governed by unruly, women-hating Taliban, as much of the media portrayed it.

"Your country is beautiful, Mr. Faiz. I am grateful you approved my visa."

Through an interpreter, Mr. Faiz and I discussed what I was interested in seeing in Kabul. He showered me with questions about my background and intentions, each one eliciting a purposeful response from me. I thought I had won him over.

"I want you to move from where you are staying at the Associated Press house," he said, "to the Intercontinental Hotel."

THE INFAMOUS INTERCONTINENTAL was where most foreign correspondents met their dreaded fate: isolation and scrutiny by loitering and watchful Talibs who gathered in front of the hotel. High on a hill overlooking the city, the Intercontinental was the one hotel still functioning in the city, and the Foreign Ministry racked up large sums of money from the few foreigners, many of them journalists, who passed through Kabul and were sent there.

The lights flickered and the lobby remained dark most of the time. The elevator did not run during the day. A chipped enamel plaque announced the directions to the pool and the spa—a harsh joke for those who remembered a time when visitors could actually wear bathing suits. Stores sat eternally locked in the lobby, their interiors lined with dust. Half the hotel had been destroyed by repeated rocket attacks during fighting between mujahideen factions, leaving one side partially collapsed, though no one paid attention to the rubble. Only the bookstore and a restaurant stayed open to serve the few guests. There wasn't a single other guest while I was there.

I browsed the bookstore and found a tattered 1970s edition of Ernest

Hemingway's *Islands in the Stream*, George Orwell's Penguin Classics, inaccurate histories of Afghanistan, and glowing chronicles of the Taliban movement. There were a couple of discarded books from departing guests in German, French, Italian, and Russian, along with a few English-Urdu and "Learn Dari in a Day" handbooks for ambitious journalists who thought they might actually get that much access to local Afghans without a guide. Later the same bookseller grew confident with me and offered up an entire selection of books banned by the Taliban—his secret stash.

I returned to my room, disheartened by the prospect of reading as my sole option to pass the time until I fell sleep. Everything was silent. I took off my clothes and stood naked on the balcony of my lonely room, under the stars. A woman. Naked. Outside. Under the Taliban. Definitely grounds for a public execution at the soccer stadium on a Friday. But I couldn't resist. The air was chilly. We were hours deep into the public curfew across the city, and people were at home, asleep, dreaming of or dreading sunrise.

I crawled into bed and stared at my meager collection of books.

OVER THE NEXT WEEK I managed to visit a women's hospital and a neighborhood bombed out by the Soviets and widows begging for money on the street. I shot fully clothed women in labor hitched up on rusting old-fashioned gynecological chairs, and Afghans traipsing through the postwar rubble. When I stopped the car where begging widows crouched all day, they got up and swarmed the window, thinking I had money. Dirt and poverty had faded their brilliant blue burqas into a sad powdery gray.

On one of my last days there, I visited with a Sudanese woman named Anisa, who ran the main UNHCR office in Kabul and had been living in Afghanistan for several years. I was relieved to see her, sitting behind a grand desk in a bare-bones office. I had been craving the presence of a female with whom I shared at least a few cultural references.

Anisa took me to a middle-class neighborhood on the outskirts of Kabul. Four women greeted us at the door. The front of their blue burqas had been slung back over their heads, revealing angular features, fair skin, and striking blue eyes. They all wore floral skirts. Their white patent-leather pumps were lined up at the door. It still surprised me to see an actual living being under the tomblike burqa. They smiled warmly and excitedly ushered us inside their modest clay home, wicker baskets and pink-and-green-embroidered sheets hanging on the walls, lacy curtains fluttering by windows covered in wax paper.

The UN had secretly hired the women to teach vocational skills—knitting, sewing, weaving—to widows and poor mothers in their neighborhood. They sat on the floor and, over the requisite tea and biscuits, began to talk. They were nothing like the women of the countryside; they were educated and had held jobs in government ministries before the Taliban came into power. They were frustrated with the restrictions on their freedoms, which, among other things, prohibited them from working outside the home.

"Before, our capital was destroyed," one of the women explained. "The Taliban has rebuilt our capital. In each house in Afghanistan, though, the women are the poorest of the family. The only thing they think of is how to feed their children. Now the men are also facing problems like the women. They are beaten in the streets if their beards are not long enough, thrown in prison for not praying. It is not only the women who suffer," she said.

"Wearing a burqa is not a problem," another said. "It is not being able to work that is the problem."

Everything they said surprised me. It had been naïve of me to think that, given all the repression women in Afghanistan were facing—their inability to work or get an education—wearing a burqa would be high on their list of complaints. To them, the burqa was a superficial barrier, a physical means of cloaking the body, not the mind.

The women also put my life of privilege, opportunity, independence, and freedom into perspective. As an American woman, I was spoiled: to work, to make decisions, to be independent, to have relationships with men, to feel sexy, to fall in love, to fall out of love, to travel. I was only twenty-six, and I had already enjoyed a lifetime of new experiences.

THE DAY BEFORE I left Kabul, I returned to the Foreign Ministry to get my exit visa from Mr. Faiz.

"Welcome," Mr. Faiz said, gesturing for me to sit. "How was your trip? What are your impressions of our country?"

I thought of Mohammed from the visa office, the working city women stuck at home, the widows in the countryside, the maternity hospital with its ghastly conditions. Mr. Faiz, in his grand office at the Foreign Ministry in Kabul, represented everything millions of women across the world have fought. In Afghanistan the Taliban granted me license to see and to do things no Afghan woman had permission to do since they took control: partake in meals and in conversations with men outside of their families, go without a burqa, work. But perhaps there were many women in Afghanistan happy with how they lived: their days spent baking bread in the countryside and caring for their families in the crisp, clean Afghan air. My own life choices must have been equally as confounding to people like Mr. Faiz.

"Mr. Faiz," I said, "I love your country. I only wish Taliban rules permitted foreigners like myself to openly engage in conversation with the locals. It is very difficult for me, and for journalists, to visit Afghanistan and have anything positive to write about, given such restrictions on our interaction with the Afghans." Mr. Faiz, of course, didn't know I had broken their rules by meeting with some Afghans on my own. "It is a culture renowned for its hospitality and warmth."

"I understand," he said.

I looked down at the last sip of room-temperature green tea in my china cup and felt oddly comfortable. I didn't want the moment to end.

"It is not time yet. When we are ready to have you meet with our women and our people, we will definitely invite you in."

I smiled, and as our eyes met Mr. Faiz did not look away. I finished the last cup of tea, and as I left I pulled my chador tightly around my head and neck, making sure it wouldn't slip from my hairline in the wind.

I returned to Afghanistan twice in the next year. Between trips I found a photo agency willing to distribute my work. But for a long time no newspaper or magazine bought them. In the year 2000 no one in New York was interested in Afghanistan.

CHAPTER 3

We Are at War

I returned to New Delhi and kept shooting, traveling throughout India, Afghanistan, Pakistan, and Nepal, focusing on human rights and women's issues. Marion and I fueled each other with story ideas and motivated each other when we were tired or frustrated or in a rut. It was also easier for us to get assignments as a team, so when Marion decided to move to Mexico in late 2000—because she had always wanted to live in Latin America, and she and John had broken up—I did, too. It was on to the next adventure.

I never considered going back to live in New York and didn't even stop home to see my family. By the time I finished college, my family had scattered across the country. My sister Lauren moved to New Mexico to paint when I was still in high school. Lesley moved to Los Angeles to work for Walt Disney when I was in college, and Lisa followed a few years later to write movies with her partner. Christmas became our time to gather as a family, a reunion we all looked forward to.

We remained close despite the geographical distance, but life abroad had its costs. While I was in India, my sister Lauren's first husband was diagnosed with lung cancer and died thirty days later. I never got to say good-bye to him or comfort her. That same year my mother was in a car accident that left her unconscious for three days; my family chose not to tell me, because I was far away and there was nothing I could do. I often lived with an aching emptiness inside me. I learned early on that living a world away meant I would have to work harder to stay close to the people I loved.

MEXICO CITY was about to empty out for a holiday weekend. El Distrito Federal, or el D.F., as Mexicans called the capital city, was a sprawling mass of concrete blocks, intricately designed bronze statues, and colonial-era buildings, some bereft of character, others lovely Latin American haciendas. A thick haze of pollution formed a perpetual milky umbrella over the city; cars, especially lime-green Volkswagen Bug taxis, choked the wide avenues. The DF's sprawl and chaos was intimidating, uninviting.

Marion already had a new boyfriend, a professional mountain biker who led tours through the countryside for semiprofessional mountain bikers. On Easter weekend, they were going to the nearby state of Veracruz, and I suggested that Marion and I go along with them. I was a tomboy growing up and didn't think it could be that hard to ride a bike. From the town of Papantla de Olarte, a dozen of us set off through countryside lush with the yellow flowers of vanilla plants. The first time I hit the front brakes at top speed, I flew over the handlebars.

I decided to spend the rest of my weekend riding in the support van. A young Mexican man with a thick mess of brown hair named Uxval was one of the guides. He spoke Spanish, English, Italian, and just enough of every other language to be able to charm women around the world. He was engaged to be married, but there was an uncomfortable chemistry between us immediately. Like most mama's boys, he was strategically in touch with his feminine side. Everything about his

personality was deliberate. When we said good-bye, I wished him well
with his marriage.

Two days later he called and asked if he could come by the apartment I shared with two American roommates. I gave him my address,
and he arrived within a few hours. He walked in the door and pulled me
close and kissed me. We stood there embracing for what seemed like
hours, and when we stopped, he turned around to leave.

"I just had to do that before I did anything else," he said and walked
out the door.

Uxval broke off his engagement with his fiancée that night. I was
apprehensive about getting involved with someone who would break
an engagement over a gut attraction to a relative stranger, but I was
attracted to his decisiveness. A few years earlier my grandmother Nina
sat me down at her kitchen table in Hamden, Connecticut, to talk about
love. I had just broken up with Miguel, who was reserved and passive,
and I was at that tender age when decisions about love and life seemed
somehow intertwined, when the questions of whom to love and what
profession to choose seemed essentially the same question: How do you
want to live? "I'll tell you a secret," she said coyly, as if she were going
to tell me that she and my grandfather French-kissed before they were
married. What she told me would stay with me for life.

"I used to go with this fellow, Sal," she said. "Years ago Sal would
pick me up from work and walk me home to my doorstep. We used to
sit on the concrete steps for hours on Sherman Avenue. We would walk
from Sherman to Chapel Street to pass the time and see the shows, the
Paramount, you know. He was funny and spontaneous, and back then
there was nothing to do but walk and go to the theater for twenty-five
cents. He made me laugh, and he would grab me and kiss me all the
time. But he didn't have a pot to piss in. He had no money. He was a
hard worker. He worked long, long hours and helped his mother out
taking care of his brothers and sisters. But he never had any money. No
future.

"We went our separate ways, and soon enough my friend Eleanor fell for him. She was crazy for him, and he liked her, too. He treated her real nice, and she was mad about him. She cooked for him all the time and tended to his every need. He was a hard worker. He always made sure that she was all right. I was already with Ernie.

"Don't get me wrong, your grandfather was a good provider. He was a good provider, and he trusted me with everything. I never had to show him the receipts from the grocery store. My sisters still do this with their husbands. Your grandfather gave me my freedom. He let me play cards on Quinnipiac Avenue and never told me I had to be back at a certain time. When his brothers came over, Ernie would sit at the table and watch us play. He didn't like to play, but he would sit and watch and talk with us.

"Eleanor and Sal were doing well. They stayed married right up until the end. I have no regrets. Your grandfather can be a little distant, but he is a good man. I hear Eleanor has Alzheimer's disease, and it gets progressively worse. I say, 'You know, Ernie, I think I will call Sal to tell him I am sorry about his wife—invite him by for coffee.' 'Sure,' Ernie says, not listening. So one day when your grandfather is at work, the doorbell rings. It is Sal. Eleanor is by now in a home, and he comes in. We talk, reminiscing of when we were sixteen years old, walking down the main boulevard in Hamden. I tell him I'm sorry about his wife, and we finish our coffee. He's on the way to the hospital. I walk him to the front door, and in the foyer before we reach the door Sal grabs me. He grabs me and kisses me like I haven't been kissed since those golden days when he would walk me home from work down the main boulevard. 'I have been waiting over fifty years to do that, Antoinette,' he says. 'I know,' I said, and I walked him out.

"His wife died three days later, and I didn't call him. I felt funny. Before a kiss I could reach out without the slightest bit of tension. It all ended with a kiss. Even a phone call was too much.

"But you know," Nina said to me, "I had forgotten the passion of a kiss like that. When a man grabs you and kisses you like he means it. It felt good. Don't get me wrong, your grandfather is a hard worker, and a good provider, but it was nice. What would it have been like? All those years with passion? I cook, and Ernie doesn't eat. I say, 'Ern, let's have coffee,' and he drinks it, but he'll never ask. We drive home from the doctor's, and I say, 'Ern, let's stop and get a cup of coffee at Dunkin Donuts.' He says we can drink it at home."

I never forgot that story. And I never wanted to regret the kisses I missed.

THERE WAS A LIGHTNESS and spontaneity and romance to my relationship with Uxval, something I'd never felt before. When I wasn't on assignment outside Mexico City, we slept in late until we couldn't possibly stay in bed any longer, or went for long walks, or loaded our mountain bikes onto his car and rode them up the steep, treacherous hill to La Virgen, a giant statue of the Virgin of Guadalupe. I loved him painfully and did anything to please him, even if it meant learning to ride a mountain bike fifteen miles uphill twice a week.

The only thing I could not give him was my photography. I was publishing pictures on the front pages of newspapers, but I had so much more I wanted to accomplish: to immerse myself in longer assignments, to work for magazines, to start shooting regularly for the *New York Times*. I wanted people to recognize my photographs, to be affected by my work—just as I had felt looking at Salgado's work in Argentina. This was just the beginning. I hadn't even set foot in Africa! The more I worked, the more I achieved, the more I wanted.

Photography drew me away from Uxval like a lover, and this was a simmering source of tension between us. Each time the phone rang he pulled away, protecting himself from my inevitable departure. He knew he couldn't ask me to forgo my work. There was no way to do my job without traveling, without physically being away from home. I never said no to an assignment—not ever.

One morning in September, as Uxval and I lingered in bed, my roommate Michael banged on my bedroom door. I knew something was amiss—none of us would ever deliberately wake the others in the morning, and rarely did anything in Mexico City require urgency. We didn't have a television with cable, so we darted up the stairs to Marion's apartment. I sat down in front of her television and saw the Twin Towers on fire. Half-asleep, I didn't realize the planes had smashed into them on purpose.

People were jumping. My mind flashed to the women in wedding gowns I had once photographed on the roof of the World Trade Center for the annual wedding marathons on Valentine's Day, where young couples, radiant with love, steeled themselves in the wind tunnel on top of the world, the brides clinging to their veils. I started crying.

Michael broke the silence. "You know what this means?"

I didn't.

"We are at war."

We spent the entire day glued to Marion's television. The words "Afghanistan," "training camps," "terrorists," and "Taliban" started getting thrown around by news anchors, analysts, and politicians. I felt the familiar knot of excitement and dread in my stomach: I would have to leave again for South Asia. I would have to leave Uxval. The story was taking root in Afghanistan and in neighboring Pakistan, and they were countries I knew.

Michael was a journalist, too, and understood what September 11 meant for me. "So when are you flying to Pakistan?" he asked.

I needed to call SABA, my photo agency, and offer to go to Pakistan. I had watched the most historic event of my lifetime on a borrowed television set in Mexico City, and I wasn't about to miss the second half of the story.

"I have to leave," Uxval said flatly, and with an uncharacteristic peck on the cheek, he left Marion's apartment, left me sitting in front of the TV, left me transfixed, as I had been since the early morning.

I hated myself for being so driven. I wanted to plead with him to stay, but I needed to concentrate. I had calls to make. All flights into New York City were canceled, and I had to figure out how to get to New York and to Pakistan. Though I was young and terribly inexperienced, few photographers had worked in Afghanistan under the Taliban as I had. I wasn't considering that I might be going to war but was instead worrying about what would happen to the civilians, to the women I had photographed sequestered in their homes in Kabul, Ghazni, and Logar.

This was the first time I had to decide between my personal and professional lives. Some part of me knew, or hoped, that real love should complement my work, not take away from it.

PART TWO

The 9/11 Years

PAKISTAN,

AFGHANISTAN,

IRAQ

CHAPTER 4

You, American, Are Not Welcome Here Anymore

I landed in New York on September 14 and went directly to Ground Zero. There was nothing left of the towers but mangled steel and ash, lines of solemn people clutching their palms to their mouths as they gasped in horror, and countless posters in search of the missing. I was devastated; New York was home. I chastised myself for not being there to cover one of the defining moments of my lifetime. The geopolitics of my generation changed with September 11; in the media Latin America was forgotten.

I raced up to Union Square to SABA, my photo agency. Marcel, my agent, offered to split the cost of the flight to Pakistan with me, and we booked my ticket to Islamabad. He then handed me a giant Canon digital camera, the first digital camera I had ever seen, along with the manual.

"You shoot Nikon, right?" Marcel asked.

"Yes. All my life," I said.

"Great. Well, Canon has the best digital camera on the market, and you will need digital to file to newspapers and magazines from Pakistan. Here is the manual and one wide-angle lens for the Canon. Learn how to use the camera during the flight."

My adrenaline surged. Uxval, Mexico, the mountain bikes, the kisses, the long lunches during the week—they were all tucked away in what was becoming the giant filing cabinet in my mind.

BY THE TIME I arrived in the hostile Pakistani city of Peshawar, dozens of journalists had already checked into its few hotels. It was September 21. Peshawar was a dusty, ominous border city—teeming with suspicious-looking, bearded men, CIA agents, and Pakistani intelligence—thirty-five miles from the border with Afghanistan. Every place in public view was conspicuously bereft of women; only the occasional white, black, or sky-blue burqa skated ghostlike through the narrow alleys. It was the type of place where everyone constantly looked over his shoulder. We all knew that the United States was going to retaliate for the attacks on the World Trade Center and the Pentagon, and we wanted to position ourselves close enough to Afghanistan so that when the borders collapsed, as they inevitably do in the chaos of an invasion, we could all rush in to report on the ground. So much of the buildup to the war in Afghanistan was a mystery to me, but it was familiar territory to my more seasoned colleagues. Were we about to have another Vietnam, with a ground war and American troops dug into trenches? Or would it be all fighter jets dropping bombs from on high? I had no idea. But I loved being close to the center.

I shared a room at the run-down, medium-sized Green's Hotel with Alyssa Banta, a Filipina-Mexican-American photographer in her midthirties from Fort Worth, Texas. Older journalists with bigger expense accounts stayed at the posh Pearl Continental Hotel. Faces I had seen only on TV darted through the lobby, striding with purpose, trailed by their enormous production crews, through the atrium courtyard. Famous writers hovered over computers in a makeshift newsroom. Alyssa and I were undoubtedly two of the least experienced "war" photographers there, but the opportunities to shoot were diverse. America had become obsessed with Islam overnight. Anything that shed light on the religion that allegedly fueled the attacks against America made the front page. Editors suddenly found news value in the Taliban, in the plight of Pakistani women, in Afghan refugees living in Pakistan—all stories I had done while living in India.

It was in Peshawar that I got my big break: freelancing, or being put on rotation, for the *New York Times* on a huge news story.

It was my proximity to the action that got me the job. When a big story broke, the *Times* would parachute in their top staff correspondents and photographers to report, but photographers were also often hired on a freelance basis. If there wasn't already a staff photographer on the ground, the photo editor would have to scramble, and so those initial hours of a breaking news story were crucial for a freelance photographer. You had to be in the right place, and available by phone or e-mail at that moment. You had to say yes.

I knew I had one chance with the *Times* to prove myself a strong choice to cover the mood in Pakistan before the war. Not only did I have to make compelling images, but I also had to coordinate them with the *Times* staff reporters. *New York Times* journalists were always on deadline, always overwhelmed, always stressed out. No matter how much they pretended they didn't care about landing a story on the front page, all *Times* correspondents fought hard to "front." They were competitive with journalists from other newspapers, even more brutal with one another. And almost no one had time to be bothered by a photographer. Instead I often had to intuit the story of the day on my own. I got up before dawn; I went to bed at midnight. I worked every waking hour so that I could be at the right place at the right time.

I also made sure I used every advantage I had. I knew from my time in Afghanistan that I had a unique kind of access. I used my gender to get inside the women's madrassas (religious schools) to interview and photograph the most devout Pakistani women. Before I shot a single image, I spoke with them at length about their political and religious beliefs. It was the first time I witnessed open hatred toward the United States, toward my government and its policies governing international affairs. The women were proud of the September 11 attacks and voiced no remorse for the innocent lives lost. They were sympathetic to the Taliban and their beliefs. They also rooted almost all their animosity in the Israeli-Palestinian conflict; to them, the attacks of September 11 were justified after years of American support for Israel and discriminatory policies against the Palestinians. Through these women I began to understand the depth of hatred this bias fostered across the Muslim world, and I wanted to explain this to readers still trying to make sense out of 9/11.

I also wanted to give readers a sense of Pakistani women's lives beyond religion. I knew that if the only image people saw in American publications was of women in head scarves and long black robes reading the Koran, it might be easier to dismiss their beliefs as something completely foreign and bizarre and specifically "Islamic." But if readers could get a sense of who these women really were—if they could see them in their homes, with their children, as they cooked meals—it might offer a more complete picture.

I became fascinated by the notion of dispelling stereotypes or misconceptions through photographs, of presenting the counterintuitive. In Pakistan I learned quickly to tuck away my own political beliefs while I worked and to act as a messenger and conduit of ideas for the people I photographed. This proved instructive for the future: While these women were the first to openly express hating my country, they were definitely not the last.

I was getting photographic material and access I wasn't seeing in other publications and decided to pitch my first story to the *New York*

Times Magazine—which was entirely separate from the newspaper, with a different set of editors. They accepted. It was another milestone for me: my first publication in a magazine, and one of the publications most renowned for powerful documentary spreads.

The period after September 11 gave young photographers who hustled—and who were willing to go to places like Pakistan and Afghanistan and eventually Iraq—an unparalleled opportunity to make a name for themselves. Those weeks in September launched an entire generation of journalists who would come of age during the War on Terror.

WE EDGED CLOSER TO THE INVASION. Ordinary Pakistanis, loyal to their Muslim brothers across the border, began sneering at us, the infidel journalists, and staging protests in the streets. Men doused effigies of President Bush in kerosene and ignited their lighters, screaming, "Down, down America." I was caught up in the middle of these protests, cloaked in my tentlike chador, one of few women among the men.

One day I went to one of these demonstrations with a handful of my male colleagues. Though I was dressed as a Muslim—respectfully, with not a strand of hair showing—the Pakistanis knew I was a foreign woman simply because I was carrying a camera, working, trespassing in a man's world. To them, that was enough to merit a quick feel on any part of my body. They perceived foreign women based on what they saw in movies, often porn movies: easy and available for sex. I tried not to make a scene in front of my peers. I didn't want my gender to determine whether or not I could cover breaking news, so I continued photographing, ignoring the sweeping of hands on my butt, the occasional grab.

Once President Bush went up in flames, my colleagues were nowhere to be found. I tried to focus on shooting, but this time there were not a few hands on my butt but dozens. And this time it wasn't a subtle feel but an aggressive, wide-handed clutch, butt to crotch, back to front. I kept shooting. A combative Western woman would elicit terrible anger from these men. I tried holding my camera with one hand and swatting them with the other. It didn't work. I tried turning around, looking the men in the eye and saying "Haram," which means "forbidden, sinful, shameful," to show them I understood that their actions were unacceptable in Islam.

It didn't work. Adrenaline was raging all around me, adrenaline of hundreds of unmarried, sexually frustrated men who had no work and little education. They hated the West for America's policies in their region, even more so for the war that was about to happen. Effigies burned around me. The masses screamed, "Down with America!" I had fifteen hands on my butt. I paused, lowered my camera with its beast of a lens— about five pounds and twelve inches long—and waited for the next hand.

The second I felt something, I did a karate back-kick I'd learned in middle school.

I turned around, "*Haram!* Don't you have sisters? Mothers? Aren't you Pakistani men Muslim? Would you allow another man to treat your sister or mother like this?"

And I whacked the man directly behind me over the head with my lens. His eyes rolled back in their sockets, and he staggered.

The men around me suddenly stopped and stared.

I didn't wait to find out what happened to him; instead I sprinted back to the car, where I found my male colleagues, lounging, all of them smitten with their afternoon's work, checking the backs of their digital cameras for their prizewinning photographs, completely oblivious to what I had gone through to compose even one frame.

THE PAKISTANI GOVERNMENT BEGAN monitoring our movements closely. At Green's Hotel the cluster of journalists sat around discussing the possibility of being attacked by fundamentalists or Taliban sympathizers in the middle of the night. It was terrifyingly thrilling. A few of us prowled the hotel looking for escape routes: back doors, the roof, our bedroom windows. I wondered about young, curious Mohammed from the embassy. Was he back in Afghanistan? Was he fighting?

Alyssa was wide-eyed and manic, convinced the Taliban were coming any minute. She chose the ledge outside our window as our escape route; if they came, she said, we would crawl along the narrow ledge and jump to the next building only a few feet over.

It wasn't enough, we thought; we need a disguise. We enlisted the help of our female Pakistani interpreter and went to the market to buy blue burqas and the golden, rubbery shoes worn by Afghan refugees in the camps. Our interpreter explained that there was an art to walking in a burqa; we couldn't just rely on the giant blue sheath to disguise us. She gave us a lesson in burqa walking. In our cramped hotel room we donned our burqas, tight netting concealing our eyes, and walked back and forth, from wall to wall.

"Not so confident," she instructed. "Hunch your shoulders. Focus your eyes on the ground. You American women are too self-confident. Humble. Be humble."

She tried to strip away the self-confidence we had spent years building up. We pretended to climb onto the backs of trucks by climbing on and off the bed, our burqas tangling around our ankles, tripping us as we crumbled to the floor in fits of anxious laughter.

ON OCTOBER 6, the night before the United States bombed Afghanistan, I got an e-mail from Uxval. "I want a girlfriend in flesh and blood," it said, "not an Internet girlfriend."

My professional high crashed. I called him immediately.

"Please, Uxval," I begged in my mediocre Spanish, which failed me whenever I was upset. "I love you. I need to stay here just a few more weeks. The war is about to begin, and I will be home soon."

"No. *No quiero esperar más.*" (I don't want to wait anymore.) He had waited for three weeks. His voice was cold.

The telephone line crackled. Alyssa was sleeping, and I burrowed myself in the tiny bathroom with the stained toilet, pleading with him to wait for me.

"Please, my love. I am working for the *New York Times*! It is so important for my career to be here. A few weeks is nothing. Just give me a little more time."

He was resolute. "I want a girlfriend who is here with me every day. Not on e-mail or on the phone." He hung up.

I cried out loud, waking Alyssa with my sobs. "What happened?" she asked. "Is everything OK, baby?"

"Uxval just broke up with me." I felt stupid even uttering the words. We were about to go to war.

"Oh, baby, I am sorry. But don't worry about him . . ." she trailed off, half-asleep. "There will be others. If he can't understand your life now, it will only get worse."

THE UNITED STATES BEGAN its aerial bombing campaign in Afghanistan. None of the journalists in Peshawar tried to cross into Afghanistan at that point; as far as we knew, the Taliban still controlled the country. It would be suicide to go in until the Taliban fell. But we knew the fall of the Taliban was imminent.

The morning after the campaign started, I returned to the mosque where I had routinely visited and photographed Pakistan's women fundamentalists. From the moment I entered, I felt uneasy. As a journalist, I assumed I would be viewed as a neutral observer, not as a propagator of American actions overseas. But in the doorway of the mosque one of the women I had photographed said, "Please. The bombing has started.

The Americans are killing our Muslim brothers. You, American, are not welcome here anymore."

I soon went off my long-sought-after assignment for the *New York Times*, claiming I needed a break, and flew almost nine thousand miles back to Mexico City. My roommate Michael greeted me at the door of our apartment with a confused look.

"What are you doing here? Isn't the Taliban about to fall?"

"Uxval dumped me last week."

"*So?* You came home for *that?*"

I wanted to board the next flight back to Pakistan. I felt like an idiot. "Yes. I need to see him face-to-face."

I put my camera bag and luggage down in my room, put on my gym clothes, trudged over to my dismal, smelly gym, and got on the cheap stair-climber. I was so confused by what I had done. I was no longer heartbroken, no longer crying. For the first twenty-four hours after arriving in Mexico, I didn't even call Uxval.

He heard through friends that I was back and showed up at my door as if nothing had ever happened and picked me up and carried me directly to the bedroom.

Uxval had no idea what I had sacrificed professionally to fly home to win him back. His life was exactly as I had left it: working during the day, riding bikes in the afternoon, drinking icy beers at night. I wanted to hate him, but I was deeply in love with him. Less than a month later, on the morning of my twenty-eighth birthday, we watched the fall of Kabul on television in Mexico City, and I imagined all the journalists I had met in Peshawar scrambling over the border to get the story. I couldn't have been farther from the action. I wasn't sure whether I had made the right decision in flying back to Mexico—whether I wanted my personal life or my career to dictate the decisions I made, where I lived, and how I lived. But I knew that I felt unsettled, watching Kabul fall on the small TV we'd bought after the attacks of September 11. I was in the wrong place.

The Taliban's only remaining Afghan stronghold was in the southern part of the country, in Kandahar. As they had in Peshawar, journalists were now camping out in Quetta, the Pakistani city closest to Kandahar, so they could rush in after the Americans attacked. I called Marcel in New York and let him know I wanted to go back. The *New York Times Magazine* put me on assignment. I promised Uxval I wouldn't be gone long.

IN QUETTA a whole new group of about a hundred journalists was holed up in the incongruously luxurious five-star Serena Hotel, one of several hotels in South Asia built by the Aga Khan, the billionaire leader of an Islamic sect. We indulged in long breakfasts, visited the horrific Afghan refugee camps, and waited for the border to open.

Quetta was even creepier than Peshawar; there were no shops or places to walk around, and two cinemas showing American movies were attacked after the bombing started. Alcohol was banned, so we drank a lot of tea, occasionally swigging some smuggled whiskey out of water bottles. World-renowned photojournalists—everyone from Gilles Peress to Alexandra Boulat to Jerome Delay—stayed in rooms just down the hall from mine. I walked around starstruck and giddy.

One morning I was having breakfast and my phone rang. It was Uxval. My eyes lit up, and I stepped away from the table to spew my daily *Te quiero*s (I love yous) before heading out to work. When I sat back down at the table, Gilles Peress, who had covered Iran and Bosnia, among many other conflicts, looked at me, expressionless, and said, "Was that your boyfriend?"

Yes.

"Do you love him a lot?"

Yes.

"He will cheat on you one day." And he walked away.

I didn't believe him. I was still naïve then. Someday I would know what Gilles meant: that in this profession relationships ended in either infidelity or estrangement. A dual life was unsustainable.

EVERY JOURNALIST at the Serena wanted to be the first to get the news of the final fall of the Taliban in Kandahar. The competition put an extraordinary amount of pressure on all of us to take risks, and it was important to be cautious, to avoid running into heavily armed Taliban fighters as they fled or getting blown away by American air strikes that might mistake us for those Taliban fighters.

Our interpreters and drivers, who had sources inside Kandahar, kept us updated on the progress of the fighting; some journalists got intel from Washington. The camaraderie at the Serena disappeared. Photographers who had been sharing the next day's itinerary became cagey and private. Everyone thought he had some exclusive details that would get him to Kandahar first.

One night the Pakistani government locked the front gates of the Serena to keep the journalists from leaving for Afghanistan. In order to prevent getting trapped inside the hotel, a group of us from the *New York Times* snuck out and drove toward a house belonging to one of our fixers inside Quetta. After what seemed like fifty phone calls to the *Times*'s New York and Washington bureaus, and the Pentagon, we decided to cross the border for Kandahar.

Our mini convoy of cars passed through the same endless brown flatness I knew from my previous trips. I shared a car with another female photographer, Ruth Fremson, and a few male correspondents, but most of the ride was silent with the anxiety of the unknown. We didn't see any Afghans, any U.S. military. None of us knew whether the Taliban had fled. We hoped we would arrive in a liberated city, but it was hard to tell what had taken place: Afghanistan looks bombed out even when it hasn't been bombed.

Inside Kandahar it was anarchy. Teenage boys walked through

unpaved streets with rocket launchers and Kalashnikovs hanging from their necks like giant rock candy. The men—anti-Taliban or possibly former Talibs who had switched sides—wore stacked turbans, dark kohl around their eyes, and Kalashnikovs and necklaces of ammunition strung around their necks and backs. Everyone strutted around aimlessly, milling around boxy, low-hanging storefronts with dirty awnings flapping out front. I was familiar with Afghanistan—how it looked both biblical and lifeless—but somehow the destruction and the armed men all seemed more ominous now.

The *New York Times* crew found several floors' worth of rooms in a shady hotel above a bakery that dutifully churned out fresh bread several times a day. In war zones most journalists lived like nomads on a college campus: We shared rooms, meals, satellite phones, cables—anything and everything—and often moved around if a better room in a better location opened up. I had been sharing a room with Ruth, also on assignment for the *Times*, and I was grateful to have her as a role model: She was wise but not patronizing, started working before dawn and finished long past dusk. Every night she helped me file my pictures to New York on the satellite phone she set up in our room. Besides one other journalist who was staying at the same guesthouse, I don't remember any other women in Kandahar at all.

The *Times Magazine* correspondent I had been paired with decided to profile Gul Agha Shirzai, an anti-Taliban warlord helping the Americans, who had appointed himself the new governor of Kandahar. The fact that he, too, had killed a lot of people in his time was conveniently overlooked by his new American allies. I assumed that the writer and I would work as a team and that he would help secure access to the story for me, because writers generally want to have good pictures for their stories. We had originally been assigned to work together in Pakistan with the intention of carrying out whatever story he decided to write when we entered Afghanistan. But once there, things became visibly tense between the writer and me. Logistical resources like drivers and interpreters were limited, and we were forced to move around together, even though we had very different journalistic needs; he needed to do extensive, time-consuming interviews while I needed to be out among the people, photographing in the streets, documenting any visible remnants of the Taliban regime.

A few days after we entered Kandahar, we stood outside Mullah Omar's house, a vast compound belonging to the Taliban's spiritual leader. The buildings were pale yellow and riddled with pock marks, and American Special Forces sifted through what seemed like top-secret bags in the courtyard next to the mosque allegedly funded by Osama bin Laden. Afghan men milled about, watching the soldiers and then turning their attention toward me, slowly gathering to stare at the bare face of a foreign woman. I was a rare sight. Most of the troops were wearing '80s-style Ray-Bans and carrying big guns I wasn't yet familiar with as they combed through the remains of the house. I stood at a bit of a distance, photographing the troops, completely enveloped in the epic scene; the light was still soft. I was thrilled to finally be out of Pakistan and documenting a moment that felt like a significant part of history.

"Ma'am, could you please not take my picture?" one of the Special Forces asked, making me feel like a paparazzo in Kandahar, something I didn't think possible. "Ma'am . . . it is for our safety," he explained as he clenched his weapon and threw out phrases in Pashto (the language of most people in Southern Afghanistan) to the Afghan men around him. I looked at my reflection in his oblong shades and wondered how he could be more worried about his safety than mine—I was an unarmed American woman in Kandahar. I continued to photograph until I felt a tap on my shoulder.

It was my colleague, the writer, and his tone was abrasive. He wanted to know if I was finished yet, as if it bothered him I was upsetting the Special Forces. It was strange he would interrupt me in the middle of shooting in such a tense environment; it would never dawn on me to interrupt a writer in the middle of an interview in a similar scenario.

Then he told me we needed to split up. He said that it was too difficult to work together under the logistical constraints of having to share resources, and that as a woman I would ruin his access. After all, Afghanistan is a male-dominated, gender-segregated country, where women did not typically work or mix with men. He suggested we look for an additional driver/interpreter team to enable us to work separately—a difficult task during the fall of a regime.

With that, he walked away. I was bewildered. *How would I find another interpreter and driver at this point? All the reputable people had been scooped up already by our gang of invading journalists.*

My survival instinct kicked in. I asked one of the interpreters from the *Times* team to help me get into Gul Agha's mansion. He smiled. He knew the new governor well.

I was soon seated beside the burly Gul Agha and sharing *iftar*—the evening meal breaking the day's fast during Ramadan—with a bunch of male villagers who had definitely never shared a meal with a woman outside of their family. The whole mansion was carpeted and without furniture, and rows and rows of men from surrounding areas had come to break their fast with their new leader. They looked as if they had walked out of the tenth century, cloaked in turbans and capes, their kohl-laden eyes fixed on me as they ate. I stayed close to Gul Agha, unsure of my boundaries. He encouraged me to take pictures. I lifted my camera tentatively at first and photographed the sprawling table laid out on the tattered carpet as the men feasted.

When the correspondent entered, I was still seated beside the governor. He gave me a faint nod, and I felt triumphant. His presence also emboldened me to move around the room, to photograph Gul Agha surrounded by villagers in various states of postprandial repose. The photographs were intimate, a new window into the lives of the conquering warlords who declared themselves in charge and whom the

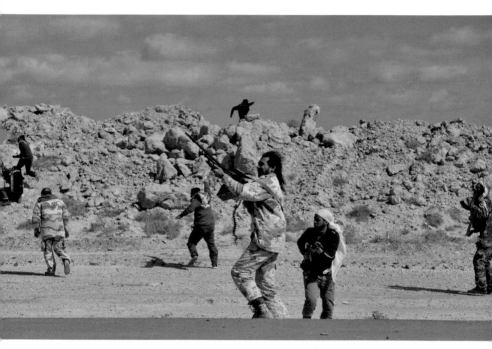

Opposition troops fire at a government helicopter as it sprays the area with machine-gun fire. The opposition was pushed back east, out of Bin Jawad toward Ras Lanuf, the day after taking Ras Lanuf back from troops loyal to Qaddafi in eastern Libya, March 6, 2011.

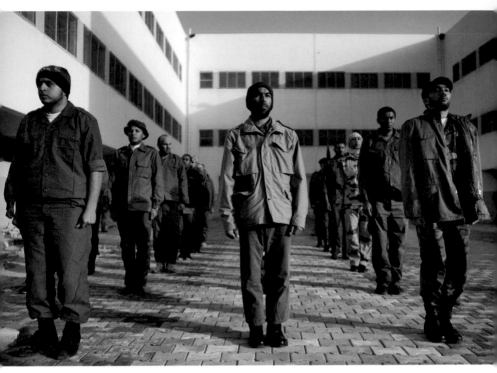

Rebels call for volunteers to fight in
Benghazi, March 1, 2011.

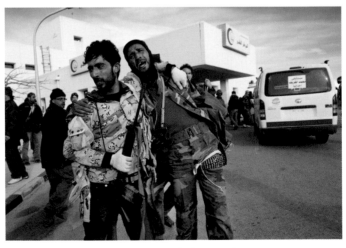

A rebel fighter consoles his wounded comrade
outside the hospital in Ras Lanuf, March 9, 2011.

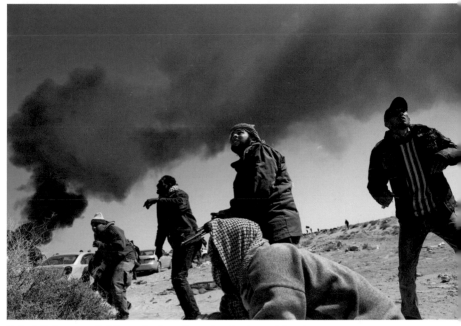

Rebel fighters and drivers look up into the sky in anticipation
of a bomb and incoming aircraft, March 10, 2011.

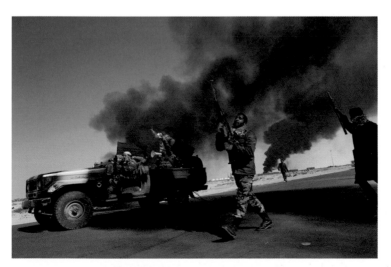

Rebel fighters push the front line forward on
a day of heavy fighting, 2011.

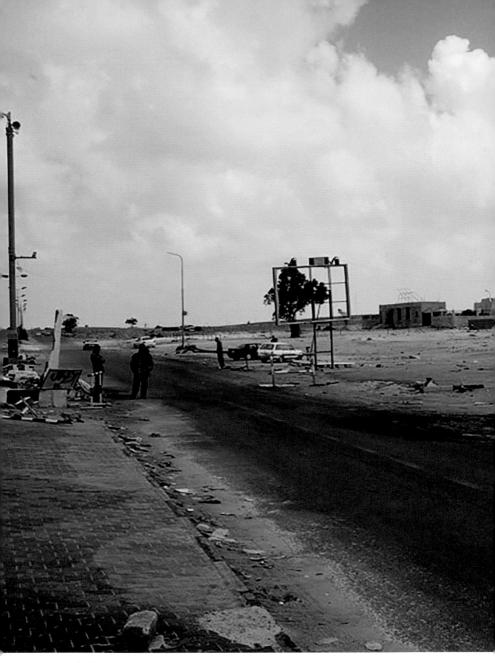

The location where we were taken,
photographed about one month later
by Bryan Denton for the *New York Times*.

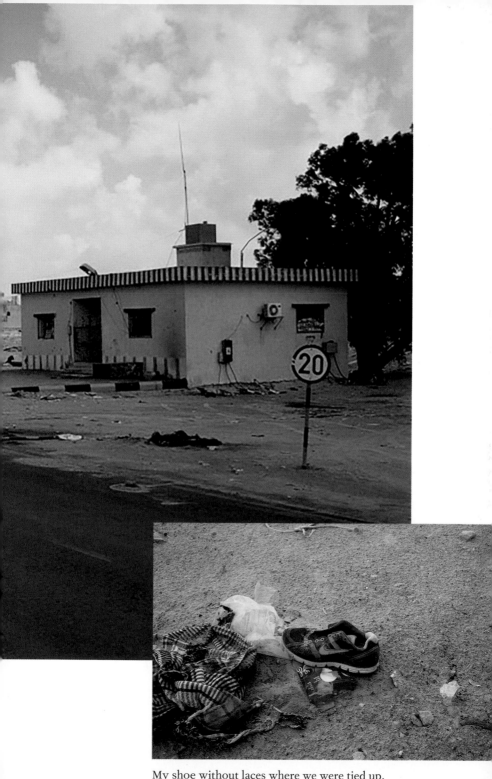

My shoe without laces where we were tied up.

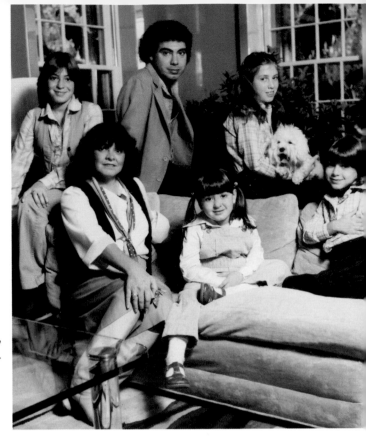

Family portrait,
circa 1976.

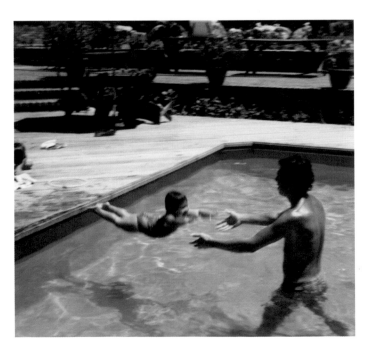

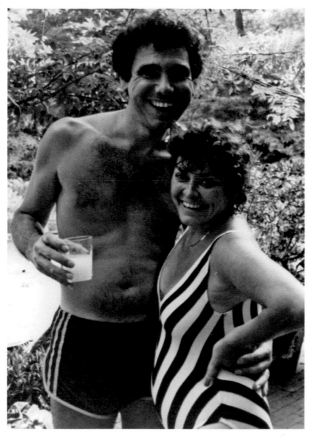

Phillip and Camille at one of the pool parties.

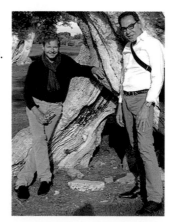

Bruce and Phillip.

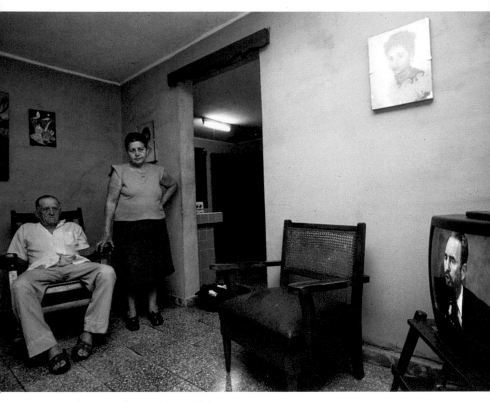

Cuban couple watching Fidel Castro
on TV at home, 1997.

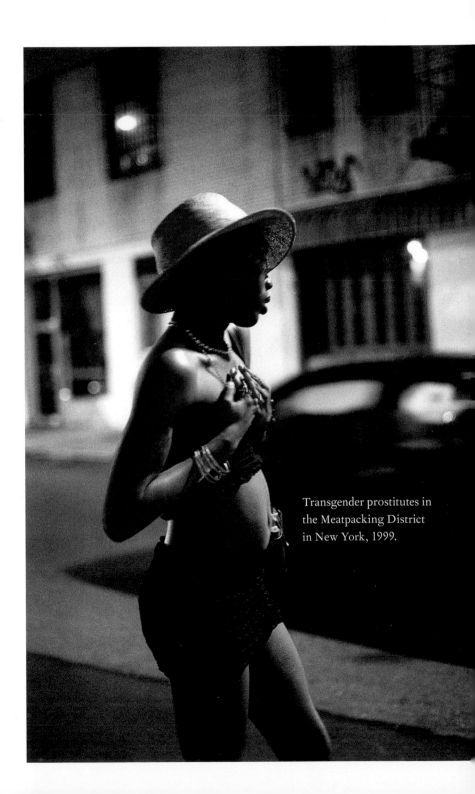

Transgender prostitutes in the Meatpacking District in New York, 1999.

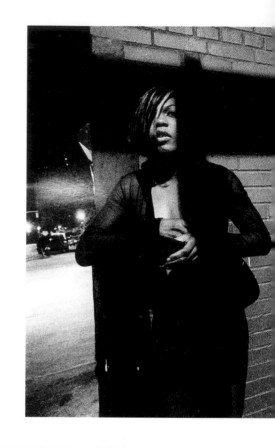

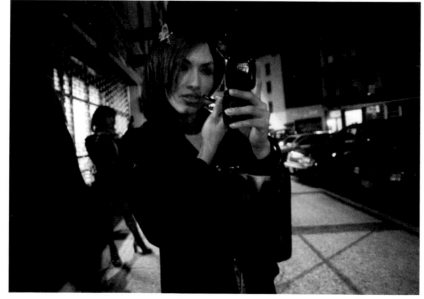

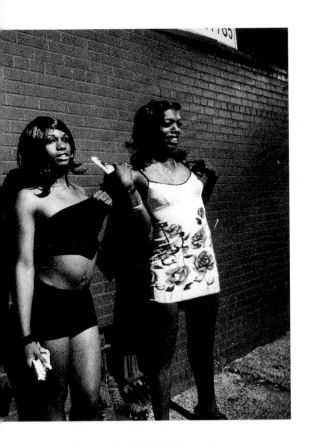

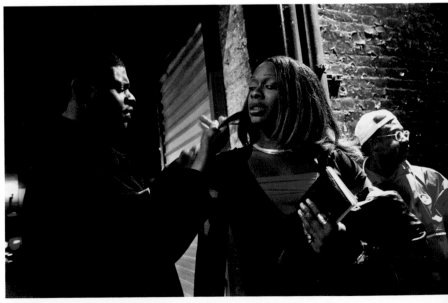

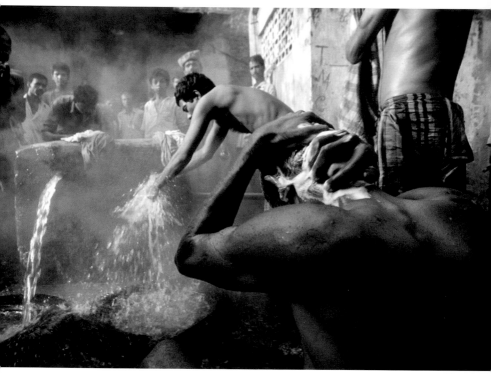

Indian men bathing on the streets
of Calcutta at dawn, 2000.

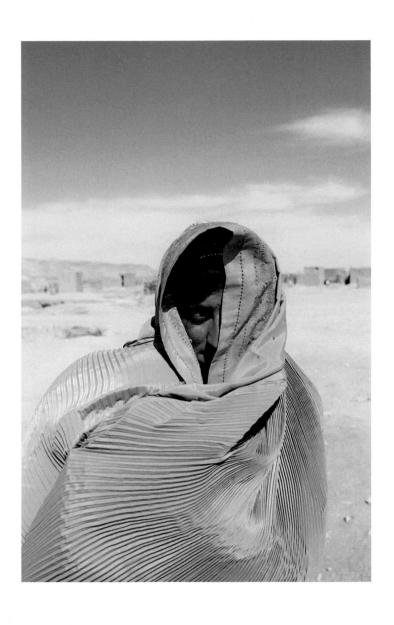

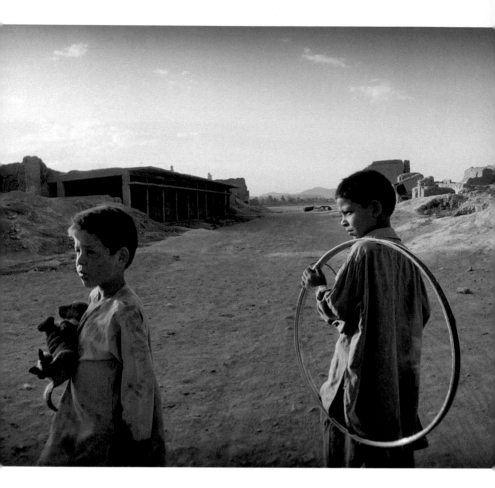

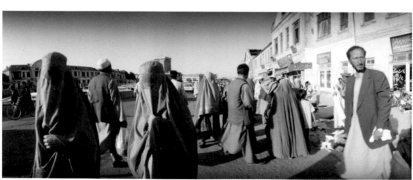

Scenes of Afghanistan while it was under
Taliban rule, May and July 2000.

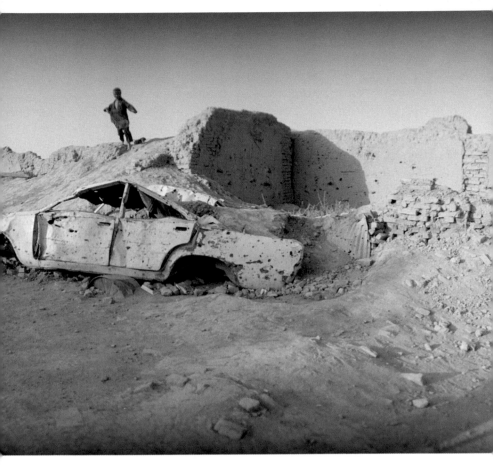

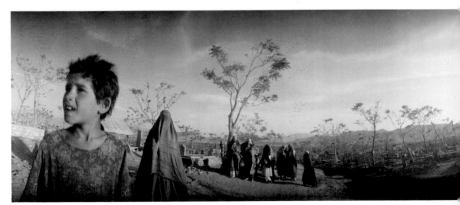

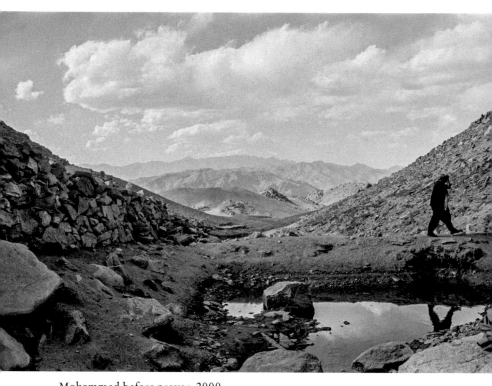

Mohammed before prayer, 2000.

Americans would eventually prop up. My editor was pleased with the candor of the images, knowing I was working under difficult conditions.

Several days later, as the city celebrated, dozens of men and boys gathered around speakers screaming Bollywood tunes that had been banned under the Taliban. It was Christmas, and I told my editors I wouldn't be able to stay on. It was time to go home to Uxval, my other life.

UXVAL PLANNED OUR CHRISTMAS VACATION in a beach village on the Oaxacan coast. Within seventy-two hours of leaving Afghanistan, where I had been swaddled in scarves and couldn't look men in the eye, I was wearing a bikini and kissing Uxval on the beach. After three weeks surrounded by thousands of refugees living in squalor in Pakistan and Afghanistan, I struggled to acclimate to the vapid world of partying Mexicans and Americans who smoked pot and drank beer all day and all night. Uxval had signed us up for surfing lessons. I was exhausted and weak from giardia, a nasty stomach ailment caused by unhygienic foods and water most probably tainted with feces, which caused constant diarrhea, burps of sulfur, weight loss, and days and nights of little sleep. But I had to step up and be a real girlfriend—an exciting, attentive, normal girlfriend—to make up for the weeks away.

I couldn't do it. I was unable to switch off my brain. I admired the lithe, smiling women, surfing effortlessly. They seemed so happy. At night I drank a few glasses of wine, and by eleven I went home to sleep. Uxval stayed out partying until dawn. I couldn't muster up the strength or desire to go out with people with whom I had little in common. By then most of my friends were photographers and journalists who shared my obsession with international politics, world events, and breaking news.

We started fighting. I was jealous of the women flitting around him. He was jealous of my job. We established a pattern of incredible romantic highs and tormented lows, where I saw an insecure side in myself

I hadn't even known existed. I knew I could never be the woman he needed. I feared this would be true for every man. My work would always come before everything else, because that was the *nature* of the work: When news broke, I had to go, and I wanted to. I knew that if I wasn't there when the story broke, another photographer would be.

My friends and family sometimes asked why photographers didn't just take fewer assignments to preserve their marriages or relationships, why they didn't simply become a different type of photographer, one who worked in some sunny studio adjacent to her home. The truth was, the difference between a studio photographer and a photojournalist was the same as the difference between a political cartoonist and an abstract painter; the only thing the two had in common was the blank page. The jobs entailed different talents and different desires. Leaving at the last minute, jumping on planes, feeling a responsibility to cover wars and famines and human rights crises *was my job*. Not doing those things was the same as a surgeon ducking out of an emergency operation or a waitress refusing to bring a customer's plates to the table. But I didn't have a boss who would glare at my inadequacies—who would fire me when the patient died or the customer complained. Neglecting any aspect of my job was like firing myself.

Even so, I always rushed home from trips to post-9/11 Afghanistan to keep Uxval happy. I shuttled from a Kabul mental hospital, where I saw naked women wandering through the garden and other women chained to the walls, to twenty-mile mountain-biking trips in Mexico, where we cooled ourselves in glittering streams. I tried to keep up, to love what he loved, to be the complete woman.

One night there was to be a meteor shower, and Uxval suggested we climb Iztaccíhuatl, a mountain outside Mexico City, to watch the stars fall out of the sky. The last thing on earth I wanted to do when I wasn't in Afghanistan, where I was climbing mountains for professional reasons, was to climb a mountain for fun, but of course I agreed. He excitedly packed the tent, our gear, and a stove and was ready in an hour.

We set out around noon and climbed twelve thousand feet. I could barely lift my legs. My temples ached. I had altitude sickness.

We stopped and set up our tent. Images from Peshawar, Quetta, and Kandahar flashed through my mind. All I wanted was to go back to South Asia on assignment for the *Times*. Around 1 a.m., Uxval roused me from a deep sleep and pulled me out of the tent into a bitter cold night. He held me in his arms, as the stars poured out of the weeping sky. I lived in that beautiful moment, not wanting to be anywhere else. But a few minutes later I was cold. My mind slipped back to the mountains of Afghanistan as we fell asleep.

IN THE FALL OF 2002, two months before my twenty-ninth birthday, on a Saturday morning in Mexico City, I sat down at my laptop. Yahoo! Mail was on the screen. There were dozens of messages from a woman named Cecilia with a similar subject line from the top to the bottom of the page: *te quiero, te quiero, te quiero*, the occasional *te extraño* (I miss you). I stared at the screen in disbelief. These proclamations of love were not for me. Uxval had inadvertently left his e-mail open on my laptop. The e-mails were to him from another woman. He was cheating on me.

My shock turned into sadness and then anger within an hour. I threw everything Uxval owned in garbage bags and put his belongings by the door with a note: "I know about Cecilia. You left your e-mail open on my laptop. Get all your stuff out of this apartment by the time I come home on Monday. Do not call me."

I couldn't eat for weeks. I forced myself to drink water and juice. My days ebbed into wide-awake nights. Depression was not something anyone in my family ever talked about, unless we were referring to friends or distant relatives. Now I couldn't get out of bed.

One sleepless night I remembered how wonderful the last year had been for my career: traveling back and forth to South Asia for the

Times, once my biggest dream, and working consistently with the paper's Mexico bureau chief; shooting stories for the *Boston Globe* and the *Houston Chronicle* with Marion. I had been so happy.

"You have your work," I told myself. I even said the words out loud to give me strength.

The next morning I called the foreign picture editor of the *New York Times* and asked if there was a region where she needed more freelance photographers. I explained that I had to leave Mexico City.

"OK, let me think about it," she said. "Give me a few days."

In the meantime I had dinner with Uxval's best friend. He told me Uxval had been cheating on me for months with this Cecilia of Yahoo.

"Who is she?" I asked him.

"She is a secretary for Telmex, the government telephone company."

I looked up. "Does she match her handbag to her shoes?"

She was predictable and present. I could never compete with a secretary who clocked in nine to five Monday through Friday, who had all her weekends free.

A few days later my *Times* editor called. "I have an idea," she said. "The paper is moving Dexter Filkins to Istanbul to be close to Iraq, so he's positioned nearby when the war begins. He is one of the paper's top correspondents, and I bet we will need a photographer there."

"You mean you need someone in Istanbul?"

"Yes, Istanbul."

I knew nothing about Turkey. But Dexter and I had been friends in India, and within months I had packed up my life in Mexico and moved to this country to which I had no ties and whose language I did not speak. It didn't matter. I would be there for the next war.

CHAPTER 5

I Am Not as Worried About Bullets

I moved to Istanbul the first week of January 2003 with two bags of clothes, my cameras, and my laptop, and was lonely from the moment I arrived. Istanbul was cold in January; there was a constant gray drizzle outside. I had pictured a biblical Middle Eastern city, more exotic than Western, with narrow alleys and mazelike stone walls. Istanbul's architecture was modern and industrial, almost cold.

I didn't know how to say hello or thank you, please or good-bye. I ate *simit*, sesame-covered loops of bread, for breakfast and lunch, because they were for sale on every street corner and I was too shy to ask for anything else in Turkish. The television in my room offered only Turkish channels, and I kept turning it on, hoping that all of a sudden I would understand the soap operas and news broadcasts.

I was biding time before the start of the war. In early February Colin Powell made his speech at the United Nations claiming that the United States had proof that Saddam Hussein had weapons of mass destruction, and we journalists were just waiting for the invasion date. Although the

United States' war in Afghanistan seemed a justifiable response to the September 11 attacks, many journalists believed that the Bush administration was fabricating reasons to go to war with Iraq. But we were riding this wave of war that was defining the first decade of the twenty-first century, imbued with the same sense of purpose I imagine war correspondents felt covering Vietnam: a desire to be with our countrymen as they were dragged into a dubious American invasion.

The *New York Times Magazine* assigned me to work with Elizabeth Rubin in northern Iraq, the Kurdish region that was opposed to Saddam and supportive of the American intervention. I was to meet Elizabeth in Iran—a country not particularly friendly to Americans at the time, but that did allow journalists to cross the border into Iraq. We would arrive some weeks before the invasion and stay to document the aftermath. In 2003 editorial budgets were healthy. Editors didn't think twice about putting me on assignment for a month or two at a time, at a rate of $400 per day, just to make sure I was available and in position as a story evolved. Those days are over.

The war in Iraq was the first time in my career the U.S. military offered journalists the chance to accompany them on the front lines of war, that is, to "embed" with the troops. So I had three options: embedding with the U.S. troops as they made their way through the desert toward Baghdad and photographing combat; renting a car and traveling without the protection of the military through the vast deserts of Iraq, which seemed slightly crazy; or reporting from northern Iraq—otherwise known as Kurdistan, home to millions of Kurds who had been oppressed by Saddam—and moving toward Baghdad only after Saddam fell. I chose the last option, because I, like many others, felt it would expose me to the least amount of combat. And it seemed the best way to cover the humanitarian disaster that might follow the invasion: a refugee crisis of Iraqis fleeing southern Iraq to the north. I wasn't sure I would be able to keep up with the soldiers physically—I still had never actually been in combat—so I decided to work around the edges.

SEVERAL WEEKS BEFORE the start of the Iraq war, I was on assignment in South Korea for the *Times Magazine*, photographing North Korean refugees who had escaped to South Korea. In the middle of the assignment, I got an e-mail from Scott Braut, one of my editors at my new photo agency, Corbis. One of his roles in the lead-up to the invasion was to ensure that all Corbis photographers planning on going into Iraq were well equipped with the necessary gear to cover the war, including combat and possible chemical attacks. I responded to him in a state of panic and bewilderment.

From: lynsey addario
Sent: Tuesday, February 11, 2003 11:25 AM
To: Scott Braut
Subject: Re: Body Armor

Scott,

I am trying to buy body armor for my impending departure for Iraq, and am starting to break out in hives. I called AKE War Outfitters like you suggested, and they put me on hold for about 3 minutes, knowing I was calling from Korea. I hung up.

I then checked out the websites you recommended, and am not sure if I just tried to read Korean. Basically, I have no idea what I am looking at— ballistic, six-point adjustable, tactical armor, etc. Please understand that this language is not familiar to me—I grew up in Connecticut, was raised by hairdressers.

Would it be possible for you to call Second Chance in the states, and explain to them that I am a photographer, I am going to either Baghdad with the US troops or into Northern Iraq with god knows which terrorists and tribal leaders, I am not as worried about bullets as I am about shrapnel, don't want anything too heavy (guess this would mean ceramic plates), don't want to spend a million dollars (though my life may be worth a fraction of that one day), and these are my measurements: (sorry if this is too much info for you, but I photographed for 13 hours today, it is 1:30am, and just want to get this planning over with . . .)

I am 5'1", I have no idea what the circumference of my head is for helmet size, and certainly have never measured the distance between my nipples. I would go downstairs and ask someone at the hotel for a measuring tape, but I don't think the people at reception would send me anything to measure my head at 1:30am, because it would take them about 3 hours with the Korean English dictionary to figure out what the hell I am asking for, and I would surely jump out my window before going through that process right now. So, let's say I have a medium head. As for the vest, my waist is about 29", my chest is 34, and I have big boobs.

Also, the NYT Magazine says that the NYT bureau in Turkey might have a gas mask and a chemical suit I can use. It will most likely be sized for a large, burly man (as most war correspondents tend to be), but at this point, I don't think I'd be able to slip my body into it within the 13 necessary seconds before the chemical gas arrives, anyway, so it should be fine. As for the camera gear, I would be forever indebted to you for an extra Nikon D1x battery, and for my feet, a pair of those warm socks you mentioned.

Thank you so much. Call if you have any more questions, and please let me know the cost of the vest before you go ahead and get it.

Lyns

SOMEHOW, BETWEEN body-armor-planning sessions and anxiously watching the news, I strung together a semblance of a personal life. Eventually I gave in to Uxval's proclamations of love and regret and invited him to live with me in Istanbul. I had one foot out the door, but I was lonely and I loved him, he was persistent, and this time he had a vision for our life together. Uxval was the son of two successful Mexican painters, and compared with them, he seemed directionless after leaving his previous job, and with an artistic calling he had never fulfilled. After we met, he started photographing, and he taught himself video to enable us to work alongside each other in Istanbul. I met him at the airport, brought him to our new home, and handed him a set of keys. The next morning I left for Iran and then Iraq, where I spent the next three months.

IN TEHRAN I met Elizabeth for the first time and was immediately struck by her attractiveness, the way she managed to remain feminine in a profession that cloaked femininity with androgyny. Early on in my career I always dressed like a man—jeans or army pants, sturdy hiking boots, a modest top. I rarely wore colors other than black, brown, or gray and tried to dress as sexless and boring as possible. When I went home, I made up for months of this behavior by wearing tiny miniskirts and high heels. Elizabeth, who had worked in this business longer than I, seemed to have realized that retaining a bit of femininity was crucial to her sense of self or maybe to a sense of normalcy. I hadn't realized yet how important that illusion of normalcy would become.

That week, we crossed into northern Iraq by road. Dozens of foreign journalists had made the journey before us, and we breezed through the checkpoints bordering the two countries. Elizabeth's ease with everyone—the Iranian officials, the border guards—reflected the fact that she had spent ten years in conflict zones: Bosnia, Kosovo, Sierra Leone, Uganda, Chechnya. She never took herself too seriously, and laughed easily with her subjects. Everywhere Elizabeth and I went, often as a friendly team of long-haired brunettes, people opened their doors to us. I wondered if they underestimated us because we were women in a part of the world dominated by men. Whatever the reason,

I found it a great advantage: Elizabeth was one of the smartest journalists I had ever met.

About a hundred foreign journalists were shuttling between the Kurdish cities of Erbil and Sulaymaniyah, and we eventually settled in the latter. Sulaymaniyah was a progressive city, with a wide avenue cutting through the center that was lined with low concrete buildings mixed with modern, glassy office towers. We took a room at the Ashti Hotel, a simple place with a dark lobby and seventies-style furniture that was chock-full of journalists. The only thing better than a nice hotel room was a nice hotel room where all the other journalists camped out: It was a way to keep up on the latest developments and conquer the boredom of our evenings.

Friendships form fast in war zones. At night, we gathered in someone's hotel room at the more luxurious Palace Hotel. I knew Ivan Watson, the NPR correspondent, and Quil Lawrence, a BBC World Radio reporter, from Istanbul and Afghanistan. We bought bottles of wine from the Ashti with labels that dubiously read BOTTLED IN EUROPE. Quil sometimes put on salsa music, and we spun around the hotel room for hours. But the invasion was looming, so few of us got out of control. Anyone on assignment in northern Iraq represented a major news outlet, and the pressure to produce stories every day was enormous.

Elizabeth, I quickly learned, worked from morning until long after midnight—until our interpreter and driver cried for mercy. To Elizabeth, our fixers were extensions of us, a fundamental part of the team. We went through what seemed like a dozen drivers and interpreters in our first month in Kurdistan. An interpreter was good but he showed up late for work. A driver was good but his car was unreliable. An interpreter was good but he didn't get along with the driver. One evening we were reporting in a remote village and got a flat tire on the way back to the city. Our driver didn't know how to change the tire. We sat in pitch darkness on the side of a road weeks before the Americans first attacked Iraq, waiting for our driver to learn how to change a tire. We had to fire him.

Eventually we ended up with Dashti and Salim. Dashti, our inter-preter, spoke Arabic, Kurdish, Persian, and English. He even learned some Spanish in a few weeks on the Internet because he would hear me talking to Uxval on the phone and was frustrated he didn't understand the language. Salim was a funny Kurdish boy who wore a mischievous smile and talked incessantly about finding love. Elizabeth talked through the story with Dashti while I gave Salim advice on romance, and they made our jobs possible. I formed an attachment to them that would last for years.

During the day we went looking for signs of U.S. military presence in northern Iraq. We kept our eyes out for Special Forces who might be wearing beards and local clothes, trying to fade into the background. I photographed the training of the *peshmerga*, Kurdish fighters ready to ally with the Americans. And we went in search of the Sunni funda-mentalist group Ansar al-Islam that was hiding in villages across the mountains. The Bush administration alleged the group was linked to both Saddam Hussein and al-Qaeda, thus bolstering the case for war.

THE INVASION began on March 19. American Special Operations troops parachuted in across northern Iraq in the dead of night. The U.S. military there wasn't looking for WMDs or Saddam; it was look-ing for terrorists, specifically Ansar al-Islam. The Americans rained cruise missiles on many of the villages and military sites throughout the region, causing thousands of Kurdish families to flee the area. We trav-eled almost daily to the area around Halabja, where Ansar al-Islam was holed up.

I didn't know the language of war. I didn't know about cruise mis-siles (which could be fired on a precise target from a navy ship stationed within range) or mortars (bombs shot out of tubes propped up on the ground) or rocket-propelled grenades (small exploding rockets that can be shot from the shoulder). If the sound came from an RPG, that meant we journalists were being targeted; if a cruise missile was dropped, it was most likely from the Americans. I needed to know these things. I needed to know who had what weapons and how they were fired off, and where they were going to land.

One morning a group of about eight journalists woke early to investigate civilian casualties and collateral damage from the Americans' attack the night before. Our massive white Land Cruisers—representing the *New York Times*, the *New York Times Magazine*, the *Washington Post*, the *Los Angeles Times*, and several television and radio channels—snaked along the road that led through the lush green foothills of snowcapped mountains toward the hostile area. Our vehicles were clearly marked with the initials T.V., for "television." The area was not pro-American. The road ahead into Khurmal, a conservative Islamic town infiltrated with Ansar al-Islam, was actually too dangerous for Westerners to traverse; the terrorists could easily target journalists from their perch in the mountains or on the roads. Dozens of civilians were fleeing in flatbed trucks, overstuffed cars, anything with wheels, their belongings strung flimsily to the roof, faces pinned to the windows as they zipped past us on the side of the road. I thought of Lucian Perkins's 1995 prizewinning photo from Chechnya, which had been etched in my mind: the hands of a young refugee pinned against the rear window of a van as families fled the fighting.

We parked our cars along the road near a checkpoint as we tried to get information about the situation in Khurmal from the civilians and to photograph their fear. Local villagers screamed at us to leave the area, to keep our flak jackets on. But there was a calm hanging around this chaos: The shooting and mortar fire between the Western-allied Kurdish *peshmerga* and Ansar al-Islam had stopped. We decided to heed the locals' advice and leave. As I headed toward our car I paused. *Had I gotten everything I needed?* I ran back for some final images.

A pickup truck full of Kurdish *peshmerga*, posing with their guns, headed toward me. I photographed them as I stood alongside a tall, trim television cameraman who held his giant camera steady on his shoulder. I suddenly felt my stomach burn, an urge to flee. I ran back to our vehicle, where Elizabeth sat waiting and pulled at my car door. It slammed, and then *boom.*

A massive explosion behind us blew our car forward. Smoke and debris clouded the windows. A mortar round? Our driver immediately hit the gas, springing us away from the scene. Behind us, all I could see was black smoke, a charcoal sandstorm billowing toward us.

"Go! Go! Go! Get out of here! Go go go go!" Elizabeth screamed.

Yes, yes, yes, go, go, go! It didn't occur to me to stay at the scene and continue photographing. An experienced conflict photographer would know to stay, to shoot the wreckage, injured, and dead, but I was young. This was my first bomb.

A few miles down the road we pulled over as cars zoomed past us. A carcass of a pickup truck riding on three melted wheels careened past, the dismembered remains of a body in the back. We followed the truck to a marketplace, where the limp body, miraculously still alive, was passed from one car to another. Brains poured out of a gash in the head. The man was one of the *peshmerga* fighters I had been photographing before I ran away. It was my first casualty in Iraq.

At the hospital, bystanders, nurses, and relatives unloaded bodies into a room with gym mats on the ground. Blood covered the floors and splashed the walls. Supplies were minimal. The injured kept coming through the doors. We heard people say the explosion had been a car bomb; I was wrong, it wasn't a mortar. I still didn't know the difference. A car bomb—a vehicle laden with explosives, sent to detonate near a specific target—could have been aiming for our line of Land Cruisers, carefully marked with the letters T.V.

I was queasy. I held my camera tight against my face like a shield and kept shooting. An interpreter who had been working with my friend Ivan arrived with his leather jacket melted onto his arms and back and blood spattered on his face and chest. I panicked, thinking something might have happened to Ivan.

"Where's Ivan?" I asked.

"I was not with Ivan." He could barely speak.

I walked out to the front of the hospital to find Elizabeth. She was standing beside Eric, an Australian TV reporter, his face and glasses smudged with blood. He, too, was in shock.

"Does anyone have a satellite phone?" he asked in monotone, to the air, as if expecting no response.

"What happened? Is everyone you were with OK?" we asked, prying, as he passed in and out of waves of consciousness, trying to gather himself. He put his hands out in front of him and gestured like a conductor—waving his hands slowly back and forth, silencing us.

"One minute," he said. "One minute . . ." His hands were still raised before him. "My cameraman is dead. Paul is dead."

I knew Paul was the cameraman who had been next to me when I fled. He had continued shooting, and died.

Eric held Elizabeth's phone, then looked at us. "Could you dial some numbers for me?"

I stood back a bit, fearing that Eric might sense my weakness. His shock was still acting as a sort of buffer; I didn't want the look on my face to shatter his calm and thrust him into the agony of loss.

A Kurdish taxi driver pulled up to the entrance of the hospital and jumped out.

"Is anyone here a journalist?"

I needed an excuse to walk away from Eric and the phone call he was about to make.

"Is anyone here a journalist?" the driver repeated. "I have the body of a journalist in the trunk of my car and don't know what to do with it."

I definitely couldn't handle that. I walked back over to Eric and Elizabeth. Eric rattled off a phone number, and Elizabeth dialed and handed the phone back to him. It was a number for the wife of his dead colleague, and the answering machine picked up. He hung up. Eric uttered another number, and someone picked up. It was his office in Australia.

"Hi. This is Eric. Paul is dead."

Just like that.

I ran around to the back of the hospital and put my face in my hands. That phone call could have been for me, for Ivan, for Elizabeth. I didn't even have any phone numbers for Elizabeth's family. We were all there minutes before the car bomb detonated. Now there was some random taxi driver with the body of a colleague folded and dismembered in his trunk, asking what to do with it. How did one transfer the body of a friend out of a country we all snuck into illegally, when there were no functioning embassies, no police, no diplomats, and the only open border accessible from northern Iraq was with Iran? It seemed so obvious, but I didn't know war meant death—that journalists might also get killed in the war. I hid behind the hospital, ashamed of my weakness, my tears, and my fear, wondering if I had the strength for this job, and wept inconsolably.

The war had begun.

ONE DAY in early April I was lying on my bed, eyes closed, in a rare moment of rest. Suddenly car horns and yelling rang through the hotel windows. I figured it was a wedding and dug myself deeper under the sheets. The commotion kept going. I walked across the hall to my colleague's room and looked out from his balcony. The entire city of Sulaymaniyah had gathered along the main avenue beneath our hotel.

We turned on CNN. A bold banner scrolled along the bottom of the screen. Baghdad had fallen. Saddam Hussein was gone. I threw on my work clothes, grabbed my cameras and lens pouches, and ran downstairs.

Outside, American flags flapped in the breeze, Iraqi Kurds kissed photographs of President Bush, and kids danced under massive cardboard replicas of B-52 bombers painted in the colors of the American flag.

"We love Amreeekaa! We love George Bush!"

I had been opposed to the invasion, but for a few moments I felt proud to be American. It seemed impossible that the war could be nearing its final stages so quickly! I wondered how much longer I would stay in Iraq.

In the aftermath we raced to get to Mosul, Kirkuk, and Tikrit, the three major cities between northern Iraq and Baghdad. The landscape shifted from green and mountainous to sun bleached and sand colored. The best reporting often happened in the fragile days after a government fell and the country opened up to the media. We scrambled to work before restrictions on media access shut us out. We trekked from the prisons to the intelligence offices, from abandoned factories to Saddam's palaces—looking for classified documents, traces of weaponry, signs of chemical warfare, and any information on the regime's secrets. We all wanted to be the one to unearth the magical evidence. We all wanted to find the WMDs, even if we'd never thought they existed in the first place.

In Kirkuk, Kurds had faces painted with red, white, and blue. American troops rode through the city, hanging out of open Humvees, bathing in rose petals and kisses. The municipal office in Kirkuk became a temporary hangout for the U.S. Army. Soldiers sat in the main reception area beneath a giant, already defaced portrait of Saddam. When I arrived, only his eyes were scratched out; by evening Kurds were gouging out his cheeks, his teeth; by morning the face was gone.

Iraqis descended on every building like ants, stripping each of them of its possessions. Men rode down the street with massive air-conditioning units—under Saddam, owned by only the wealthiest Iraqis—on their bicycles. Furniture was piled high on people's heads. Chairs, couches, beds, and tables all appeared to be walking around the streets. Young men swam in the artificial lakes surrounding Saddam's massive marble palaces while families picnicked on the lush grounds and toured the stately palace atriums.

We headed to Mosul to meet with General David Petraeus, the U.S. commander of the 101st Airborne Division, which had set up a major base in one of Saddam's palaces. Security was lax. Many Iraqis loved the Americans then, and Americans loved Iraqis then, too. I was so home-sick for conversation not filtered through an interpreter that I spent the afternoon flirting with the strapping and dirty eighteen-year-old sol-diers, regressing to my high school vocabulary and demeanor and pag-ing through well-read copies of *Maxim* magazine. A cafeteria with hot food was erected in the rose garden. Dozens of high-level officers sat behind computer screens and satellite feeds running off generators. It was an incredible display of technology in a country that had little run-ning water and unreliable electricity since the invasion. It was also a symbol of victory: hundreds of U.S. troops operating out of one of Saddam's homes.

I was set up with a cot alongside about thirty soldiers in a giant room. It opened up to a grand terrace overlooking the city. I stepped out to the balcony to work under the stars and enjoy the cool breeze. I had a good day of shooting behind me and another one ahead of me. I just smiled out there, alone on the balcony, and knew that this feeling could sustain me forever.

UNLIKE THE REST of the press corps that descended on Baghdad, in addition to my assignment with Elizabeth I had been asked by *Time* magazine to stick around and work in the north in the weeks immedi-ately following the fall of Saddam. Salim, who stayed on as my inter-preter, was forced to live vicariously through the sensuous, alluring dispatches from his best friend, Dashti, who had traveled to Baghdad to continue as interpreter for Elizabeth. For many young Kurds, Baghdad was a chance to experience big-city life, despite the fact that most stores were still closed, the electricity was still cut, and Arabs and Kurds didn't always love each other. The prostitutes of Baghdad were an irre-sistible temptation for Dashti and Salim, whose sexual experiences were limited to fleeting moments of soft porn on satellite TV.

"Can we please go to Baghdad already?" Salim pleaded day after day. "Dashti is there, and he says there are so many beautiful women!"

"Salim, I am on assignment, and they want me in Mosul. As soon as this assignment ends, we can go." I wasn't about to compromise my work so my interpreter could lose his virginity. But this experience with interpreters, I was learning, was a typical one: We were living with them day in and day out, and they became close friends, often like family. There were few other people I spent such extended periods of time with, day and night, and I worried about their desires, hardships, and needs as much as they did mine.

Dashti called several times a day. "A friend has arranged four sisters in this brothel . . . I have met all of them . . . I will make sure they are ready for you."

Soon enough I was off to Baghdad to shoot another story with Elizabeth. Salim began preparing himself, squirming in the passenger seat with excitement. As we drove along endless stretches of barren desert highway my satellite phone rang relentlessly with Dashti on the other end: "The sisters are ready for Salim!"

Dashti, the ultimate fixer, had done the necessary groundwork for his best friend's deflowering, as if he were arranging just another interview.

I felt some sense of responsibility. I had spent the last two months consumed with anything but the normalcy of life: arranging drivers, preparing vehicles with spare tires and extra containers of gas, looking for hotel rooms with south-facing windows for satellite reception, trying to wake up early enough on three hours of sleep to take advantage of the soft morning light and its long shadows. As we approached Baghdad, my thoughts, my responsibilities, shifted to Salim and the loss of his virginity.

Where the hell did one start explaining the birds and the bees to a twenty-three-year-old Iraqi Kurdish boy who has never kissed a woman? I started with condoms and AIDS.

"There's no AIDS in Iraq," he said.

"Well, OK, but do you know what to do?" My voice trailed off. I couldn't explain foreplay to a Muslim man when I was unmarried and allegedly a virgin. I let it go. I just hoped Salim would make it to work the next day in time for the early morning light.

I HAD BEEN ANTICIPATING arriving in Baghdad for many months, but by the time I pulled into the Hamra Hotel, where many of the foreign journalists were staying, I barely had the energy to familiarize myself with a new city. Baghdad was relatively prosperous in 2003. Under Saddam it had a proper infrastructure, with roads, electricity, and water; green spaces and private clubs; and riverside fish restaurants along the Tigris. Compared with Afghanistan's, Iraq's population was well educated. Arabs had traveled from across the Middle East to attend the university in Baghdad. Those first few weeks life went on in a surprisingly routine way. The city didn't feel particularly dangerous. Civilians were out; shops were open; there were cars on the streets. Electricity and water functioned in select neighborhoods.

Elizabeth and I stayed at a rented apartment across from the Hamra, in a residential neighborhood named Al-Jadriya. In the beginning the social life of most journalists revolved around the Hamra pool, drinking beer and wine and watching the muscular correspondent for the *Christian Science Monitor*, Scott Peterson, do pull-ups from the fire escape in a teeny-weeny black Speedo. A few times a month a vivacious, blond California native named Marla Ruzicka, the founder of an organization that counted civilian casualties in Afghanistan and Iraq, arranged salsa parties for all the journalists and aid workers who didn't have security restrictions. The BBC radio correspondent Quil and I would dance for hours on end until it was time to return to our respective rooms.

During one of the first summer parties, a correspondent asked, "Who has gotten separated since the start of the war?" and almost everyone in the room raised their hand. There were so many divorces after the fall of the Taliban, many more after the fall of Saddam Hussein. Our partners got tired of waiting, and rightly so. Many accused us of cheating, but more often than not we were cheating with our work. No other period in our careers would ever compare with the importance of those post-9/11 years. But some were also taking advantage of the double lives we led as journalists, and Baghdad, especially, became a laboratory for reckless romance. Home was a sort of parallel existence: our ever-present real life versus this exhilarating temporary one.

When I got back to my room, I always called Uxval. I recounted scenes from the day and tried to keep him involved in my life from a distance. But while my heart missed him, my passion had shifted to Baghdad. I was too busy, too absorbed by the rapidly evolving news, too enthralled with Iraq to devote much time to something or someone beyond my immediate grasp.

In fact, the hardest part of those early days was deciding what to cover first. A dictatorship's secrets had been spilled into the streets of Baghdad. We needed to document the truth.

At a mass grave called al-Mahawil, sixty miles south of Baghdad, men and women weaved aimlessly around the open ditches where dozens of bodies had been dug up. Laid neatly in rows were plastic bags containing the remnants of each body, its tattered clothes, its strands of hair. Some had identification cards, some did not. Women in black *abaya*s, the floor-length, curtainlike scarves worn by conservative women all over the Middle East, shuffled from grave to grave weeping, screaming, arms thrust into the air. They were the widows and mothers of the disappeared men that Saddam's loyalists executed during the Shiite uprising of 1991.

I was unable to photograph. I had no idea where to start. I tried to imagine what they were feeling. The wailing women were dramatic but a cliché I had seen from mass graves before; as still images they could never convey the depth of what I was witnessing. Could the anguish of seeing a loved one after more than a decade—decayed in a plastic bag, with nothing more than strands of fabric for identification—ever translate into a single frame? My mentor Bebeto's words rang in my ears: Observe, be patient. My dangling cameras beat against my stomach, and I walked clumsily through the dust, waiting for the right moment to capture the women's grief. I had been shooting for almost ninety days without a break. This day proved it was worth it. All the doubts I had about the war were temporarily quelled. I suspected the American government was lying to us, but on that particular day I didn't care.

IN THE MONTHS AFTER Saddam was deposed, Iraq fell apart. A population that had been silenced for decades was suddenly able to express itself any way it wanted. Throngs of Iraqis lined up for hours outside banks to withdraw their money, screaming with frustration as they struggled to get through the doors. American soldiers shot off their weapons above the crowds, sometimes punching the very men they were there to "liberate." Fires raged as looters prowled the streets pirating electrical wires. Checkpoints began popping up around the city.

Nothing made sense. American troops allowed the looting of the National Museum but protected the caged lions at the house of Saddam's son Uday. To the media, the troops proudly displayed the Hussein brothers' sex dens—decorated with heart-shaped love seats and littered with pornography—while basic services like water, gas, and electricity failed to materialize. The superpower couldn't provide for a basic quality of life. Then the head of the Coalition Provisional Authority, L. Paul Bremer, disbanded the entire Iraqi army, leaving thousands of trained soldiers angry, jobless, and unable to feed their families.

One morning I came upon crowds of Iraqis agitating under the scalding sun, waiting to get their propane tanks filled for cooking. They had been in line for hours and were losing their patience. The American troops were gassing them with a strange, bright-green gas. I photographed the mayhem: ladies in black *abaya*s shoving one another and clanging against American tanks; men in line, exasperated, behind barbed wire; American soldiers screaming at the crowds until the veins along their necks popped out.

Suddenly one of the Iraqi men jumped out of line. A group of American soldiers picked him up and threw him to the ground. One had his knee on the guy's chest; another started punching him in the face. Iraqis screamed in protest.

I kneeled about eight feet from the scene and photographed, shocked by what I was witnessing. What happened to "liberating the Iraqis"? I was waiting for one of the soldiers to step in and stop the madness when I noticed an old woman in an *abaya* in the right corner of my frame. She was about sixty years old. She raised a propane tank over her head and smashed it on a crouching soldier's neck. I kept shooting. No one even noticed me.

The Americans didn't understand the value of honor and respect in an Arab culture. Young American soldiers, many of whom had never traveled abroad before, much less to a Muslim country, didn't realize that a basic familiarity with Arab culture might help their cause. During night patrols, fresh-faced Americans in their late teens and early twenties would stop cars jam-packed with Iraqi family members—men, women, and children—shine their flashlights into the cars, and scream, "Get the fuck out of the car!" Armed to the teeth, they busted into private homes late in the night, pushing the men to the floor, screaming in their faces in English, and zip-tying their wrists while questioning them—often without interpreters and while the children stood, terrified, in the doorway. They would shine their flashlights on women in nightgowns, unveiled, track their dirty boots through people's homes, soil their carpets and their dignity. For an Arab man, foreigners seeing his wife uncovered brought shame and dishonor to the family, and it merited revenge.

BY MAY I was used to life on the front, and it was the world outside that had begun to feel unfamiliar. I received an e-mail from Vineta, my college roommate. She was still living in New York, like so many of my old friends. Her e-mail began: "I was sitting at the boat pond in Central Park today reading the paper . . ."

I stopped. People really did spend their days relaxing in a park, reading an actual copy of the newspaper. I couldn't remember the last time I'd had a morning like that, where I didn't wake up and run to the roof to look for smoke from that morning's bombs, or wasn't following some desperately sad woman looking through tethered plastic bags for the remains of her son. I couldn't remember the last time I had even held or seen a real newspaper, for that matter.

A few days later I left Iraq. I needed a break, and I needed to see Uxval, who had been idling in Turkey, waiting for me to get back. I drove back up through Iraq, through Sulaymaniyah, and into eastern Turkey. Now going home felt like leaving home, too.

In Istanbul my mornings were languid. I slept as long as I could. I didn't stress about morning light, shadows, alarm clocks, car bombs, or whether my driver would turn up on time. I made my own coffee. I listened to Billie Holiday and Nina Simone without worrying whether whoever I was sharing a room or a house with would mind the music.

Uxval and I made love in the afternoon but to a different rhythm. Uxval was the same, but I was more complicated. He was frolicking around in the Istanbul sunshine, and I was a caged animal, incredulous that life was proceeding as usual outside Iraq. I marveled at the women around me, Turkish and foreign, decked out in colorful clothes that revealed their bare arms, their legs, their cleavage.

Only a few days passed before I found pictures in a drawer of a blond woman with gold-rimmed sunglasses staring flirtatiously at the camera, bathed in soft sunlight. She was sitting on the red tram that rode up and down the street outside our apartment window. It was an intimate look I knew all too well.

"Who is this?" I asked.

"Oh, that's Claudia," he said dismissively. "She was in my Turkish class . . ." (I had assumed she was Turkish, but she was Mexican. Only Uxval could manage to find and conquer a Mexican woman in Turkey in three months.)

Turkish class that I paid for, I thought. And probably in my apartment, and in my bed, and rolling around in my sheets. All on my dime. Uxval had moved to Istanbul for us to be together, and we both knew that his options for earning a real living there would be limited at best. I had wanted to make sure things were taken care of while I was away, so I paid the rent, the bills, and left spending money for him each time I left for Iraq. In return, he was there when I came home. That was our deal, and apparently it had consequences.

I put the photo down and looked at him. I didn't have the energy to go through it again. "She's attractive," I said. He knew that I knew. And he and I both knew I no longer cared. The arrangement worked for us. As I began to understand the new rhythm of my life in Baghdad and on the road as one of permanence, I accepted my relationship with Uxval for what it was. I loved him, and I didn't want to come home from long stretches away to an empty apartment. Though I knew he was dating other women while I was off for months at a time, I accepted his philandering as one of the compromises of the work and lifestyle I had chosen. We left for a romantic weekend on the Turkish coast the next morning, and three weeks later I was back in Iraq on assignment with Elizabeth, happy to be back to the world I understood. In Iraq I didn't have to worry about finding pictures of strange women in my drawers or wonder why no one cared that a war was going on.

I RETURNED TO FIND that the war had changed. As the Americans became more aggressive, the Iraqis retaliated with more improvised explosive devices, or IEDs. The first time I witnessed an IED attack against Americans, I was in the car with my Iraqi driver "cruising," a term coined by my colleague the photographer João Silva. Cruising meant driving around aimlessly in search of street photos when news was slow. That day I saw a Humvee in flames under a bridge and asked my driver to pull over.

"*New York Times* . . . photographer . . . I am American . . . journalist . . . ," I yelled to the Americans from across the street. I didn't attempt to take any photographs until they knew who I was. We had learned from the killing of a Reuters photographer on the balcony of the Palestine Hotel that a long lens could be mistaken for a rocket-propelled grenade.

I ran across the street toward the soldiers and said, "I am so sorry for your loss. Can I speak with the commanding officer? Who are you guys with?" I looked at the patch sewn onto his uniform and recognized the soldiers as part of the 82nd Airborne. I knew no one could authorize anything but the commanding officer, and I didn't want to waste time. I flashed my press credential. I had finally acquired the proper U.S. military–issued press pass they required for access to any scene that involved the military. It was a simple press card with a photograph, issued by the Coalition Press Information Center, and ensured that the journalist had been screened by the Americans' provisional government in Iraq.

The young man repeated the name of my organization with a sneer: "Oh, the *New York Times*." They thought we were all lefties opposed to the war. The commanding officer arrived and authorized me to shoot. Three soldiers accompanied me as I ran back across the highway in order to photograph from a distance.

I raised my camera to shoot and framed the smoldering tank and the soldiers standing guard, including the same three soldiers who had watched me clear access with their commanding officer and had escorted me across the street. They suddenly looked at me as if they had never seen me before. Then they raised their guns and lowered their eyes to the scope. They were aiming at me. At me? I held my viewfinder to my eye, my entire body shaking. Would they really kill me,

my own countrymen? Would they kill me because I was photographing a place where one of their men had been injured in an IED attack—
one of *our* men? I held my eye to the frame and paused. Was this a game
of chicken? I pressed the button three times.

"YOU FUCKING BITCH!"

One of the soldiers began screaming at me, waving frantically, with
his gun dangling from one arm.

"Get the fuck out of here, you fucking bitch," he said again. He had
an M16 automatic rifle, and he waved it in the air. The other soldiers still
had their guns pointed at me. They could have shot me in that moment
and made up some excuse, that they didn't know I was a journalist. And
I knew it. I went back to the car. The Americans wanted to bring democracy to Iraq, but a convenient form of democracy that allowed them
to censor the media. Iraqi insurgents had begun attacking Americans.
And American journalists—who had every right to take pictures of
these public scenes—were beginning to face censorship. We were allowed to cover only what the people with guns wanted us to see.

I STAYED IN IRAQ for most of the summer of 2003, as the tenuous
peace following the fall of Saddam continued to unravel. Bombings became more and more commonplace, and I grew inured to the violence.
That November, the morning after I celebrated my thirtieth birthday, I
was back in Istanbul, lying in a hangover slumber in Uxval's arms. The
familiar sound of a bomb jolted me awake. It was a sound I had grown
used to in Iraq. But I didn't believe it.

Uxval shook me. "That was a bomb!"

"Are you crazy?" I was annoyed. *As if he knows what a bomb sounds
like*. "We are in Istanbul." I had finished my last glass of wine only a
few hours ago.

He jumped out of bed, ran to the front room, and craned his neck in
search of smoke.

"There is debris in the air. That was a bomb. Get your cameras."

Within minutes we were out the door. It was the fastest I had ever arrived at a bomb scene, because it was only a few streets over from mine. The tiny street was normally dark, shadowed by the grand nineteenth-century buildings of the old city, but today it was bathed in dusty shafts of light. The faces of the buildings had been torn off. Bloodied, motionless bodies lay contorted and half-naked in the rubble. Broken pipes spewed water in every direction; black soot and ash charred the road and the other buildings. Metal poles and pieces of wood fell across the street curbs. Crowds of Turkish men started to gather. I photographed.

A body lay across the sidewalk. I didn't realize it was a body at first, because it was missing a head. Another body, a man, looked as if he had been blown out the front door of a shop. His shirt was on, intact, and his shoes were on his feet, but his pants were gone. He was wearing blue plaid boxers.

I worked quickly, before the Turkish police came to remove us all from the scene. Men rushed past me carrying a man on a makeshift stretcher. He was barely conscious, his face pale and green, blood streaming from a hole in his leg. The police arrived, and they came right for me—the woman. In the Middle East I was always the first one removed among my male colleagues. I rushed home to file.

Al-Qaeda claimed responsibility for the bomb. The target near our home was a synagogue.

A few days later the headquarters of HSBC, the British bank, was bombed in a neighborhood about twenty minutes away. Uxval and I again grabbed our cameras, which were ready this time, and ran toward a taxi stand down the street. As we were running, there was a massive explosion only a few hundred yards to our right, and we pulled out our cameras to shoot. A fresh plume of smoke and debris rose up to cloud the pristine blue sky.

Traumatized pedestrians who had just narrowly escaped death were fleeing the scene toward us, many with blood trickling down their faces. Uxval said that the explosion had come from the British Consulate.

Some people were still in the same position they had been in when the bomb went off. One man in a suit stood on a second-story window-sill of a now-faceless shop building. Dismembered bodies lay every-where, under layers of bricks, broken sidewalk, dust, and ash. Survivors checked them for pulses. The outer wall of the British Consulate had collapsed on top of a car, and dozens of men frantically tried to dig it out from under the rubble.

I tried to dodge the police as I continued documenting the scene. They pushed me away again. I tried a different angle. I knew I had to shoot as much as I could—this was terrorism on a world scale. They zeroed in on me again, the woman. I watched a handful of Turkish male photographers shoot freely inside. Uxval was inside.

And then, suddenly, I desperately wanted to call my mother. I reached into my camera bag in search of my cell. It was gone. Someone had stolen my phone amid this death and horror. While bodies lay bleeding on the cement. The very thought broke me down. I felt sick to my stomach. I walked over to a telephone booth and shut myself inside. I couldn't stop crying. Istanbul, my haven that wasn't. The fence I had halfheartedly slung up between my work and my home had finally col-lapsed.

CHAPTER 6

Please Tell the Woman We Will Not Hurt Her

By 2004 the streets of Baghdad were more familiar to me than those of Istanbul. I came to think of Baghdad as my home. The *New York Times* house there had two stories, with four bedrooms upstairs, two downstairs, and two more in the basement. The upstairs bedrooms had nice light, and two were connected by an outdoor balcony. The house was large enough to accommodate five foreign correspondents—including a bureau chief, who decided what correspondent would cover what stories—three or four photographers, and a staff of interpreters and drivers. Unlike U.S. government employees, who lived behind the checkpoints and blast walls of the infamous Green Zone, the journalists lived in the city, the Red Zone, among the civilian population, and relied on Iraqis for everything. Downstairs there was a dining room and an office where the Iraqi staff and the foreign correspondents made calls and toiled away on computers. The kitchen was ruled by a chubby, gay Iraqi cook and an equally chubby cleaning lady who we eventually learned was having an affair with one of the drivers. I went in there only to make coffee and grab a banana before heading out in the morning. The rest of our meals were served at the dining table, where we usually ate dinner together every night.

The roof took on a life of its own. When bombs became frequent, we all ran up the three flights of stairs to the roof to see from which neighborhood the smoke would rise; if the explosion seemed big enough, we would immediately grab a driver and jet out in whatever car was available. Newspaper reporters and photographers had to get to the event as quickly as possible, before the authorities roped off the bodies and before a rival newspaper grabbed some vital piece of info. That was normal for newspaper journalism. What was not normal was the frequency with which such urgent explosions compelled us to respond. Life felt like a pinball machine, some explosion perpetually flinging us this way or that. When we realized that the war wasn't going to end anytime soon—and certainly not after President Bush announced that "major combat operations in Iraq have ended"—we installed a makeshift gym with a cheap elliptical machine, a bench, and some weights on the roof. It almost never rained in Baghdad.

Eventually the *Times* house became a fortress, with concrete blast walls more than fifteen feet high surrounding the perimeter and a staff of fifteen armed Iraqi guards standing watch twenty-four hours a day. We imported two expensive treadmills from Jordan. Our lives became progressively more sheltered and separated from the city we had grown to love. Unlike the early days of swimming and salsa parties at the Hamra, these days we stayed indoors when we weren't on reporting trips. They, too, grew more and more infrequent. Baghdad became too dangerous for us to even do our jobs. Every time we wanted to report a story we had to arrange an additional car with another driver and two armed guards to follow us, in case one of our cars broke down or we faced any trouble along the way. All this meant that we spent most of our free time with other *Times* correspondents.

A colleague once said that journalists got one romantic free pass in a war zone, a get-out-of-jail-free card: one mistake, one regret, one person we are ashamed to acknowledge. There was a fair amount of sex in Baghdad: a lot of cheating, a lot of love, and a lot of mistaking loneliness for love. I was guilty of this miscalculation, guilty of confusing the intensity of war with genuine feelings. The reality was that most male war correspondents had wives or faithful girlfriends waiting at home for months on end, while most female war correspondents and photographers remained hopelessly single, stringing along love affairs in the field and at home, ever in search of someone who wasn't threatened by our commitment to our work or put off by the relentless travel schedule.

I had never dated an American male. Before Iraq, I don't remember actually having dated anyone who spoke English as a first language. But somewhere between the bombs and the early morning coffee-and-banana breakfasts at the bureau and the long days in the backseat of the car driving around Baghdad while reporting stories—the weddings, the funerals, and a surreptitious stop at the amusement park in the Al-Mansour district to ride the Ferris wheel that towered over Baghdad—I fell for a colleague.

Matthew had come from Atlanta to work in Iraq. He looked like the quintessential American, with a perfect white smile, light brown hair, an angular jaw, and the typical foreign-correspondent stubble. He wore rimless glasses smudged with fingerprints. He was always smiling, as if friendliness would mask his ambition.

We became a good photographer-writer team. Almost everything we did landed on the front page. For several months we were inseparable, collaborating on articles, talking through ideas, inspiring each other. Week after week we stayed up late into the night, going over the leads of his stories on deadline, sneaking from room to room through the outdoor balcony. We shared the same cultural references, the same sense of humor, the same enthusiasm for our work. It was effortless, unlike my disintegrating relationship with Uxval. Matthew and I both had tenuous commitments to other people, but it never occurred to me that they could endure, given the depth of our feelings for each other.

When Uxval arrived in Baghdad to visit me, I went through the motions. It all would have been so romantic—his heroic arrival in Baghdad in the middle of my long, intense shooting stint. But I felt nothing. I told Uxval to go back to Istanbul, move out of our home, and move back to Mexico City. I gave him all the cash I had on me—around $2,500—to help pay for his trip home. And with this petty alimony he disappeared. It was the first time in years I felt free.

TWO OR THREE BOMBS went off every day. We got used to it. My judgment of danger became increasingly skewed. I lost a sense of fear. I was no longer running away from explosions but running directly toward them. I just wanted the lasting, indelible images of the war to sear the front pages of the newspaper so our policy makers could see the fruits of their decision to invade Iraq. I wanted this at any cost.

Car bombs and roadside attacks against American troops had grown so frequent that the soldiers were terrified and shot almost preemptively, blindly. The Americans set up impromptu checkpoints along the roads and erected stop signs in English—a language and script not all Iraqis understood. Cars that failed to stop before the checkpoint were fired upon. I witnessed two entire families killed at the same checkpoint within twenty minutes of each other.

The Iraqi insurgents grew more organized, unleashing a new kind of fury against their invaders. In late March the American Blackwater security contractors were murdered, set on fire, and strung up with electrical cables on a bridge in the western city of Fallujah. It seemed like a turning point in the war. Blowing up soldiers and fleeing was one thing; desecrating civilians and displaying them for the world to see was another.

One morning I put on my *abaya* and wrapped my hair under a black head scarf and climbed into the backseat with Matthew. I often based how conservatively I dressed, or how much I covered, on the level of danger. We were traveling down a known smugglers' route, so I opted for the most all-concealing *hijab* I could wear, just short of covering my face. We had decided to chase a story on a rumor that an American helicopter had gone down near Ramadi. We pored over a map with our drivers and security staff and called other journalists and drivers for advice. We wanted to travel on the side roads, because the marines had closed off all main roads in preparation for a siege of Fallujah, and Fallujah was on the road to Ramadi.

It was a sunny spring day in April 2004, neither hot nor cold, and I had spent the wee hours of the morning photographing the funeral of a Shiite man who had allegedly been killed by Americans in Sadr City. I had returned to the bureau, and we immediately headed out again. Waleed, our driver, was six foot four when slouching, his head hanging huge over his body. His Sunni family was from an area near Ramadi, which was helpful for reporting the story; in Iraq tribes and familial ties mean everything. Khalid, a Sunni originally from Palestine, was our interpreter that day. He was barely in his twenties and overweight and proudly introduced himself to everyone in accentless English as "Fat Khalid" or "Solid Khalid." He was always joking, as long as we didn't interrupt the American movies he watched on his laptop or his incessant Internet chats with women from God knows where.

We set out at 11 a.m., heading west around the Abu Ghraib prison on the outskirts of Baghdad, around small towns marked by soda stands and little else, sunken green fields of crops and long grass surrounded by palms. Though the road was unfinished and bumpy, I was happy to be coasting down a small, quiet road out of Baghdad and through the lush farms. Matthew and I huddled in the back together. He commented on how serene the villages looked; I joked that we shouldn't talk about safety until we arrived at our destination. The sky, approaching midday, was luminescent without being harsh. We were in rural towns, so the farms essentially made up the towns. There were no main city centers. Waleed and Khalid talked in the way they often did when they were trying to shield us from their concern about something.

And then they went silent. I noticed a few Iraqis with AK-47s standing along the side of the road. By now American checkpoints controlled so many roads and areas of Iraq that the presence of men in black with AK-47s could only mean one thing: lawlessness. There were no American troops in the area.

"We are on the smugglers' route," Khalid said.

What he was trying to say without sounding scared is that we should turn back. We went over our alibis again: that no matter what happened, I was Italian and Matthew was Greek. Under no circumstances were we American. There were more men with guns. It was too late.

We rounded a corner, and a lanky, scruffy man walked close to my window, gun in hand, like a hunter on the trail. He stared at our car: two foreigners in a Sunni stronghold. The Western enemy traveling in the heart of the insurgency. I looked at Matthew—his Americanness— and threw a shawl I had lying in my lap over his head. A sky-blue minivan careened out in front of us, cutting off the road. Dozens of armed men swirled around our vehicle, frenetic and edgy with their new find.

"We are going to die now," I said.

I thought of the four journalists who had been ambushed along the road between Kabul and Jalalabad after September 11. They had been killed. Now it was us, encircled by gunmen in a village called Garma, about forty minutes from Baghdad.

I couldn't see the green fields anymore. Men opened Khalid's and Waleed's doors, pulling them out of the vehicle and out of our view. Our own doors were locked, and our windows were blocked by men with faces wrapped in red-and-white- and black-and-white-patterned keffiyehs, who screamed and unleashed entire magazines of bullets into the air. Our car was armored, bulletproof, with windows as thick as encyclopedias but vulnerable to the arsenal of weapons in this village.

One boy no older than twenty, a rocket launcher strapped to his back, vibrated with skittish energy, as if he himself might explode.

"We are going to die," I said. "We are going to die." I could think of nothing else to say. We were utterly defenseless.

A few men tapped on Matthew's door with the tips of their AK-47s.

"Please don't open your door," I said. "Please don't open your door."

Khalid came to the window, all three hundred pounds of him panting and sweating, and said, "Matthew, get out of the car."

They wanted the man. Matthew unlocked his door, and they led him out, hoisting their guns to his chest, leaving me alone in the backseat. Two men remained at my door, guns raised at me, but were clearly confused about how to proceed. I was a Mediterranean-looking American woman in full Iraqi Arab attire: Was I Iraqi? A Muslim? Did I speak Arabic? My olive complexion and almond-shaped eyes have afforded me relative anonymity in countless countries, and the kidnappers couldn't tell whether or not I was one of them.

I watched Matthew being led away from our car toward the blue minivan, an American male, kidnapped alone in the Sunni Triangle. He would be tortured, perhaps killed. I knew the only way through this was as a team. We were in the Muslim world, where the greatest respect was reserved for women and children. I jumped out of the car and walked ten feet over to where Matthew was being held in the middle of the road. The gunmen looked slightly startled at the sight of me. I rubbed my index fingers together, symbolizing the union of a man and a woman in my made-up version of sign language, trying desperately to convey that he was my partner, and said in English, "He is my husband, and I am not leaving him." They didn't understand English but understood that I was not to be deterred. They half-led me—half-followed me—into the minivan alongside my "husband."

Waleed and Khalid were still caught up in a flurry of activity outside the van. I sat next to Matthew, both of us now inside the truck—still parked diagonally across the road, its sliding door open on the passenger side. In the front seat two masked men faced us, pointing their guns. I rubbed the sides of my forehead with two fingers, repeating "Oh, my God," over and over to myself, trying to hypnotize myself out of hysteria. Matthew was calm. I realized that I had left all my belongings behind: my cameras, my waist pack, my laptop, both of my American passports, my IDs, my satellite phone, my everything. I looked up, hoping to see an opportunity to retrieve at least my passports so I could hide them before they were discovered, and saw an insurgent, his face wrapped in red and white, driving off with our car down the village's main road.

Would I ever use my cameras again? What were the last images I shot? Were they good? Would anyone see them? Would I even live to know?

My passport. Oh, God, my American passport. How could I have been so stupid?

"Oh my God oh my God oh my God," I whispered, rubbing my forehead. I tried to keep my eyes down. "Our passports. OhmyGodohmyGodohmyGod."

The minivan started along the main road in the village and pulled around to the back of a house. Dozens of masked men swarmed around, weapons cocked. Our door slid open to let in the commander, who had a calm face and wore a cheap set of AmberVision sunglasses. He didn't seem as if he would kill us.

He introduced himself in slow, halting English as the commander of the village and asked Khalid to translate. Matthew answered all the questions, steady and sincere. All I could think about was our passports.

"Where are you from?"

"Greece and Italy."

"Are you American? Are you with the coalition?"

"We are Greek and Italian, and not with the coalition."

"Give me your passports."

"We left them in Baghdad," Matthew lied. "We don't have them."

I was sure they would find them and that we would be killed.

"Why are you here?"

"We are journalists, here to tell your side of the story. The Americans have closed the roads in and around Fallujah, and we want to tell your side of the story. We are here for you. We want to write about the civilian deaths, what the Americans are doing to the Iraqis."

The truth always sounded so convincing. I kept my head down, kept rubbing my temples. It seemed to keep me calm and focused on staying alive.

"Where are your press IDs? Who do you work for?"

"Our IDs are in our bags in our car. We work for the *Times*." He left out the *New York* part.

I asked: "Could you bring the car back?"

"Where do you live?"

"We live at the bureau, in a house in Baghdad."

"Where is it, and what is the phone number there?"

He took Matthew's Thuraya satellite phone. Rebel groups and journalists around the world carried Thurayas, smallish satellite phones that could make calls anywhere east of London and north of a satellite floating in the sky above Madagascar. Thurayas enabled journalists to operate in remote areas not linked to a mobile network. The commander started to dial the number of the house, when they suddenly decided they no longer trusted Khalid, our Palestinian-Iraqi interpreter. Poor Khalid was so scared, he was sweating and stuttering. The commander kept asking him whether he was lying, because he could barely get two words out of his mouth. They brought in Gareib, their own interpreter, a Palestinian Brit who claimed to work as a journalist but was clearly part of the insurgency. His hair was like a mop, and his eyeballs were jumpy. They asked Khalid to get out of the car, and the commander and Gareib continued.

"What is the phone number at the *Times* house? And where, exactly, is it?"

We gathered they were trying to confirm whether we were lying about not being part of the American-led coalition, whether we really lived outside the Green Zone. Matthew described where the house was, along the Tigris River, near the Palestine Hotel, and gave the phone number of the bureau. They dialed but didn't call.

Gareib asked again: "Where are you from?"

We stuck to our alibis.

"If you are lying about your nationality, just say it. Just tell us the truth."

I started sweating. I was sure he would give us away, and finally I raised my chin and made eye contact with both the commander and the dicey translator.

"We are not lying," I said firmly.

Gareib softened. He told us that he, too, was a journalist, working with another British journalist, doing a piece on the insurgency. I was sure he was anything but a journalist.

The commander asked whether I had taken any photos since I arrived in Garma.

I said no.

Matthew had a point-and-shoot camera, with photos from the previous few months in Iraq, and offered it up to the commander to prove we had spent our time in Iraq in the company of Iraqis, not Americans. He scrolled through the memory card: Shaima and Ali, an Iraqi couple we had been following during the lead-up to their wedding for a feature story, Matthew smiling along the side of the road in Baghdad, pictures from the day the contractors were killed in Fallujah. Memories.

At that moment our car reappeared, and the commander motioned for me to get out and retrieve our things. My legs were rubbery. I gathered in my arms all our gear: my waist pack with my IDs and one of my passports; my cameras; a backpack with my computer, satellite phone, and a two-year American passport I occasionally carried when I needed to apply for visas while in the field. It had inadvertently been tucked into an interior pocket of my backpack, which was among Matthew's belongings. The masked men drilled their eyes into me and watched me carry everything from one car to another, still confused by my existence.

The commander snapped at them to help me.

I placed our bags in the minivan near us and sat back down beside Matthew. The commander walked away for a second, as did the men with their guns pointed at us. Matthew slipped his passport to me, and I put both of ours into my underwear, beneath my *abaya*. I thought of the time when $7,000 made it through Iraq in my underwear when Elizabeth and I were held up at gunpoint. It was one place they just wouldn't go.

The commander returned with the guards, and he looked over my stash of cameras, pleased that I was actually a professional photographer. He asked to see the contents of the digital cards on my two camera bodies. I had woken up at 6 a.m. and spent the morning in Sadr City, photographing the Mahdi Army outside Moktada al-Sadr's office, the other insurgents dancing, their faces wrapped, their weapons in the air.

"Where is this? When was this?" The commander's interest was piqued.

I explained that the Americans had killed several people in Sadr City the day before, and I went to photograph the funerals and the protests at dawn that morning in Sadr City, in Baghdad.

"Where are your press IDs?"

It was more important for us to show proof of being journalists than to worry about which companies we represented. I reached into my bag and pulled out my press identification cards from Turkey and Mexico. Matthew, who had hidden his IDs in his sock when they first led him into the minivan, took off his shoe, pulled his *New York Times* ID out of his sock, and handed it over to the commander. He studied the IDs. Even after seeing these, they didn't question our nationality again.

The situation seemed to be easing, and I finally raised my eyes. I looked around the car. The gunmen were still perched in the front seat, peering at us from behind their weapons, and I noticed the one on the right relax. I took the liberty of staring for a few seconds and then offered a weak smile before returning my fingers to my temples to rub the sides of my face.

Matthew muttered under his breath, "Stop rubbing your forehead. Relax."

"Shut up," I said. "I am nervous, and it is better if they know they are making a woman nervous."

Khalid was back in the car, and I was relieved to have his familiar, fat presence nearby. One of the gunmen mumbled something out loud, and Khalid translated: "Please tell the woman we will not hurt her."

See? I thought. *The forehead rubbing worked.*

A man came from inside the house, carrying a dented silver bowl a bit larger than a fist, and handed it to the commander.

The commander offered the dripping bowl to Matthew and me. "Drink."

In Iraq, offering water was a sign of hospitality—a decisive moment when one went from being an enemy to a guest. I took a sip and turned to Matthew. "Drink as much as you possibly can."

I knew we would live.

The commander, pleased with his new friends, then said, "We want to offer you Pepsi as a sign of Iraqi hospitality."

We smiled.

Before the Pepsi emerged from the house, all the men surrounding the car started scurrying around the grounds of the headquarters.

"We are about to launch an attack on the marine base nearby," the commander said proudly. "Watch, we will fire rockets."

Before the words escaped his mouth, piercing booms ripped through the air above our heads, punctuating the silence. The commander instructed us to leave the village at once.

GAREIB ESCORTED us out of town. We were driven in the minivan back to the main road into madness. Insurgents rallied around a rocket launcher, firing off successive rockets. Others unloaded bullets from their Kalashnikovs into the air. They had lost interest in us.

Waleed was back in the driver's seat of our car, waiting for us to be transferred from the minivan to our armored car on the side of the road.

We grabbed our things and started across the street toward Waleed. I whipped around.

"Commander!" I called out to the man in AmberVision sunglasses who had just authorized our release. "Can I take pictures?"

He stared at me. "No! Go. Now!"

"But I am a journalist . . . ," I said. "And you are attacking the Americans."

I was somewhat shocked at my own request, but the words flew out of my mouth before I even had time to think about them. The fact was that we were genuinely trying to show their side of the story, and we were sitting in an insurgent's den in the midst of a very photogenic battle. I only half-expected to get permission, but I would have been disappointed in myself had I not asked.

He smiled. And then he refused.

I ran back toward the car.

Gareib again led us out of town in a separate vehicle as the commander had instructed. His car moved suspiciously slowly. About two hundred yards down the road, Gareib's driver pulled over, got out, and motioned to Waleed and Khalid. Matthew and I sat in the backseat, too scared to talk.

"You cannot leave this evening," Gareib said. "You must spend the night somewhere in the village, and you can leave in the morning."

"No way," Matthew said. He was fiddling, anxious, almost angry. "We are leaving. The commander told us we can leave. We have been released. Let us go!"

Gareib explained that the insurgents had just launched an attack on the Americans, and if the Americans happened to counterattack—and fire on the area from which they had received fire—everyone in the village would assume it was us who told the Americans where to bomb.

Matthew was getting angry. "That is ridiculous. We are leaving. We are not spending the night. No. Way."

I whispered softly, "I don't think we have a choice. We are kidnapped, remember?"

Gareib called me out of the car. He leaned in close. "You better tell your friend to relax and keep his mouth shut."

I apologized and said that we were scared.

"Just tell him to stay quiet. He is pissing me off."

I turned to Khalid and Waleed. "This is your country, your culture. You understand the situation much better than we do. What do you guys think we should do?"

"We are *leaving*," Matthew said again.

"Matthew, just be quiet for one minute. Khalid and Waleed will tell us what to do—they speak Arabic, they know these guys, they will tell us what to do. We really don't have much of a choice."

"If we spend the night, they will kill us in the morning," he said. He was losing it. "It'll give them time to think and plot. They will kill us."

He was probably right.

"I think we should do whatever they tell us to do," Khalid said. "They know where our house is in Baghdad, and Gareib is saying that if the Americans really counterattack, the guys from this village could bomb the *New York Times* bureau."

We closed our doors, Gareib got back into his car, and we continued driving along the narrow streets, farther and farther into the residential area of Garma. We pulled up to a house, where the gates opened almost immediately, and pulled right up to the living room door. There was no chance any neighbors even witnessed our arrival.

The owner of the house, a short, stocky man with a tightly trimmed beard and dark brown eyes that showed the exhaustion of war, greeted us in the driveway. Gareib handed us off to a new captor and disappeared.

The room was a typical Iraqi sitting room, with a rug-lined floor and long, overstuffed cushions against the wall. I had been in Iraq long enough to know that they would try to separate me from the men and put me in a room full of women who spoke no English and whose questions revolved around whether I was married and had babies. I couldn't handle the thought of such mundane conversation when our lives were all at stake. When the inevitable offer came, I refused politely, explaining that I just wanted to stay with my husband and that I would sit with the men. I wanted us to be together. The owner's son, no more than eight, brought us tea and cookies—the irony of hospitality while being detained in Iraq.

Matthew and I reversed roles. I was calm; he was slipping into a trancelike panic, convinced we were going to be killed. It was about 5 p.m. now, and we had only a few more hours of daylight before it would be impossible to travel back along the dark roads from Garma into Baghdad. Our fate depended on Gareib. Matthew stopped talking almost entirely. I asked our captor (the owner of the house) about his family. We sat. We drank tea. It got darker. Waleed, looking incredibly oversized in the claustrophobic room, made small talk with our new captor. I wanted the AmberVision commander back.

An hour later Gareib returned with a British reporter I didn't know. The only thing we could deduce was that Gareib had basically gotten the British journalist embedded with the insurgents, and because we had stumbled upon them and hadn't arrived invited and vetted, we were kidnapped, whereas he was allowed to work. But the British guy had no idea we were being detained, and he spoke to us as if we were sharing a beer in a bar. We could hear mortars, rockets, and small-arms fire in the distance, and the pair was about to go to report on the battle from the perspective of the insurgents. Matthew and I asked Gareib if we could tag along. He refused.

The British reporter, who was either oblivious or stupid, tried to make small talk. "So, where in America are you guys from?"

I looked at him with daggers in my eyes. "We are not from America. I am from Italy."

Fortunately Gareib was talking with Waleed and Khalid. I mouthed to the reporter to stop mentioning the words "America" or "United States." I wanted to kill him.

I wondered what the chances were of our getting hit by air strikes from the marine base nearby.

Gareib and the British journalist left, and we pleaded with them to come back before dark.

Time inched on, and our captor became loquacious. He asked us about our time in Iraq and was pleased to hear that Matthew and I had traveled extensively around the country, that I had been in Iraq since well before the war and was very sympathetic to the locals, as well as against the occupation. At a certain point the man launched into a solil- oquy on the fundamental differences between Ali Babas, a colloquial name for bandits, and insurgents, who were fighting against the occu- pation of their country. No better time for a philosophical discussion. He was worried that Ali Babas gave the insurgents a bad name. I shared with him that I had been held up at gunpoint very close to Garma and that the men who held me up were clearly different from the men in his village. He said the insurgents were not bad people but had been pro- voked and humiliated by American hostility and violence—to the point of no return.

"Wouldn't you fight a man who came into your house in the middle of the night, touched your women, stole your belongings?" he asked. "Who humiliated you in your own country? Wouldn't you fight him?"

We all agreed.

Matthew was so stressed that he lay down beside me and improbably started dozing off. I had an idea and whispered to him, "We could always tell them that I was pregnant and feeling ill. Perhaps they would release us if they thought we were having a baby, no?" He closed his eyes.

I knew it might be interpreted as sexual, or improper, to lie down in front of strange men, so I sat there upright, envying Matthew's sleep. I wanted to curl up next to him and wake up to the familiar sound of birds outside our Baghdad window.

The captor asked if I would like to meet his wife, and he led me through a dark room and into the kitchen, where his wife sat on a stool, watching the children play in front of the house. She stood up, over-joyed at the sight of someone new to speak with, and the man walked away, leaving us women time to get acquainted.

I had been through this process an infinite number of times, and though my Arabic was minimal at best, I knew that women needed few words in common to communicate.

"Are you married?"

"Yes." I pointed to the other room, where Matthew lay sleeping.

"Children?"

I held my stomach, gesturing as if I were pregnant. I thought there was no better time to start the rumor than with the wife.

She looked me over, and as many village women who have met few foreigners do, she decided she wanted to look at my clothes and my body beneath the *abaya*. She opened my black cape to see tight jeans and a tightly fitted T-shirt. She smiled and started patting down my thighs, running her hands over my stomach, laughing.

Her two sons burst into the kitchen, giggling. They stood before a mirror to my right, repeatedly wrapping their faces in a keffiyeh like the men in the village. They were playing dress-up.

It was now almost dark, and Gareib reappeared in the room, breath-less, back from monitoring the progress of the attacks on the Ameri-cans. He summoned the stocky owner of the house and stepped back out the main door to the outside. Matthew sat back up, groggy and ready for the end.

The door to the room where we sat was ajar, and partially through the crack and partially through a small window we could see our captor negotiating with a new man, dressed in all black, with a Kalashnikov slung around his back. They were obviously discussing our fate, and they went back and forth in disagreement. Matthew was convinced again that we were going to die.

But Gareib came back and told us we were free to leave. They just wanted to use our Thuraya phones to call our office in Baghdad and confirm that we were really who we claimed we were.

We went outside and stood beside our car, waiting for the unknown. The driveway door opened, and Gareib asked for Matthew's Thuraya once again and the number of the bureau. There was a palpable tension between our captor and Gareib. They seemed to be fighting over what to do with us.

The man in black approached and looked us over.

"I want to marry a foreign woman," he said, looking me directly in the eye, smiling with tarnished, crooked teeth. Khalid was translating.

"Thank you," I put my hand to my chest, "but I am married. I have three sisters though . . . Perhaps I can introduce you to one of them the next time I am here . . ."

Our captor suddenly decided he had had enough of both Gareib and the man in black. He turned to us and directed us back into our car. "Everyone get in the car!"

He ordered me to lie down across the floorboard in the backseat, out of view, and ordered Fat Khalid and Matthew into the backseat and Waleed into the passenger seat. He wrapped his face with the keffiyeh and got into the driver's seat. I felt us backing out of the driveway, the sky darkening with every second, and we drove slowly through the town toward the main highway leading to Baghdad. I raised my head just enough to see that every ten feet or so an insurgent stood, poised with his weapon along the side of the road. They were building trenches with explosive devices for the next arrival of American troops to the village, our captor proudly explained.

We had reached the highway. He tapped Waleed on the shoulder, motioning him to take his place once again behind the wheel, and with that he jumped out of the car and ran across the street, back toward the village. Our captor had saved our lives.

We were on our way home.

I sat up to see the sun setting over darkened fields. We drove in a superstitious silence. No one wanted to speak about our fate until we were home. Our cell phones didn't yet have service, and we didn't dare stop long enough on the side of the road to make a satellite call with our Thuraya. Matthew and I clenched hands, no longer ashamed to show our feelings in front of Waleed and Khalid. Forty minutes passed in a blur until we entered the periphery of Baghdad and Waleed's phone started ringing. I heard him cooing typical Arabic expressions of love and affection: *ayooni* (my eyes), *habibti* (sweetheart), *galbi* (my heart).

I thought only of my parents and hoped they hadn't been told anything.

WHEN WE ARRIVED AT the *New York Times* house, our office manager, Basim, started toward us from outside the front of the house, where a crowd of about twenty staff members had gathered. The formalities between men and women in the Arab world disappeared, and we embraced, one by one. It was dark, but I could see proud Basim weeping like a child. He sent me reeling into fits of tears as the gravity of the last few hours overcame me.

"Your parents have all been called by the New York office," a colleague said. "You should call them."

I went directly up to the roof, one of the few places where I found solace in Iraq, in search of the stars and the open sky. My hands were too nervous to dial; my throat was dry and cracking. I couldn't remember phone numbers emblazoned in my memory since childhood. I scrolled through the cell phone in search of "Mom" and dialed her first. I got her voice mail and started crying at the sound of her voice.

I then scrolled to "Dad." He never answered his phone. What day

was it? Wednesday. He was working. I called his salon, my memory
returning. The squeaky voice of their receptionist answered at the hair
salon on the other end, and nothing came out of my mouth.

"Is my dad there?" *They knew who my dad was, right?* "Is Phillip
there?"

"Yes, yes, honey, yes." Her voice was urgent, and I knew she knew. I
was immediately flooded with guilt for the pain I had caused my parents.

My dad picked up the phone, and he couldn't speak. I could only
hear him whimpering on the other end, struggling, like me, to form a
sentence. It was one of the first times in my life I elicited a trace of emotion from him; I felt his love for me in the absence of his words.

"Dad? Daddy? It's OK. I am fine." I was crying so hard I could
barely get the words out, but I wanted to sound strong for him.

"Oh, baby. Please come home. Please come home."

I looked up into the black sky, sobbing. "OK. I will come home soon."

I promised I would go back, but when the paper asked me if I wanted
to pull out of Iraq, I didn't. I knew that trauma accompanied the work
of a conflict photographer—we had all heard about the drinking,
drugs, and suicides of the previous generation of war correspondents—
and I wanted to take control of my own response. I was in touch with
my feelings enough to process what they meant; I did not want my response to kidnapping to be escape. Matthew and I discussed options,
and we decided we would give it a week or two more and then leave. I
was shaken but not deterred by what I knew had become my mission in
life. I accepted fear as a by-product of the path I had chosen.

I did, however, create a will. The kidnapping in Iraq was the first
time I really thought I was going to die, and though I didn't own anything other than my pictures, I had finally recognized my own mortality. After the kidnapping, back in the United States, I made an
appointment with a lawyer I met through a mutual friend in New York
to declare that I would leave my money to my mother and the income

generated from resales in my archive to my sister's children. It was all laid out, but I needed to sign the final documents. I arranged for two of my editors at Corbis to stand as my witnesses.

That day Corbis had just received a new shipment of body armor for its photographers to take to Iraq. I was trying on a flak jacket and helmet. It seemed only appropriate to sign my death papers while wearing my protective gear—a good omen, I told myself.

So I signed my first will in a flak jacket, holding my helmet in my left hand.

MATTHEW AND I HAD endured so much together, but the question of us, our future as a team beyond Iraq, loomed large. I had dealt with relationships at home and had dealt with relationships in the field but had never tried to combine those two very distinct worlds. I also couldn't fathom how he or I would be capable of returning to an old lover after all we had been through.

We spent one final weekend at the Four Seasons Hotel in Jordan, where so many journalists shacked up in luxurious rooms and rolled around in thousand-thread-count sheets, wrapping up their illicit affairs before heading back to their real lives. The brunch room was a who's who of infidelity. Matthew went home to the United States, and I went off to Thailand by myself to decompress, to wade and swim in the still, blue sea.

Each morning on a minuscule island off the coast of Koh Samui, Seoul, my narrow-framed boatman with leathery skin and sunken cheeks and dressed in a colorfully decorated sarong, met me on the shore in front of my beach hut to take me to a nearby desolate island, where a long white stretch of pristine sand was surrounded by clear, calm turquoise waters. Seoul didn't speak much English, and I was thrilled I didn't have to make small talk with him every day. I was coming down off the wire of anxiety, stress, and near-death experiences, and I felt a cavernous emptiness. The adrenaline that had soared through my veins for months suddenly dissipated, and I was aimless, like a wayward dog, reading book after book to try to fill my mind with other people's experiences to replace my own. My heart ached. Seoul picked me up each morning, dumped me on the lonely stretch of beach where I read and swam each day, and returned around 3 p.m. to take me back to my hut. I paid him the equivalent of about $5 for this specialized service.

One morning, five days into my stay in Thailand and five days into the chaos of my mind, wondering whether Matthew would come back to me or stay in his comfortable relationship back home, Seoul spoke:

"Madam?" he asked.

"Yes, Seoul?" I answered, turning my eyes briefly to him and then engaging the horizon again.

"Why no husband?" Seoul asked.

I turned back to Seoul and smiled. "I am busy, Seoul. No time for husband."

One year later, after months of vacillating between his two prospects, Matthew married his first love. He returned to familiarity, to security, and to a life with a woman he adored. The reality was that I could offer little to a man other than passionate affairs and a few days a month between assignments. Romantic feelings in a war zone were exaggerated by the intensity of every day; one month in Iraq alongside someone was equivalent to six months in the normal world. Our love never would have flourished anywhere but in Iraq.

BEFORE I LEFT Iraq for good, I made a push to widen the scope of my coverage. I was in Istanbul when *Life* magazine had called with an assignment to photograph injured American soldiers. The father and grandfather of the reporter, Johnny Dwyer, were both doctors in the military. We would have five days in the field hospital at Balad Air

Base, where hundreds of soldiers would be coming directly out of battle, en route to the U.S. hospital at Ramstein Air Base, in Germany. As far as I remembered, the military had never given journalists that type of access to photograph injured soldiers. The human costs of the war had been carefully concealed.

The military rules of coverage stipulated that we not attempt to photograph or interview anyone who didn't agree beforehand. I had to get a signed release from every soldier I photographed, and if a soldier was unconscious, I was allowed to shoot but could not publish the image until he regained consciousness and signed the release. Almost every soldier I photographed signed the release. In fact, they were so thrilled with the idea that their contribution to defending America was being recorded in *Life* magazine that many begged me to take their picture. The censorship was coming from above, not from the soldiers themselves.

I was finally photographing the wounded Americans I'd been prevented from photographing. I was sure that the series of images would enlighten Americans to the reality of the war in Iraq. They would see the images and protest our presence there. These were things they hadn't seen before.

The story was slated to run in mid-November, but it was held by *Life* magazine for weeks, and eventually months, through Bush's inaugural speech in January. In February 2005 I received an e-mail from my photo editor at *Life*. She explained regretfully that *Life* would not publish the essay of injured soldiers coming out of Fallujah, because the images were just too "real" for the American public.

I was a freelance photographer. I walked a fine line between being assertive about my work and not so high-maintenance that no editor wanted to work with me again. But on a story like this, where as far as I knew no other still photographer had had access to the injured soldiers at Balad—where the soldiers themselves were eager to have their stories told—I was devastated that the images wouldn't be seen.

Almost five months after I shot the story, they finally did run in the

New York Times Magazine, but something in me had changed after those months in Iraq. I was now a photojournalist willing to die for stories that had the potential to educate people. I wanted to make people think, to open their minds, to give them a full picture of what was happening in Iraq so they could decide whether they supported our presence there. When I risked my life to ultimately be censored by someone sitting in a cushy office in New York, who was deciding on behalf of regular Americans what was too harsh for their eyes, depriving them of their right to see where their own children were fighting, I was furious. Every time I photographed a story like the injured soldiers coming out of Fallujah, I ended up in tears and emotionally fragile. Every time I returned home, I felt more strongly about the need to continue going back.

PART THREE

A Kind of Balance

SUDAN, CONGO, ISTANBUL, AFGHANISTAN, PAKISTAN, FRANCE, LIBYA

CHAPTER 7

Women Are Casualties of Their Birthplace

Even before the experience with *Life* magazine, at thirty years old, I had started stepping away from America's War on Terror. That summer of 2004 I had covered the transfer of power into Iraqi hands and had known it was the moment to make the transition to other types of coverage. I needed to branch out beyond the daily demands of breaking-news photography. I had learned how to work quickly and effectively, but it would always be difficult to experiment and grow as a photographer when working under the violent, restrictive conditions of Iraq. I wanted to see what else I could do, and for that I needed to try a different region. It was time to move on, from Iraq and from the destructive love affairs of my youth. I was single for the first time in many years, and ready to be.

My attention turned to Africa. For years I had imagined it a continent where I could lose myself in the people, the stories, the light, the colors, the heat, smell, dust, grime—and my photos. But I had been so wrapped up in the post-9/11 wars in Iraq and Afghanistan that it had remained a distant dream until *New York Times* correspondent Somini Sengupta e-mailed me with an idea: Darfur. The war in Darfur began in 2003 when rebel militias made up of ethnic black Africans began attacking the Sudanese government—composed primarily of Arabs—to protest institutional racism and injustices against their tribes. The Sudanese government retaliated without mercy. They bombed and attacked their own people across Darfur with air strikes carried out by antiquated Russian aircraft called Antonovs and then sent in armed militias on horseback, known as the janjaweed, to rape and murder villagers and pillage their homes. The conflict was ethnic but also over access to land and water. Wars often had as much to do with resources as tribal, religious, or national hatreds. Darfurians from the Fur, Masalit, and Zaghawa tribes organized themselves into two main rebel militias, called the Sudanese Liberation Army (SLA) and the Justice and Equality Movement (JEM), to fight the Arab government's attacks. By 2004 the rebels were completely entrenched in fighting the Sudanese government, trying to help civilians flee into neighboring Chad, and strategically working with journalists who sneaked across the border into Sudan's Darfur region to help them document the charred countryside littered with bodies.

It was a perfect opportunity to start working in Africa and to focus on a story with a strong humanitarian angle. I was getting steady work with the *New York Times* and *Time*, and I had managed to save a little money during my long stints in Iraq, when all my expenses were paid for by the paper. It was the first time in my adult life I wasn't consumed with anxiety over the next assignment and the next dime, and I could afford to take a risk.

I had no way of knowing then how important Sudan would become to me. I would return for five consecutive years and would establish a deep connection to the country and its people. My work in Africa would change my career, and my life.

SOMINI AND I MET up in Ndjamena, the capital of Chad, and flew to Abéché, a Chadian town close to the Sudanese border. Our French military aircraft was manned by two extremely good-looking French pilots, who invited us to sit in the cockpit and watch the stretches of desert beyond the panorama of the windshield. I had never seen endless swaths of unpopulated, virgin land. The pilots showed off for us, tilting their aircraft to the left and right, and I ended up puking into a bag for the entire second half of the flight. So much for being a freshly single, veteran photographer and impressing the good-looking soldiers.

In Abéché we spent the night at a UN guesthouse before traveling by four-wheel drive to the remote village of Bahai, where refugees were arriving in droves from across the border in Darfur. In late 2004, there was little infrastructure at the refugee camps: The Office of the United Nations High Commissioner for Refugees and the international aid groups were so overwhelmed by the sudden influx of tens of thousands of refugees that most had not received shelter or food and were accessing water through emergency water bladders set up in the desert by the NGOs.

As we traveled to Bahai I realized what a punishing journey it would be for refugees, with nothing but sand from horizon to horizon. I saw makeshift tents populated by malnourished civilians with fresh terror in their eyes. Skeletal villagers who had arrived seconds ago nestled under spindly trees with tattered fabric hung in the branches as sunshade. They were hungry, thirsty, and too listless to beg or move. I instantly reverted to the reserves of my memory for similar images: James Nachtwey's images from the famine in Somalia, Tom Stoddart's images from South Sudan, Sebastião Salgado's workers from around the world, Don McCullin's images of the Biafra famine. Darfur was not a famine, but it was the first time I had seen people who simply didn't have food and were so weakened by their escape that they could barely walk.

I moved around the desert camp self-consciously, a white, well-fed woman trudging through their misery. The people understood that I was an international journalist, but I was still trying to figure out how to take pictures of them without compromising their dignity. As much as it would be natural to compare this misery to that in Iraq, it was impossible. Iraq and Darfur were two different worlds, yet my role was always the same: Tread lightly, be respectful, get into the story as deeply as I could without making the subject feel uncomfortable or objectified. I always approached them gingerly, smiling, using their traditional greeting. The Sudanese spoke Arabic in addition to their local languages, so it was familiar to me. "Salaam aleikum," I would say, and then, "Kef halic? Ana sahafiya." (How are you? I am a journalist.) "Sura mashi? Mish mushkila?" (Photo OK? No problem?)

And they would nod, or smile back. They never refused.

The crisis in Darfur was a fast-developing story, and the international community had begun throwing around the word "genocide." Few photographers had shot the refugees at that point. By then I had seen how our devastating photos from Iraq had forced policy makers and citizens to be cognizant of the failures of the invasion. I hoped that heartrending images from Sudan—especially on the front page of the *New York Times*—might motivate the United Nations and NGOs to respond more urgently to this crisis. As the Sudanese government continued to deny wrongdoing in Darfur, photojournalists could create a historical document of truth.

THE SUDANESE GOVERNMENT wasn't issuing journalist visas for Darfur, so the only way for a journalist to cover the situation at the time was to sneak in illegally from Chad. The SLA had almost no financial support and its logistics were minimal, but journalists sometimes crossed the border with them. The SLA's leaders were wise enough to understand that media coverage might help their cause, so they used their every last resource to accommodate trips into Darfur.

Like most rebels, the SLA used tattered Kalashnikovs. Often a dozen fighters shared one dilapidated truck. For my visit to Darfur, the SLA grouped four foreign journalists together—me, Somini, freelance photographer Jehad Nga, and Jahi Chikwendiu of the *Washington*

Post—oblivious of the competition between teams of journalists vying for exclusive stories. It was a hodgepodge of a group. Jahi was a charismatic and talented African American photographer who had traveled extensively around Africa and called all the rebels "my brother," grinning widely. Jehad stood over six feet tall, weighed about as much as me, and rarely uttered a word.

The plan was to drive to the edge of Chad, then walk a couple of miles through the no-man's-land between Chad and Sudan and meet the rebels in Darfur. We knew we would have to carry everything on our backs while in Darfur, so we minimized our kit, leaving behind lenses, batteries, clothes, shoes, and, not so intelligently, several bottles of water. We set forth on our five-day journey across the Sahel, the southern edge of the Sahara.

The heat was brutal. Even the small amount of weight we each carried seemed too much under the desert sun. Soon after setting out, we came across some nomads with a string of camels who kindly offered to strap our water, tents, and anything else we could manage to the humps of their herd to lessen our load. We formed a little convoy of man and animal, trudging through the sand. Not a single nomad drank even a sip of water over the three-hour walk. I plowed through the first of two bottles I carried. We should have carried more water.

The Sahel was laced with wadis, gullies that filled up during and after the rainy season with fresh streams of muddy water. They flowed like arteries through the desert landscape. We were tempted to drink from the wadis, but they were brown and viscous, sure to induce an immediate case of diarrhea. When we arrived at the edge of the first mini river, chest high and muddy, our improvised guides formed a human chain and passed our things from one side to the other. I stripped off my shoes, sunk my toes into the clay-colored muck, and made my way, holding my passport and cameras high above my head.

Once we reached the other side, a few miles into Sudan's rebel territory, we met the SLA rebels—a collection of lithe, sinewy young men, most wearing brightly colored turbans and old American basketball jerseys and T-shirts they could have picked up from a Goodwill in Minnesota. The "vehicle" we were promised in Chad turned out to be a pickup stripped of almost everything but the wheels and the frame and sagging with the weight of seventeen rebel fighters. Their clothes, sleeping gear, pots and pans, giant jugs of water, gasoline, and Kalashnikovs formed a mini mountain five feet high above the bed of the truck, and it was all held together by crisscrossing ropes tethered to the sides. They motioned for us to climb on. I wondered how long we could endure the ride, clinging for our dear lives to the shoddy ropes as we plowed through the sand toward emptiness.

I used the pidgin Arabic I'd learned in Iraq to talk with the Sudanese rebels, and Somini tried her French, but we mostly communicated through incoherent attempts at sign language. At night we slept wherever the rebels slept, hoping to find refuge under a beautiful, beefy African tree—rare in the landscape we were traversing. Somini was generous enough to let me share her tent with her; in Chad insects had spit acid on my skin, leaving long, watery blisters up and down my arms by morning. Jahi had brought a single-man tent and set up alongside us. Poor Jehad slept upright in the passenger seat of the truck and was devoured by the mosquitoes.

On our second day we were low on water, and there was no well in sight. We had assumed there would be someplace to buy bottled water in Darfur. We were stupid. There were no proper stores in the villages we passed, and the air was hot and dry like a blow-dryer on our faces and throats. Somini, Jehad, Jahi, and I shared a "food bag," in which we pooled what we had brought from Chad: pasta, cans of tuna, protein bars, biscuits, and sugary pineapple- and orange-flavored drink mixes. It wasn't enough food, and we were always hungry and always thirsty. I was convinced we would dehydrate and meet our fate in the middle of the desert, trying to ascertain whether Darfur was a genocide or a civil war.

Every couple of miles the truck would sink into the sand, its wheels spinning, digging deeper into the abyss. Or the truck would simply break down, because it was old and overworked. We then sat for hours as one or two guys fiddled with the motor with a screwdriver or a tool from 1965 while the others splayed out, happy in the sand. They ate out of communal bowls full of *asida*, a grain-based dish that looked like a ball of plain oatmeal. Some would hunt for gazelles—a gourmet lunch—while the others would nap. Miraculously the truck always restarted, but it took us almost three days to travel just twenty miles into northwestern Darfur.

At every water source the rebels would stop and fill their bottles with brown mud mixed with water, but we knew that this would make a *khawaja*, foreign white person, deathly ill. We rationed the few bottles of water we had brought and wondered what we could do as the signs of dehydration—exhaustion, lethargy, headaches—plagued us. I became obsessed with finding water. I had never been in a situation where there were no taps, no wells, no clean streams—no sources at all, really. The sun seared our light skin, and liquid evaporated from our bodies faster than we could sweat. The rebels were so busy drinking pure mud from streams, they barely noticed our desperation for anything remotely resembling water. They just kept pilfering our empty water bottles as we tore through them. In Darfur plastic was like gold, and money was almost worthless.

Finally, on the third day, we arrived at a rebel base in Shigekaro, a tiny village of more sand and emptiness, interrupted by a few thatched huts and one tiny shop that sold flavored drink mix, salt and sugar, pasta, and little else. A dried-out wadi rimmed the village, its trees providing fundamental cover for what had become a natural toilet. No water.

The SLA had a mini training camp in Shigekaro, and we camped out and photographed the soldiers in formation doing training at dawn and dusk. Our fighters regrouped and rested. I walked around the village in search of water as a vampire hunts for blood; I might have pounced on a child if she had water. Then I saw words I never thought I would be so happy to see in Darfur: SAVE THE CHILDREN.

It was a well! I couldn't believe my eyes. I leaned over the edge to see if there was actually water in the well, and indeed the rust-colored, stagnant water looked leaps and bounds cleaner than the muddy stream. Save the Children, an aid group headquartered in my little hometown of Westport, Connecticut, would save us from dehydration.

We spent the afternoon trying to devise a water-purification scheme: Jahi and Jehad found a villager with a bucket and another with a cooking pot—there was actually only one woman with a pot in the entire village—and we spent about five hours each day, with the help of villagers, fetching water, boiling the water, and pouring the water into the plastic bottles that kept mysteriously disappearing from our stash and reappearing among the heap of the rebels' belongings tethered to the back of our truck.

Most of the rebels had never received a formal education past grade school, but they listened to the BBC on shortwave radios and could rattle off the names of every single international figure involved in the Darfur conflict, from the UN to U.S. government officials to Sudanese bit players. They were eager to show us the toll of the war, including scenes of devastation that hadn't yet been accessible to many international journalists: burned-out villages, abandoned and looted. In one a charred pot sat upright amid the charcoaled remains of the town, and I could imagine the scenes of panic and fear as the villagers were chased out of their homes by the janjaweed, many women raped as they tried to flee. Skeletons were scattered across the ground, some still fresh, with leathery skin in varying states of decay stretched across the bones; some had clothes, some didn't, but most of the dead's shoes had been removed and stolen. Good shoes were always valuable in war.

Every so often we'd come across civilians en route to the safety of the camps in Chad. It was a long, difficult walk under the intense summer sun, and people spent the hottest part of the day cowering under scrawny trees. Everyone was terrified of the janjaweed. But the trees provided only psychological cover from them at best.

One day we stopped in a village, and when I got off the back of the truck to shoot, a little girl about three years old took one look at me and started screaming in terror. She tore off, running for the horizon. I was confused.

"What happened?" I asked Mohammed, the interpreter who was accompanying us.

Her female relatives were laughing, which was doubly surprising to me. "Is she scared of the camera?" I asked.

"No," Mohammed explained. "Your skin is dark for a *khawaja*. She thinks you are an Arab."

My Italian American, olive-hued skin had never been a liability before. I watched with horror as the little girl continued running, wondering what atrocities she must have witnessed at the hands of Arab militias.

For the next five years I returned to Darfur for about a month a year, for the *New York Times*, for the *New York Times Magazine*, and later with a grant from Getty Images. As the situation in Sudan worsened, the Sudanese government became more stringent about issuing visas to journalists. Visas weren't the only obstacle to covering the conflict in Darfur; the bureaucracy of permits, useless papers, stamps, and photocopies was nearly insurmountable. But I was persistent and patient with my visa applications and paperwork and became one of the very few photographers to consistently cover the conflict there from 2004 to 2009.

In Darfur, I understood the conflict intimately, understood how the players operated and how to maneuver within the system to get my work done. Over the years I photographed the plight of refugees, villages on fire, ransacked homes, victims of rape. As my images appeared in the *Times* and the *Times Magazine*, the combination of photographs and beautifully reported articles by my colleagues elicited significant reactions from readers, from UN and aid workers, and from policy makers. It was one of the few times I actually witnessed the correlation between persistent coverage and the response to that coverage by the international community.

Darfur—unlike Iraq and Afghanistan, which were wars instigated by an invading foreign military—exposed me to the kind of war where people killed their own people, on their own land. It was a war that perhaps started as a genocide but eventually devolved into a civil war, where every side was responsible for murder, for rape, and for pillage, and all the players were guilty.

Over the years I forced myself to be creative in how I covered the same scenes over and over. I started shooting refugee camps out of focus, sometimes in abstract ways, to try to reach an audience beyond the typical *New York Times* readership—an audience geared more toward the visual arts. As ugly as the conflict was, the protagonists were beautiful, wearing brilliantly colored fabrics and, despite the persistent hardships, wide, toothy smiles. The Sudanese were lovely, friendly, resilient people, and I wanted to show that in my work. It seemed paradoxical to try to create beautiful images out of conflict, but I found that my more abstract images of Darfur provoked an unusual response from readers. Suddenly I was getting requests to sell fine-art prints of rebels in a sandstorm or of blurred refugees walking through the desert for several thousand dollars.

I was conflicted about making money from images of people who were so desperate, but I thought of all the years I had struggled to make ends meet to be a photographer, and I knew that any money I made from these photos would be invested right back into my work. Trying to convey beauty in war was a technique to try to prevent the reader from looking away or turning the page in response to something horrible. I wanted them to linger, to ask questions.

BETWEEN THESE VISITS to Darfur, beginning in 2006, I made frequent trips to another civil war, in the eastern part of the Democratic

Republic of the Congo. Hundreds of thousands of civilians had been displaced from their villages in the east and were living in overcrowded camps across North and South Kivu provinces. Attacks from both government and rebel soldiers left millions dead and a countless number of Congolese women sexually assaulted. The soldiers raped women to mark their territory, to destroy family bonds (rape victims were often ostracized from their families), and to intimidate civilians as a way of establishing power. They forced the families of the victims to watch the rapes. And they gang-raped women and often used their weapons to tear them apart, causing fistulas, or tears between the vagina and anus from which feces and urine leak. The stories were unbearable. As a photojournalist, I felt there was very little I could do for the women in the DRC but record their stories. I hoped awareness of their suffering might somehow save them. I returned the following year.

In 2008 I was given a grant by Columbia College Chicago's Ellen Stone Belic Institute for the Study of Women and Gender in the Arts and Media to document gender-based violence, and rape as a weapon of war. The roving exhibition, "Congo/Women," consisted of work from the DRC by photographers James Nachtwey, Ron Haviv, Marcus Bleasdale, and me, which traveled to more than fifteen venues across the United States and Europe and raised funds to help women in the DRC get surgery for fistula repair. It was my first grant—the Getty grant for Darfur came a few months later—and the first time I was able to go to a place and focus solely on one project, without the responsibility of deadlines and covering breaking news.

I spent two weeks traversing North and South Kivu, interviewing and photographing women who were victims of sexual assault, surprised by how many women agreed to speak openly about their experiences. Some spoke about how they became infected with HIV, or how their husbands left them upon learning they'd been raped; some spoke about how they were abducted and kept as sex slaves for up to several years, forced to bear the children of their rapists. It amazed me that all the women had the maturity and strength to love their children regardless of the circumstances out of which they were born.

So many women were casualties of their birthplace. They had nothing when they were born and would have nothing when they died; they survived off the land and through their dedication to their families, their children. I interviewed dozens and dozens of African women who had endured more hardship and trauma than most Westerners even read about, and they plowed on. I often openly cried during interviews, unable to process this violence and hatred toward women I was witnessing.

BIBIANE

She had three children, though only two by the time I met her. One had just died, most likely from malnutrition. She recounted her struggle to earn money. A woman she knew offered to pay her to carry cassava flour through the forest, and it was here that she came upon the three men. She couldn't run away. They held her for three days and raped her repeatedly. Her husband returned from a trip, and when he heard she'd been kidnapped and raped, he abandoned her. Then she found out she was HIV positive, and pregnant. If she delivered the child tomorrow—at eight months pregnant, and thin as a bamboo tree—she couldn't pay for the delivery. She didn't even have sugar. All she had was the disease the men had left her with. I asked her whether she was on HIV medication, and she opened her plum-colored satchel to reveal some pills and a potato—her lunch. She was a street woman now, she said, and that was why she was crying.

VUMILA

She was sleeping when she heard a knock at her door. Nine men speaking Kinyarwanda, the language spoken in Rwanda, kicked the door open, entered, and used strips of clothes and rope to tie her and her children's hands in order to rob them. Her husband wasn't home. Once they gathered the things, they untied Vumila and made her carry her own belongings on her back deep into the forest. When she fell from exhaustion from walking up and down hills and through the woods for about a week, they kicked her. They arrived at the first rebel checkpoint, and men—some in uniform, some in tracksuits—untied her hands. At least nine men raped her and several other women in a large, open room while the other men watched. The commander of the camp chose Vumila to be his "wife," and she was forced to stay inside his house day and night. She was raped over and over and over for eight months. When she had to go to the bathroom, they put a string on her like an animal and followed her to the river. Those who tried to escape were stabbed to death, and their bodies were displayed before the other prisoners. Eventually one of the men who had been detained with her was sent back to the village to find three cows to exchange for each person's release. He found only two cows per person. Vumila and the others were beaten, whipped, kicked, stripped of their clothes, and finally told to run away. They arrived back in their village naked, exhausted, and injured. By the time Vumila's husband returned to the village, she was pregnant with the commander's child. Her husband was angry at her for carrying the child of a Rwandan Hutu militiaman and told her she had to go back to her family. Vumila now wanted only one thing:

"All I want is that they accept my children to school. We used to have livestock that help us pay for the school, but now we cannot pay for school, and the government said that they [were] going to help everyone with tuition, free education, but now they sent the children home with no education. What kind of a country will Congo be with uneducated children?"

MAPENDO

SHE APPEARED to be dying from AIDS-related complications. I had heard that she had been gang-raped and had been sick for some time after but had no money or transportation to get to the hospital. We arrived unannounced and found her sitting with her mother and sisters outside their hut. She was shivering in the hot sun, covered in a skin rash. Her skin, once black and shiny and beautiful, was muted and splotched. She was thin and weak and could barely shake my hand. It had been five months since Mapendo had escaped back to her hut after being kidnapped by five soldiers who also spoke Kinyarwanda. She had never gone far from her village before she was taken and had no idea where the men had come from. She knew only that each of them had raped her many times, that they had left her with some illness that caused painful sores all over her body. She lay back down on the wooden plank she used as a mattress. She was tired.

In this last case, I didn't want to monopolize her energy with my questions, but I couldn't just walk away, either. We did a brief interview, and I took a few photographs of her lying down. The closest hospital was two hours away, and my car was full of Congolese aid workers, UN staff, and others who had tagged along in hopes of getting some sort of tip for their help. I told the crew of people I was traveling with that we would take Mapendo to the hospital, and to my astonishment, they protested. They called themselves aid workers and were refusing to help a dying woman. I told them that they could either share the car with Mapendo and her leaking fistula or they could sit on the roof of the car, but she was coming with us. I helped Mapendo's mother lay her ravaged body inside our giant SUV, and we drove her to Bukavu, where she was admitted to the hospital.

CHAPTER 8

Do Your Work, and Come Back
When You Finish

With each new assignment—whether I was in Congo, Darfur, Afghanistan, or elsewhere—I felt more fortunate to be an independent, educated woman. I was thirty-one years old, and I cherished my right to choose my love, my work. I had the privilege to travel and to walk away from hardship when it became too much to bear. Most people on earth didn't have an exit door to walk away from their own lives.

The trials I faced now seemed surmountable simply because I now knew there were people who had overcome much greater hardship. Suddenly my childhood in Connecticut, which I had thought to be the most normal childhood in the world, seemed lavish and full of opportunity. My mother had always told me I had no patience for anything— for waiting in line, for traffic, for my career to take off. Perhaps the years of working in the developing world, where daily frustrations and delays were an integral part of life, gave me the patience and perspective I never had as a young woman. The sadness and injustice I encountered as a journalist could either sink me into a depression or open the door to a new vision of my own life. I chose the latter.

And the more I saw of the world, the deeper my commitment to my family grew. Travel and distance meant it was difficult to see them regularly, but Christmas remained sacred family time. No matter what was going on, I knew I would get on a plane to spend ten days with the people who mattered most to me. It was the only time of year I would turn down covering the biggest news stories, like the 2003 Bam earthquake in Iran or the 2004 tsunami in Indonesia. I needed that time to recharge. I traveled more than ever, but the concept of home became more important, more essential to my sense of balance.

By 2005 I had lived in Istanbul for almost three years, the longest I had lived anywhere in my adult life, and the city had become my home. I rented my own apartment in the fashionable Cihangir neighborhood and for the first time actually bought a few pieces of furniture—a desk, a chair, a couch—and even some accessories, like silverware, coffee mugs, and carpets. My financial woes were behind me; I opened a savings account. In between assignments I had somehow created a life.

My social crowd in Istanbul felt as familiar and intimate as friends from high school or college. There was Behzad, a Marxist Iranian professor at Ramapo College in New Jersey, who spent his sabbatical in Istanbul writing books and dating beautiful women half his age; Ansel and Maddy, a young, witty American couple who had been living in Istanbul for about five years; Ivan, the NPR correspondent I had known since northern Iraq, with whom I could transition easily from working together in Baghdad to watching him play air guitar in his underwear in Istanbul; and Karl, the *Washington Post* bureau chief, who on the weekends invited all of us for sleepovers at his house along the Bosporus. There was also Paxton, an American filmmaker and writer from Connecticut, who had moved to Turkey fifteen years earlier to make a documentary about the Silk Road; and Jason, my weekend sidekick, who was inexplicably flush with cash. (We wondered if he was CIA.) Eventually an American journalist named Suzy showed up from New York, and we would effortlessly talk for hours—a reminder of how much I missed girlfriends with all the same New York references. Then came Dahlia (Sudanese) and Angry Ali (American and French, but from Palestine), career academics who moved to Turkey with a beautiful newborn daughter. That's how we spent our weekends in Istanbul: sprawled out on my living room floor with a narghile and several bottles of wine, laughing and arguing and confiding in one another all night long.

So when Opheera, a reporter friend based in Sudan, asked me to look after Paul, the new Reuters bureau chief for Turkey, I was more than happy to induct him into our tight posse of friends.

Paul flew in from Ankara to Istanbul, and we made plans to meet at Leb-i Derya, my favorite restaurant, which was perched on a steep hill and had glass walls overlooking the Bosporus. I was leaving for Tehran in the morning and preoccupied with preparations for my trip. At the time, I was dating an Iranian actor named Mehdi and couldn't wait to see him again; he was so handsome that some mornings I would just watch him sleep, wondering how I had pulled off an affair with such visual candy. I wasn't in love with him, and I was as consumed by my work as always. But some part of me still enjoyed these passionate love affairs I knew would never last.

Paul and I met on the street, and one word came to mind: Euro. He was handsome, too clean-cut and sharply dressed for my taste, and wore a flashy watch. He had a strong English accent (in fact, his mother was Swedish and his father British). Dark brown hair fell every which way around the top of his face, and I could tell his beard had been trimmed neatly to number 4 on an electric shaver. Paul was extremely self-confident, bordering on arrogant, but dinner was pleasant, and I sensed that he, too, was obsessed with work.

"I have great contacts all over the Middle East and North Africa," he bragged. "Before coming to Turkey, I reopened the Reuters bureau in Algeria. It had been shut for almost a decade because of the civil war and the death of the last Reuters journalist based there. I was in charge of Algeria and all of North Africa. Before that I was in Sweden and Panama City and also spent time in Peru covering the Japanese hostage crisis in Lima."

"Why are you based in Ankara?" I asked. Most foreign correspondents based themselves in Istanbul, the bigger, more beautiful city.

"Because the Reuters main bureau is there, close to the politicians," he said. "Ankara is the political capital of the country, and I have to work my contacts there."

He was inquisitive, like most journalists, but ultimately interested in talking about himself. We both intermittently checked our BlackBerries when there was a lull in conversation. I gave him a few tips about Turkey, passed along contacts for a bunch of friends, and left the next morning for Tehran.

By the time I returned to Istanbul a month later, Paul was already part of our regular crowd. Everyone loved him. He was funny and smart and a dedicated and talented journalist. Over the course of the next few months, Paul and I—both in long-distance relationships—ended up spending many weekends together. We would go out for dinner or make buffalo wings at Jason's, and stay up late into the night talking and drinking far too much. All of my friends had each endured endless conversations with me about my doomed future with Mehdi, and they were bored out of their minds by my love life. Paul stepped in to alleviate the burden of playing love therapist.

By February 2006 Mehdi and I and Paul and his girlfriend had broken up. It was four months after Paul and I had dinner for the first time. Because of my string of failed relationships, along with the ever-increasing demands of my work, I was sure I would spend the rest of my life single. It was the one subject that filled me with a sense of failure.

"You were dating an Iranian, you've been dumped, and you can't get a visa back to Iran to try to win him over," Paul said with conviction. "I think it's time you move on."

By May, Paul and I spoke on the phone almost every night, catching up on the day's events, the news, our respective personal lives. Paul had started dating a Turkish woman. I was dating everyone from New York to Istanbul. I must have logged 100,000 miles in a few months: From May through June 2006, I went from Istanbul to Beijing to Chicago to Florida to Mexico City to Istanbul to Damascus, photographing everything from investment bankers in Hong Kong to the former Yankee catcher Joe Girardi in Chicago to the presidential elections in Mexico. And almost every evening my phone would ring, no matter where I was, and it was Paul on the other end.

I started anticipating his calls. I felt a little flutter when the phone would ring in the early evening, knowing he had carefully calculated my time zone and when it would be convenient to call within my work and sleep schedule. I had never dated anyone who understood how my work and personal life were intricately bound.

Then the words "beautiful" and "kiss" started appearing on my once-platonic BlackBerry, and I was confused. I wasn't sure I was even attracted to him.

"Marry your best friend," my mother used to say. "You don't want to marry for passion, because the passion fades. Marry someone who makes you laugh, who you can spend time with. Looks fade. Passion fades."

Not that my mother, or I, had ever had much luck in love, but she did, on occasion, offer sage advice. And clearly the passionate route that my grandmother Nina had advised had not proved successful for me yet.

One day Paul came to Istanbul for work, and we went for dinner as usual. But something had changed between us. Jason didn't tag along, I got dressed up, and Paul booked a table at an expensive sushi restaurant. When he walked me to my door that evening to say good night, we stood under the street lamp longer than usual, as if we might actually kiss.

Just then Ivan walked by. He looked at us, stopped, folded his arms across his chest, and stood on the corner across the street from us.

"You two cannot kiss!" he yelled. "Because if you get together, Lynsey is inevitably going to break up with you, and then we can't be friends with Paul anymore. Lynsey only dates assholes, and you are too nice and normal for her. And we like you, Paul. So I am not leaving this corner until Paul walks away and gets into a cab."

That's how much faith my friends had in me when it came to men. My years of putting work first or having dalliances with manifestly unreliable people—all of it had affected them. Ivan stood there for ten minutes until Paul finally went home.

A FEW WEEKS LATER Karl had a weekend-long slumber party in his house along the Bosporus. We gathered there on Saturday to swim and barbecue, and every few hours Paul texted me from a friend's wedding in Rome. I didn't reply to all of them. On Sunday he called from the airport in Istanbul and came directly to Karl's house.

We were all in the kitchen cooking dinner. I was washing lettuce when he slipped up behind me, pressed his front side against my back, put his hands on my waist, and leaned into my ear: "I am taking you home tonight."

An electric jolt passed through my body. In all the months we had been friends—all those up-all-night boozy conversations—Paul had never touched me. The simple act of his hands on my hips, with his body pressing against me, changed the dynamic.

"No, you are not."

"Yes, I am. And you are not arguing with me."

His confidence that we would be right for each other removed the question marks in my head.

And at the end of the evening—it was the night the French soccer player Zidane had head-butted the Italian player Materazzi, leading

Italy to the 2006 World Cup—Paul and I got in a taxi together and went back to my apartment. The next morning, as we sat drinking coffee on my little balcony overlooking the green mosque in Cihangir, I knew we would probably spend the rest of our lives together.

I HAD NEVER DATED someone I could envision marrying before. Paul, like me, was completely driven by his career. He was constantly dealing with deadlines and understood my own long hours. He worked as a foreign correspondent in places like Algeria and understood the challenges and allure of covering big, often dangerous stories. I never had to explain to him why I was away for several weeks out of every month or why I had to stay up on my computer, editing and filing, late into the night. With every assignment that took me off to Darfur or Congo or Afghanistan, he simply said, "I love you. I am here. Do your work, and come back when you finish. I will be here waiting for you."

It wasn't just that Paul was accepting of my work—he was energetically supportive, excited to help me plan my reporting, fascinated by the next possible story, and visibly proud of my accomplishments. Few men were this engaged in their girlfriends' careers. I couldn't help but be suspicious.

A few months before I was taking him home to my crazy family for Christmas, I wanted to make sure he would be fine with hanging out with gay men as well as loud Italian Americans. Socially Paul was an affable, relaxed guy, but he was also somewhat refined, in that European, proper, polite sort of way. I explained to Paul that everyone was bound to ask him a million questions. I joked that if he had any secrets, he needed to tell me, because my family was capable of prying anything out of anyone. He got a bit fidgety.

"Well, I have something I should probably tell you," he said, in his forest-green V-neck sweater. "I have a title. I'm a count."

"You're what?"

"I am a count."

He explained that his great-grandfather was the adopted son of a Jewish Austro-Hungarian baron, Maurice von Hirsch, a wealthy banker who lent money to King Edward VII and made a fortune building the first railways connecting Turkey to Europe. Hirsch was also a philanthropist who donated his money to programs for the settlement of the persecuted and impoverished Jewish people living in Russia and Eastern Europe. As Baron de Forest, Paul's great-grandfather became a British MP, was a close friend of Winston Churchill's, and later became a citizen of the Principality of Liechtenstein, where he was given the title of count by the prince. In 1944 he set up a charitable foundation for the protection of the natural environment, which Paul's father runs to this day. Paul spent his childhood living in a castle in Roquebrune-Cap-Martin, on the French Riviera, next to Zairean president Mobutu Sese Seko's villa. Paul's father airlifted one hundred endangered lemurs out of Madagascar to their home and set up a private zoo that stretched all the way to the sea, full of mini monkeys that terrified Paul as a child.

I stared at him. What would I tell Nina, my Italian grandmother who rode the boat from Bari, Italy, to Ellis Island and struggled her entire life to provide for her family? Nina frowned upon people who had their success handed to them on a silver platter. And would Paul frown upon my middle-class family? I was unsure what the count title meant in present-day translation—were people supposed to curtsy in front of him? Did he wear a kilt? Did his family live in actual castles? Before I could formulate a reaction, words flew out of my mouth.

"Don't tell my family," I said.

I SHOULDN'T HAVE WORRIED; Paul fit into my world just fine. At first it was I who had a problem fitting into his. A few months into our relationship I was planning a trip back to the Darfur refugee camps in eastern Chad and flying through Paris. Paul, coincidentally, had to be in Paris for his best friend Oscar's thirtieth-birthday party. I had a backpack with camera gear and a satellite dish and another, carry-on-sized bag in case we had to catch a UN flight to the border—they always restricted luggage weight. I packed a few linen tunics, a pair of jeans, cargo pants, head scarves, a bug net, a headlamp, wet wipes, antibiotics, running shoes, and one set of workout clothes in case there happened to be a gym in the hotel in Ndjamena, the capital of Chad. Paul told me the weekend would be casual, so I stuffed a few dressy tops into my bag. In New York, a birthday party often called for fitted jeans, a stylish top, a pair of high heels, and some silver jewelry. But I had never hung out with Swedes before.

When I arrived at the restaurant to meet Paul, Oscar, and about forty of their friends, I knew I was in trouble. Everyone was a statue of blond, elegant perfection. The women were wearing semiformal gowns made of fine fabrics that somehow gathered gracefully on their curveless bodies. Their hair had been styled professionally into rolling, blond curls. They all carried Chanel, Prada, Gucci, or Louis Vuitton bags. Glistening diamonds hung from their earlobes. The men sported Gucci loafers, Prada suits, Audemars Piguet watches, labels I didn't know.

And there I was in my Zara top, my Levi's jeans, and my Nine West heels, on my way to Darfur.

As Paul introduced me to the men and women, they looked me up and down, and then turned their backs and walked away. No one cared who I was, what I did for a living, or that I was going to Darfur to document a war so people like them could have a clue what was going on in the world outside Stockholm or Paris. I started sinking into insecurities I didn't even know existed. The next day I raced to Zara, scrambling to find something fancy enough to wear.

"But you are a tough, successful woman—a war photographer who has traveled around the world," Paul said. "You really care about these women?"

There was a second dinner scheduled for the following night, and I was dreading the disapproving glances by these women who had never worked a day in their lives. I was still a woman, and I still cared what I looked like; no matter what I accomplished with my career, nothing eliminates those stinging insecurities you develop as a child or teen. And for better or worse, these people would occasionally pop up in Paul's life. I would have to deal with them again, which made me question Paul's judgment, too: How could he like these people? Did I want to be a part of this world?

Maybe I was so upset because I actually wanted this relationship to last. Something about Paul's eccentric background mirrored my own. It made him flexible about my time-consuming profession, and capable of embracing this crazy, weird life of mine. We had found familiar ground in the wilderness of our familial abnormalcy: our love of our work. He respected my industriousness and drive. The love between us was organically unconditional, allowing us to be ourselves, without any limitations. It reminded me of the love my family gave me. Suddenly, standing at that stupid Swedish party, I realized that Paul was different from any other man I had ever known.

That evening, I sat alone at a table while everyone cavorted around me, when one of the Swedes approached me for the first time and asked if he could sit down.

"Sure," I said, surprised.

"My name is Carl. I think you are the only other person here with a job."

I laughed. The next morning I sprinted off to Darfur, where I felt completely comfortable.

CHAPTER 9

The Most Dangerous Place in the World

In 2007 the war in Afghanistan dragged on, the prospects for peace diminishing every year. The Taliban insurgency spread throughout the countryside, and America, distracted by Iraq, was paying the price for neglecting a country all too familiar with an occupation. Car bombs and suicide attacks occurred weekly; NATO troops retaliated, killing a large number of civilians in the process. My relationship with the country had already spanned seven years, and as more and more lives were lost on both sides, I felt I needed to document what had gone wrong.

In August Elizabeth Rubin—my old partner from Iraq who had become a close friend—and I were searching for the perfect embed with American troops, one that would involve combat and explain why so many Afghan civilians were being killed despite the Americans' advanced and supposedly precise weaponry. We talked almost nightly, going over the options.

Elizabeth suggested that we go to the battle-ridden Korengal Valley, which was near the border with Pakistan and one of the most dangerous places in the country. Korengalis were renowned for their toughness;

the area was called the "cradle of jihad" because they were among the first to revolt against the Soviets in the 1980s. "I want to figure out why so many civilians are dying," she said. "Did you know 70 percent of bombs in Afghanistan are dropped in the Korengal?"

I was eager to dive into a good story with Elizabeth, and I was familiar enough with her work to know that anything she produced from the field would be brilliant and have journalistic impact. By 2007 I had done more than a dozen embeds; I was comfortable traveling with the military and prepared for battle conditions. We wanted to find an embed where we could stay longer than a week or two, unlike my previous stints with the military, to get a sense of the rhythms of war.

The embed permission was approved in mid-August. I went ahead to the Kandahar Airfield, a NATO and American base, to begin shooting troops with the medevac teams, and waited for Elizabeth to arrive. Elizabeth and I checked in regularly while I was at KAF, and she was still in New York.

"When are you getting in?" I asked, quietly hoping my persistence might push up her arrival date. She was already late, and I feared any further delay might wreak havoc on my carefully crafted assignment schedule.

"I'm sick," she said. "Probably another week."

"You're sick? What kind of sick?"

"I have a flu," she said. "And I'm three months pregnant."

"What? Pregnant? Are you sure you want to do this?"

"Yeah, I'll be fine. I just need a little more time here, and I will be fine."

Pregnancy was always a terrifying idea to me. In our line of work few women got married, much less had children. Only college friends back home, people with "normal" jobs, were pregnant. I had no idea how babies grew, even less about the stages of pregnancy, what women felt like, how they looked.

"Do you look pregnant?" I asked. "How are you going to hide it?"

As far as I knew, there was no rule that a pregnant journalist couldn't go on an embed, but most likely the military had never been faced with such a proposition. She assured me that it was too early for the pregnancy to be detectable, that she was comfortable with the risks, and that physically, she felt great. I assumed that the military would never allow our embed to last more than a month and that we would leave Afghanistan before Elizabeth would be far along. My philosophy had always been that people must make their own decisions, and I wasn't about to judge what Elizabeth was doing with her life and with her body. She was one of the most dedicated journalists I had ever worked with. Though the pressures, endless travel, and risks of our jobs made raising a child nearly impossible, I knew she was getting older, and wondered if she didn't want to miss this opportunity to have a baby. I was sworn to secrecy.

Elizabeth looked the same as she always did when she joined me in Afghanistan in early September and we made our way to a base in the city of Jalalabad, from which journalists were sent off to military bases across eastern Afghanistan. We met with the public affairs officer in charge in a mobile trailer media office, which was set up amid tents and a mess hall. Everyone gave us that familiar look that male soldiers try to conceal without success: Ugh, girls.

The public affairs officer clearly didn't want us to go to the Korengal because, as he argued weakly, the sleeping quarters and bathrooms weren't fit for women. Elizabeth told him we could handle whatever the men could. He looked dubious, but a few days later we were given permission to make our way to the Korengal.

Our first stop on our way was Camp Blessing, a small base in the stunning Pech River valley, where stone buildings crawled up lush mountains at impossibly steep angles. Blessing was the battalion headquarters of the 173rd Airborne. There were buildings, rather than tents, for lodging—unusually luxurious for a remote base—as well as a small gym, male and female toilets and showers, a mess hall that vaguely reminded me of a Vermont lodge, and an area for the mortar team to fire off mortars across the valley. The more accessible bases had some sort of "bird," or helicopter, arriving from Kabul or Jalalabad every day; Camp Blessing was a remote base and saw a bird every three days if they were lucky.

We were at the heart of the war in Afghanistan and immediately got to work. The officers allowed us into the Tactical Operations Command center (the TOC), where an entire wall of screens provided real-time feeds of hostile activity all over the battalion's area of operation. On infrared drone-feed screens, the commanders were able to distinguish between living and nonliving things based on their heat signatures. The TOC was also equipped to receive feeds from AC-130 gunships, the attack aircraft flying above the fighting, as well as from Apache helicopters, which maneuvered better than planes. Classified maps were pasted and tacked to almost every available wall space. Bundles of Ethernet cables, laptop chargers, hard drives, and telephone wires were taped down on desks and strung up to the walls, snaking up and down columns from floor to ceiling. White paper printouts of phone numbers, extensions, and codes were taped alongside the maps. A massive sheet with acronyms and initials decipherable to only a few lined the wall at the back of the room. A group of high-level soldiers gathered in the TOC, watching their troops in action on the ground through video feeds, while other soldiers on the phones fielded calls from remote bases as well as from the joint terminal attack controllers, or JTACs, soldiers of the air force who served in army units so they could liaise between the troops on the ground and the aircraft flying above. When combat becomes too intense, the army often needs a plane to come in and blow up everything in the area. The JTACs make the call.

It seemed impossible that we couldn't win the war with the Taliban, an enemy who had little technology—or electricity—and who ran around the mountains in flip-flops, wielding rusty Kalashnikovs and makeshift mortar tubes. But they were formidable fighters and had a lifetime of knowledge of the terrain. At almost any given time in the fall of 2007, there was a fight going on somewhere in the valley, lighting up the screens in the TOC like Rockefeller Center at Christmas.

As a rule, photographing screens, maps, or documents with classified information was always a delicate matter because the images could end up in the hands of the "enemy," that nebulous term the military used to refer to the Taliban and the anticoalition militants who wanted to eject the West from their country. I explained to the officers that there were ways I could photograph the room without revealing what was on the screens—by altering the focus or blurring an image or avoiding the screens altogether. I wanted to capture the intensity of that room. I was given permission on the condition that G2, or military intelligence, could look over my images from the TOC to ensure that I wasn't transmitting highly sensitive info. It was almost unprecedented for the military to ask to look over my images, and I agreed on this occasion because they were giving me access to the kind of scene—a glorious blinking panorama of the West's sophisticated technology—I had not yet seen in print.

After I finished shooting, the G2 officer and I sat in a side room, and as we scrolled through the photos of the TOC—soldiers in gym shorts watching the screens, fielding phone calls, and making split-second decisions about whether or not to drop five-hundred-pound bombs—he casually dropped the question "So how many months pregnant is your friend?"

I was shocked. How could he have known? We had both made phone calls the night before from our Thuraya satellite phones, and maybe Elizabeth had made some reference to her pregnancy while they surreptitiously monitored our calls.

"She's not pregnant." I kept my eyes trained on my computer screen. I had never been a good liar, but I had always been a loyal friend. Elizabeth reminded me several times a day that I could never utter a word about her pregnancy, and I obliged.

The officer quickly dropped the question, but I remained worried that others would find out.

We didn't stay long at Camp Blessing. The night before we flew out to the Korengal Outpost, we gathered in the TOC to watch U.S. troops pinned down as the Taliban fired mortars at them from a roof. The commanders considered dropping bombs from planes and discussed the potential "collateral damage"—civilian casualties—that five-hundred-pound bombs might cause. The fighting dragged on. The troops remained pinned down. And eventually Lieutenant Colonel Bill Ostlund, the battalion commander sitting in the TOC, called in an aircraft bomber and dropped one of those five-hundred-pound bombs on the area. Taliban fighters disintegrated on the screens in front of us. The combat wasn't different from what I had covered in the past, only this time I was watching it unfold on a screen, which oddly seemed more ominous than being on the ground. I noticed something else: In Iraq and in other parts of Afghanistan there were long lulls between battles. In the Korengal it was a constant barrage, day and night.

IN THE KORENGAL VALLEY the Americans had established several small bases, called forward operating bases (FOBs), and smaller combat outposts (COPs). They were dug into some of the most hostile territory in Afghanistan, in the heart of the insurgency as well as the heart of the country's timber trade—which helped fund the insurgency. The Korengal Outpost, or KOP, was only six miles south of Camp Blessing, along a narrow mountain road littered with IEDs. It was an easy target for the Afghan fighters positioned high up in the surrounding mountains. We chose to fly in on a Chinook, a slow-moving boat of an aircraft that was a larger target and less agile than, say, a Black Hawk. I always feared we would be shot down.

The minute we touched ground we were escorted directly to the medic's tent. The commander at the KOP, Captain Dan Kearney, greeted us, but our attention quickly shifted to the scene inside. Afghan boys had been brought to the base practically in shock, with superficial lacerations on their faces and bodies. Their families told the army medics that the wounds were from shrapnel from the evening before—presumably from the bombs we had watched explode on the screens at the TOC. We had flown into the very scene we had wanted to document: the effects of the war on civilians.

I spent most of my time photographing a young boy named Khalid, whose eyes were bloodshot and glassy, his fair skin spattered with scrapes and mud. Dirt had collected in the corners of his red lips, and he rarely blinked. As part of the counterinsurgency campaign to win the hearts and minds of the people, army medics often treated the injured Afghans. But they acted skeptical when the Afghans told them they had been injured by American bombs.

That night, we slept on cots in cavernous bunkers dug into the ground, lightbulbs strung up above us by precarious wires. There were fleas. Elizabeth's torso became a patchwork of bumps and splotches; no part of her stomach was spared. The fleas—perhaps detecting her pregnancy hormones—feasted on her. (They didn't seem interested in me at all.) Elizabeth went several times to the medic to get something to allay her misery, and each time he sent her away with ibuprofen and flea repellant, but there was little she could take that wouldn't be harmful to her pregnancy. She writhed all night in discomfort.

CAPTAIN DAN KEARNEY was only twenty-six years old, handsome and solidly built. Sometimes he was a gentleman, other times he was a hard-ass: autocratic and demanding of his troops. He was always gracious and helpful to us, ordering his troops to give up their cots for us or providing us with extra blankets as the late summer weather turned wintry. The troops weren't thrilled to oblige Kearney's requests.

I suspected that the soldiers rarely took us seriously and were entirely confused by why two women would voluntarily subject themselves to the hardship and the dangers of the Korengal Valley. I preempted their suspicion that we, the chicks, might hold them up in the field by being overly prepared, physically and mentally. I trained religiously for assignments, I made sure I had all the gadgets I'd need in my kit to be as self-sufficient as possible, and I tried not to show fear. As on any other assignment, I wanted to blend in here and be as inconspicuous as possible. There were some troops who struggled with the rigor of the daily six-hour patrols—primarily because they were carrying dozens of pounds of ammunition—and I was sure many doubted we would be able to hold our own alongside them.

I knew from previous experience that the soldiers went on these patrols almost every day looking for the "enemy" and establishing a presence in the area; sometimes they went geared up for a firefight. Several times a week, they walked into potentially hostile places like the villages of Aliabad and Donga, a series of houses made of thin stone slabs and stacked one above another from the bottom of the valley up the mountain. The patrols sometimes lasted seven hours. The terrain was practically vertical.

For the first few weeks Elizabeth didn't seem hindered by her pregnancy, aside from the fact that she had to stop to pee several times during the course of each patrol. After years of trying to get soldiers to overlook our gender on embeds, I cringed each time we had to ask the platoon leader, Lieutenant Matt Piosa, to hold up an entire string of troops in unfriendly villages while Elizabeth scampered off into an abandoned house or behind a tree to empty her bladder. We were also both weak and not accustomed to climbing directly uphill, especially in the thin mountain air. At home I ran almost six miles a day, and I still had a hard time scaling the slopes. I couldn't fathom doing it with a baby growing inside me.

One day we set out for Firebase Vimoto, another army outpost that served as a strategic overwatch point. It was named after an army soldier who had been shot and killed on one of his first patrols. We set out in the morning and walked straight uphill until we got to the base, which was little more than a few firing positions and a ditch for sleeping, surrounded by sandbags. It seemed a miserable place to spend a few months. On the way back daylight faded into darkness, and we, unlike the soldiers, didn't have night-vision goggles. Less than fifty yards from the base, Elizabeth let out a yelp, and I heard the crackle of bushes beneath her feet. She tumbled head over heels straight down the mountain.

I was close to panic. I knew nothing about pregnancy, but I guessed that any abdominal impact could be dangerous.

"Are you OK? Did you hit your stomach?" I gasped, fearing the answer.

She barely answered. We were already so nervous about merely getting home alive. The fact that Elizabeth was also pregnant was so absurd that we didn't even know how to react.

But Elizabeth took things in stride. Sometimes she would complain that the iron plates in her flak jacket put too much pressure on her chest and belly, so I switched my lightweight ceramic plates with her outdated steel ones. And we set off on patrols as usual—she weighted down by the growing baby, I by my cameras and her cheap steel plates.

After several weeks, I left for a stint at home to spend time with Paul. Elizabeth stayed in the Korengal Outpost and continued reporting. While I was gone, she sent regular dispatches of the happenings there, careful not to reveal any tactical information, and I felt a constant, gnawing guilt for having left her alone on the embed while I regrouped and decompressed with my boyfriend. One night Elizabeth called to say that she had gone on an overnight patrol and gotten so dehydrated that she needed two IVs on her return. I knew it was time to go back. I packed a bag full of winter gear for both of us, extra protein bars, and maternity jeans for Elizabeth.

WHEN I RETURNED, we traveled to the even more remote Firebase Vegas, which sat vulnerably on a ledge cut into the mountain and faced a wide, stunning valley. Vegas was the humble home of First Platoon. There was a roofless plywood church, some sandbags, a wooden table, and an outhouse with a very crusty copy of *Maxim* magazine strategically placed next to the hole in the ground that was the toilet. A few months before we arrived, the platoon sergeant had been shot in the head and killed in the space between the toilet and the living quarters. Every trek to the toilet was an ominous sprint. There was nothing to do at Vegas but eat military meals out of envelopes—MREs, or meals ready to eat—gossip, play cards, sleep, and patrol.

One day, we talked with the troops about their personal lives, why they had enlisted, what they were doing before they ended up in the middle of nowhere, in the Korengal Valley.

"This is my sixth tour between Iraq and Afghanistan since September 11, 2001," Staff Sergeant Larry Rougle, or Wildcat, told us. Rougle was one of my favorites. He had dark brown hair that grew into a bowl around his big brown eyes the longer he stayed at the remote Camp Vegas. His chest ballooned to form his beefy frame, and his arms were tattooed from wrist to shoulder. He was thoughtful and articulate and spoke with an ominous wistfulness, as if he feared his sixth tour might be tempting fate too much. He had once been part of a gang in South Jersey. When he shot someone and ended up in juvenile detention, he spent his time learning Russian and reading. When he got out, he joined the army. He had a girlfriend he wanted to marry. He always spoke about his mother.

Some of the guys played games and wrote e-mails on their laptops. Many read old magazines and recycled books. It wasn't long before I finished the reading material I had lugged along, and in those pre-Kindle days I ended up reading a miniature copy of the New Testament I found lying around on the base.

And every morning, day after day, in the early-light dawn we went on the patrols. We first all gathered around for a briefing from the platoon leader, the soft-spoken and painfully shy Lieutenant Brad Winn.

Then we loaded our day packs with water, protein bars, MRE snacks, and our headlamps, and I checked my camera gear to make sure I had spare batteries and as many flash cards as I owned, just in case we got locked into hostile activity overnight.

We would walk single file along a goat path through the tall cedar trees, making our way from hostile village to hostile village. The platoon leader generally put Elizabeth and me together between two soldiers, and I pestered Elizabeth constantly about whether she was drinking enough water as we trudged dutifully along the narrow paths. Our directive was to stay roughly twenty feet behind the person in front of us—allowing space between soldiers would lower the number of casualties in an ambush or land mine explosion. If attacked, we were to do whatever the soldier "assigned" to us told us to do. This was usually "Get down!" or "Run!" A part of me always quietly hoped for a brief gun battle; there were only so many pictures I could take of troops standing guard with their guns and talking with villagers. But when the bullets started flying, I prayed only for the battle to end.

During the weeks we spent hiking through the valleys, laden with flak jackets, helmets, water, and food, Elizabeth and I grew strong and determined. Our gear totaled forty pounds—mine even more with camera equipment—but we kept up with the six-hour patrols on the demanding mountains of the Korengal Valley. We grew accustomed to the incoming whistle and crash of mortar rounds directed at the base, which often landed off-target in the middle of nowhere. We scrambled for cover in a cinder-block shelter or behind massive sand-filled Hesco barriers without fanfare. Incoming rounds from Kalashnikovs or Russian-made machine guns, called Dushkas, became routine. The racing heart that at first accompanied the sound of bullets subsided into something as regular as the sound of roosters at dawn anywhere in the world.

Elizabeth's belly grew as the month passed, but in tandem with the temperature dropping; her layers of clothing increased with the size of her belly, hiding any trace of the baby. With what seemed like every cramp or headache, I got out my Thuraya satellite phone and called my sister Lisa in Los Angeles, careful that none of the soldiers could hear us.

"Lee, what does it mean when Elizabeth has cramps?" I asked. "Is it OK if she walks for hours a day? Will the weight of a flak jacket be a problem for the baby?"

My sister, accustomed to years of her little sister on the front line, and somewhat resigned to not imposing her judgment on me and my colleagues, didn't respond with a lecture about the dangers of being pregnant in a war zone or on a military embed. She was an ever pragmatic mother of two and assured us repeatedly of babies' resilience.

"Just tell her to drink a lot of water," she said. "The worst thing you can do is allow yourself to get dehydrated."

THAT AUTUMN in the Korengal, Battle Company had been gearing up for Operation Rock Avalanche, another battalion-wide mission to root out senior Taliban fighters. By mid-October the preparation was in full swing. We knew Rock Avalanche was going to be dangerous. The soldiers were hoping to lure the Taliban out of hiding to fight.

This time, two more journalists, the photographers Tim Hetherington and Balazs Gardi, were coming along on the operation. Captain Kearney gave each of the four of us the choice of which platoon we wanted to accompany for the mission. Kearney would hang back from the fighting with what was called the overwatch team, but First and Second Platoons were going to be on the front line. They would enter the villages, search the homes, and be on the offensive if attacked. The first destination, the village of Yaka China, was almost vertical in layout. If we were to accompany them, we would be walking at night, with all our gear, straight up through steps of irrigated land at a seventy-degree angle. We would be responsible for carrying our own food, water, sleeping gear, work equipment, clothing—everything we would need for a week of patrolling, camping, and trekking in the mountains—while hunting and being hunted by the Taliban.

Elizabeth suggested that we stick with Captain Kearney and the overwatch team, and Captain Kearney encouraged us to do the same—to hang back. I wanted to go with Second Platoon, on the front line, but wasn't sure we could keep up. Elizabeth decided to run the debate by Balazs, telling him what she needed for her story and also that she was pregnant. He seemed slightly taken aback, and his response was firm: We should definitely stay back with Captain Kearney and the overwatch team, who would position themselves behind the platoons' fighting in order to monitor and command the operation. We decided to stick with Captain Kearney.

I thought about Paul and was grateful he wasn't aware of what I was about to do. Though we were talking over my satellite phone almost every day, I was prohibited by embed rules from mentioning any tactical or strategic information in case an insurgent was listening. Our conversations were relegated mostly to what protein bars and MREs I ate that day and what was happening back in Istanbul with his work and our friends.

THE EVENING OF OCTOBER 19 we piled onto Black Hawks bound for the mountains overlooking Yaka China. I was terrified. Foreign troops hadn't attempted to enter the area in years. The Black Hawk hovered above the rugged mountainside, and we were prompted to jump into the blackness, several feet above the rough terrain. I leaped out of the helicopter, struggling to keep my cameras from smashing into the ground, and landed amid a contorted mess of soldiers. We lay there momentarily, a disheveled pile of humans and gear, as the Black Hawk flew off into the darkness, spraying us with weeds and dirt. I hoped my cameras didn't break in the fall and wondered whether Elizabeth and the little one were OK.

I had no idea what we were supposed to do next. Captain Kearney had lent us night-vision goggles, and I struggled to reposition mine on my helmet in front of my eyes. Within minutes Kearney got word from the TOC at Blessing that a small group of armed men was making its way toward us. The Black Hawk had given away our location. Kearney spoke to the JTAC, who then communicated with the air force to send over an AC-130. Soon we heard the sounds of planes above, the thunder of ammunition nearby, and knew the insurgents had been reduced to dust.

On the side of the mountain overlooking Yaka China, the over-watch team unpacked cumbersome machines that looked as if they had been airlifted in from Vietnam. My adrenaline, which usually kicked in at this point, was mysteriously gone. We were thousands of feet up into the October air, and the chill had sunken into my bones. There were no tents, no walls, no roof above our heads, just some brush and trees with gnarly roots and patches of dirt on the side of a mountain for us to sleep on under the stars. I unpacked my sleeping bag while Kearney and the JTACs communicated with airpower, and I fell asleep in the middle of another battle, my Nikons sitting faithfully next to my head.

Sometime later Kearney woke me up, excited: "Addario! Check out the sparkling!"

Through my goggles the JTAC soldier stood silhouetted in a green, night-vision glow as he beamed a giant laser from a flashlightlike device down onto the village below. An AC-130 circled overhead. The JTAC was helping guide the attack aircraft onto the target by "sparkling" the target. It was like a mile-long light saber out of *Star Wars*. There was a constant hum of communication among Kearney, the JTAC, the overwatch team, the Taliban intercepts, and the men in the command center at Camp Blessing.

I picked up my camera, put my night-vision goggles in front of my lens, and shot from my horizontal position, trying desperately not to fall back to sleep. I drifted in and out of slumber with my goggles on and my camera in hand. The next morning, when I awoke in a haze, they were where I had left them, still working. I wondered if anyone else had slept. In the quiet moments I soaked up the sun, trying to warm my shivering body, as the Taliban continued talking over the intercept to each other.

"We have the Dushka ready." An interpreter was speaking the Taliban's words. "We see them across the valley."

They were talking about us, the overwatch team, and they had a giant Russian machine gun poised with .50 caliber bullets ready to fire on us. I started looking around for a place to hide if our position got sprayed with bullets that could effortlessly slice through a brick wall. There was nothing but bushes, barely even a ditch deep enough to conceal us. We were wide open.

As day turned to dusk, Kearney focused his attention on the activity in and out of a house in the valley below. The overwatch team could see it with their night-vision goggles; they were also being fed information through drone feeds. Attack aircraft—Apaches and AC-130s flying overhead—waited for directives on what to shoot. Insurgent chatter was continuously spewing from the radio. Kearney's commander back at the TOC, Lieutenant Colonel Ostlund, radioed him the go-ahead to attack. Minutes later the sky rumbled with firepower.

But the hostile chatter and the activity continued in the house across the valley, like a little bees' nest. Before dawn a B-1 bomber swooped in and dropped two two-thousand-pound bombs on Yaka China. I lay on my back, listening to the guttural sounds of combat, the bombs, the smashing and crackling, the roar of a jet engine. I was so frustrated by my inability to work, my inability to photograph in the blackness of night, I decided to go back to sleep.

By daybreak Lieutenant Piosa, who was in charge of Second Platoon, radioed from the village that there were civilian casualties. And there I was, stuck with the overwatch team clear across an impassible valley, unable to document the human cost of war. I was there to bear witness but not witnessing anything at all. I envisioned my colleagues

Tim and Balazs documenting the bodies of the civilians, the destruction of the houses, the terrified women and children, while I sat on the side of a mountain freezing my ass off, photographing the overwatch team and their ancient forest-green equipment.

I begged Kearney to get me across the valley. *Couldn't we just patrol across?* I was so physically strong from weeks of hoisting thirty, forty, fifty pounds on my back and walking up and down mountains for hours a day that I was sure I could endure anything but the prospect of missing *the* photo. Kearney refused: It was completely hostile territory, and there was a vertical drop we couldn't pass. I was twitching with anxiety. The day inched on, and the Taliban intercepts continued: They were watching us, they were getting closer to our positions, and they were going to spray us with machine-gun fire from across the valley.

Kearney, a new father, was gutted by the news of civilian deaths and trying to figure out what to do next. In his normal area of operation, he met regularly with the village elders and worked hard to gain their trust and explain their mission. Yaka China was an openly hostile village that his men had never before entered, and now he had to contend with having killed and injured women and children the night before. I couldn't imagine how he handled the weight of these decisions, how he was responsible for both the lives of his troops and Afghan civilians, at the tender age of twenty-six. Aware that Elizabeth had years of experience in Afghanistan and a solid understanding of the culture, he turned to her for advice. Elizabeth talked through options with Dan and recommended that they fly into the very village they had bombed the night before and explain to the village elders why they attacked. Captain Kearney and Lieutenant Colonel Ostlund decided to heed Elizabeth's advice. The plan was to explain to the Afghans why they had attacked and to apologize for the casualties. They were going to work on winning the hearts-and-minds-of-the-Afghans part of the war.

Our helicopter landed on the dung roof of a Yaka China home, spraying villagers' hay and fodder and crops around like a tornado. Everyone gathered in a residential courtyard surrounded by homemade clay walls—Afghan men with craggy faces, Lieutenant Piosa, and his men from Second Platoon. I linked up with Tim and Balazs, who looked as if they had been through hell and back but were happy with their work.

"How was yesterday?" I asked.

"It was pretty bad." Balazs was a man of few words.

Tim explained that all the men's bodies had been removed before they arrived, but injured women and children were laid out for them to see.

I felt like a failure and sensed the limitations of my gender. Capturing civilian casualties of war was a fundamental angle of the story I hadn't yet been able to illustrate. A good photographic essay, and a truly lasting historical work of documentation, would have images of the entirety of what happened in the Korengal, from the American soldiers to the Afghan villagers. Afghans dying was an enormous part of that reality, and I was just failing to witness it. I knew that had I been stronger—had I not been a woman with finite physical limitations and with a partner who was almost six months pregnant—I might have opted to go with First or Second Platoon and attempted to scale the vertical terrain with my gear alongside my male colleagues. A writer and I functioned as a team, and when I was with a partner who encouraged me to challenge myself beyond my natural capabilities, I often went along, and relied on him for occasional support. But when I was coupled with someone whose physical condition I was worried about, I didn't feel empowered to take on the challenge, even though Elizabeth would never ask me to compromise my work on her account. We went into the embed as a team, and I felt we needed to stick together, even if it meant I couldn't make the dramatic images that Tim and Balazs had made.

Tim and Balazs were careful not to rub it in. Unlike most male photographers who covered conflict, they were thoughtful and sensitive, not arrogant or brash. Balazs and I had met previously in Afghanistan, but Tim and I met for the first time there in the Korengal. Several times over the course of the almost two-month embed, in between patrols and

shooting scenes on the base, we found ourselves immersed in some philosophical conversation about the effectiveness of photojournalism, or our
similar desires to broaden our work beyond still photography. As still
photographers, we covered the same scenes over and over again, and it
was a challenge to repeatedly engage the viewer. Balazs shot powerful,
painterly images, mostly in black-and-white. Tim had been innovative
with mediums and subject matter, often experimenting with slower, more
cumbersome medium-format cameras in war zones or combining still
images with sound or working in a totally different medium, like video.
I had recently seen a series of his simple, poignant portraits from Liberia
and admired his ability to step back from the chaos and find beauty
in simpler things. Unlike breaking-news photographers, who simply
reacted to the action in front of them, he was able to capture original,
intimate stories when nothing was happening at all. With every conversation, we learned how much we had in common, especially in terms of
our personal desire to be thinking photographers rather than reactive
ones. My impulse to write Tim off as just another thrill-chasing war photographer was proved wrong.

That night we were airlifted to the Abas Ghar ridgeline—another
cold, lonely, pine-filled stretch of land in the mountains. We trekked uphill in search of a place for Kearney and the overwatch team to set up. In
the few months that we were with Battle Company, we had grown accustomed to seeing the world through night-vision goggles and could navi-
gate the awkward depth of field and jagged rocks and shrubs as seen
through the goggles' green haze. The walk up the mountain seemed interminable, but we were stronger and more agile than when we first arrived. Everyone was so exhausted, underrested, and stressed at this point
that each soldier worried primarily for himself.

Elizabeth was still going strong, and I helped her carry some of her
gear when she wasn't too proud to let me. No one uttered a word as we
trudged along—we always assumed the enemy could be lurking
nearby. The silence was broken by the whining sobs of a private first

class. He was weak, pale, and pudgy when he arrived and was continually hazed and insulted by fellow troops who had long endured the miserable conditions and rigorous patrols in the Korengal. He must have been carrying a hundred pounds' worth of ammunition rounds. Something in him snapped. Through the fuzz of my goggles I could see his large black silhouette fall out of the patrol line and drop to his knees. He began weeping aloud.

"I can't do it anymore. I can't walk anymore. I give up."

I pitied him, but in the darkness I was secretly relieved it wasn't us—the *girls*—who'd broken down first.

The soldiers surrounded the soldier and kicked him, screaming at him for his weakness. They dragged him back to his feet. I thought it was pretty stupid to jeopardize our safety by whimpering loud enough for the Taliban to hear, but then the soldiers started reprimanding him, further jeopardizing our safety. He continued sobbing, saying he couldn't go on, and the other soldiers continued pushing him to move forward. The Taliban would have gotten a laugh out of that scene.

The terrain felt more navigable than in Yaka China, and the distance between where we were and Second Platoon was an easy thirty minutes away. On a crisp, sunny day Captain Kearney sent us on a patrol down to meet frontline soldiers, and we were relieved to finally be with them. The platoon was spread out, relaxing after several strenuous days, trading Skittles and M&M's. The communication devices whirred with Taliban voices, including one the soldiers nicknamed "the whisperer," who repeated in a hushed voice that "he was getting closer" and that "he saw hair," which we assumed was either Elizabeth or I. We knew it was only a matter of time before the Taliban attacked.

The ridgeline where the soldiers had gathered ran along a steep mountain face at roughly a seventy-five-degree angle. The angle made it almost impossible to find a place to pee, which I had been holding off on doing all morning. I took off my helmet, placed my cameras next to Elizabeth, and climbed up the mountain on all fours. About forty feet up, a monstrous tree had fallen among the sinewy pines, creating the perfect place to go to the bathroom. I jumped over the log, and before I'd even unbuttoned my pants I heard the familiar snap of AK-47 rounds—the gun of choice for the Taliban.

I dropped to the ground and lay flat behind the cover of the log. I was straight up above the troops along the ridgeline, out of their sight and all alone. I tried to dig myself as deep as possible into the ground—to get as much cover from all sides. Bullets *whooshed* past, over the cover of the tree, from several different directions. In the midst of an ambush it was always nearly impossible for me to tell what direction the bullets were coming from, or which deductions I made stemmed from reason and which from fear. Bullets snapped all around my head, that miserable sound of them slicing through the air: *Bizoom, bizzzzoooom, bizoom* . . . I could tell that the Taliban was shooting from nearby.

I felt the rise of panic from the pit of my stomach into my chest: What if the whisperer came from over the top of the mountain and stumbled upon me first? Would he take me prisoner? I was alone, and as far as I knew, none of the soldiers below had any idea that I had run off to pee. I started saying my Hail Marys in an attempt to redeem myself as a good Catholic. I pleaded with God to keep me safe, making all sorts of promises I knew I would never keep.

Or what if my fellow Americans shot up at me in a friendly fire incident? They could have easily started shooting in my direction if the Taliban were behind me. I continued praying. I knew I had to get down to the ridgeline, where Elizabeth, Tim, Balazs, and the Second Platoon were taking cover.

"Lieutenant Piosa!" I screamed. The rules of an embed are that journalists obey the commanding officer or whoever is assigned to track us; if all hell is breaking loose, however, we are no one's responsibility.

"Elizabeth!!" I screamed thinly into the bullet-ridden air. I couldn't even hear my own voice. I burrowed myself in the space behind the log, knowing I had to muster the courage to reach the others. Agonizing minutes passed until there was a brief lull in the shooting. I jumped over the log and lay prostrate on the ground, stretching my arms above my head like an Olympic diver, and rolled all the way down the mountain to where the others were. I first reached Sergeant Tanner Stichter, who was standing beside another soldier.

"*Get behind cover!*" Stichter screamed as bullets continued all around me. "*Find a tree!*"

"I need my cameras! And my helmet . . ."

I spotted Elizabeth, crouched behind several other soldiers in the forest below, hiding behind the baby pines, each with trunk diameters of no more than six to eight inches. The Taliban, ever professional fighters and masters of their terrain, were ambushing us from three sides. I cowered behind Elizabeth, once again forgetting to photograph, and looked around to get my bearings. To my right and a few feet away, Tim was filming the scene: He was perched up against a slender pine, holding his video camera steady, a picture of calm amid the panic.

Then a terrified voice came over the radio: "Man down! 2-4 is hit!"

Everyone had a call sign, and Sergeant Kevin Rice was 2-4. Piosa gave steady directives over the radio, trying to get a sense of the situation unfolding.

The panicked voice came over the radio again: "Wildcat has been hit!"

Piosa made his way forward. Elizabeth, Balazs, Tim, and I, the medic, and a few other soldiers followed behind. The sustained fire had abated.

We came upon Specialist Carl Vandenberge, who had been shot in the arm. His chest and thighs were covered in blood. As he lay in the brush semiconscious, Sergeant Stichter stood over him, pouring a bag of fluid into his mouth while warming Vandenberge's body with an instant chemical heating pack to try to prevent him from going into shock. I stopped. I sat down next to them, surrounded by a blanket of vast forest and tall pines. The others continued pushing forward.

"Hey . . . sorry . . . ," I said, my voice hushed in case the Taliban still lingered nearby. Stichter looked over at me briefly and continued tending to Vandenberge, who was on his back in the brush.

"Do you mind if I photograph?"

"Yeah, no problem," Stichter answered for both of them. He was calm, focused, as if a battle hadn't just taken place.

"You're gonna be fine." Stichter was talking to Vandenberge, who had lost massive amounts of blood through the artery in his arm. "Tell me about the car you're going to buy when you get home. What color is the car?"

"Am I gonna make it?" Vandenberge asked. "Am I going to live?"

Stichter was standing over Vandenberge, straddling him, emptying the final drops of the IV envelope into his buddy's mouth.

"What color is the interior of your car?" Stichter asked.

I wondered if Vandenberge's last thoughts were going to be on the color of the interior of the new car he was going to buy back in the States. I sat with them in silence, photographing, relieved to be in the illusion of a safe place, away from the hysteria. I didn't want to get up.

Once Vandenberge rehydrated and regained enough energy to walk, the two soldiers stood up and walked toward the medevac helicopter landing. I headed once again toward the front, where Sergeant Rice and Staff Sergeant Rougle had been hit. As I walked forward, I saw Sergeant Rice, who had been shot in the stomach. He hobbled along, carrying his own IV bag, as two soldiers accompanied him toward the medevac zone. Rice had been shot before, and he appeared less traumatized than the soldiers accompanying him.

"Hey, Rice," I said, approaching him with my camera slightly raised in front of my chest, as if asking for permission without words. "Is it cool if I take your picture? Is it OK?"

"Yes." He nodded as he continued walking toward me.

I walked with them for a while, photographing as we walked, when Rice paused.

"Hey," he asked, "do you think you could e-mail me some of these photos?"

I laughed out loud. "Yeah, Rice. Of course I can e-mail you some of these photographs. It's the least I can do. What's your e-mail address?" I asked, having learned that it's much harder to try to get these things after the fact. Rice spelled out his address for me as we lumbered toward Vandenberge ahead.

As we neared the medevac point, I saw Captain Kearney running at top speed down the mountain toward us from his overwatch position. His gun was slung over his shoulder, and tears streamed down his face. "Rice!" Kearney wrapped his arms around him, and they all stood there and wept, soaking up the incredibleness of the ambush.

I photographed Rice and Vandenberge walking across the bleak terrain, covered in blood, arm in arm with their comrades. It was the first time I felt as if I were as much a part of the story as I was bearing witness while covering a war. But I was so consumed by adrenaline, I wasn't even processing my emotions. Rice and Vandenberge were loaded onto the Black Hawk, and I watched them take off into the dust kicked up by the propellers.

Seconds later I heard, "We have to go get the KIA."

The KIA? I asked myself. The KIA. The. Killed. In. Action. Fuck. "Wildcat"—Rougle—had been hit, and he was still missing. Rougle, who had just been telling Elizabeth and me that he was going to propose to his girlfriend when he went home on leave, who had survived almost six tours since September 11, 2001.

Other members of the scout team, Sergeant John Clinard and Specialist Franklin Eckrode, emerged carrying Rougle's body in a body bag. I couldn't believe Rougle—so vibrant and alive just an hour before—was now dead, in a thick, black, rubbery bag, being carried to the first of so many stops along the way home to his final resting place. Clinard and Eckrode were openly crying as they walked toward me, the limp body dangling between them. A bunch of young Americans who should have been out drinking beers at bars back home and living up their early twenties were instead carrying the lifeless body of their dearest friend through the lonely mountains of Afghanistan—a place that no one would care about twenty years from now. I wondered what we were doing there when so many others had failed to occupy Afghanistan in the past. Were we trying to influence and change a culture that was hundreds of years old? We were in what seemed like the most desolate place on earth, with no people around, neither Afghans nor Americans, and I wondered why we were there, fighting in a forest in the name of democracy. We were giving our lives for a policy that wasn't working—something completely intangible.

I raised my camera in a gesture to ask permission to photograph. I felt horrible asking, but we had been with them for two months, and I knew it was important to document Rougle's death. They all said yes as they knelt down momentarily and paused for a rest. What would it feel like to carry your best friend in a bag? Did they question the war the way I did? The four scouts who carried Rougle's body each bowed their heads and cried. I photographed through my own tears, sitting nearby. The hum of the second medical evacuation helicopter approached to collect "Wildcat."

The minute Rougle's body flew away from the Abas Ghar ridgeline, I knew I had to get out of there. I was spooked, convinced we were about to get ambushed again and not confident I would survive. Every time I walked over toward the team translating the Taliban intercepts on the radio, my sense of urgency grew. Kearney and the commanders of the 173rd Airborne back at Camp Blessing retaliated for Rougle's death with a series of two-thousand-pound bombs on the villages surrounding our position. Everyone was ready to kill, to avenge Rougle's death and Rice's and Vandenberge's injuries. It was only going to get bloodier.

"Kearney? Is there any way to get me out of here?" I cringed as I asked him to also deal with me: a freaked-out girl who was pleading to be extracted from the middle of a hostile ridgeline, where every Black Hawk flight in risked getting shot down by an insurgent on the mountain.

"I'll see what I can do, Addario," Kearney said. "There isn't much air willing to come in here. It's hot."

That night I lay awake, my heart pounding, my eyes wide open through the night as I listened for any sound of an ambush. Elizabeth, meanwhile, was undeterred. She was determined to stay until the end of the mission in order to see the story through, to see the soldiers arrive back at the KOP safely. She was not interested in flying out with me on any helicopter.

As a photographer in a war zone, I didn't have a weapon. I needed to get as close as I could to the action in order to get the photographs, but I also needed to stay alive. And the only thing that had kept me alive during Iraq, Afghanistan, Lebanon, Congo, and Darfur was my inner voice that told me when I had reached my personal limit of fear. It told me when I needed to pull back to preserve my sanity, and possibly my life. Elizabeth and I as a team were often willing to take the same risks, and this symbiotic relationship was a fundamental part of a successful partnership in war zones. But I was definitely the conservative one, perhaps because of her many years of experience or perhaps because she was braver. Her fearlessness, her commitment to the story, and her boundless energy to take notes every waking second were only some of the things that made her such an incredible journalist. I couldn't bear to listen to the whisperer saying they were going to attack again.

Rougle's pack and I ended up coasting over the desiccated landscape toward Camp Blessing the next day.

When I arrived at Camp Blessing, I went into the TOC, the command center where Elizabeth and I had begun our journey into the Korengal almost two months before, feeling the weight and sadness of war. For six days I hadn't taken my jeans off my body, combed my long, scraggly hair, washed my face, looked in a mirror, slept on anything other than the side of a mountain. I greeted the clean, coiffed men navigating the maps, screens, and drone feeds in the control room, and they all stopped and stared at me when I entered. Perhaps it was the sight of my face, blackened with dirt and streamed with tears, or maybe they were slightly shocked that Elizabeth and I were able to hold our own during such an intense mission. Whatever it was, I felt as if we had finally gained their respect with our experience in Rock Avalanche.

I dumped my pack in a tidy, lonely room with a bed at Blessing and went directly for a shower. The hot water ran long over my naked body for some time, breaking all the rules of limiting water use on the base, and I watched the dirt make dark little rivulets around my feet into the drain. I went back to the room, which seemed like paradise compared to the Abas Ghar ridgeline, and began the long process of downloading my discs. I had hours of work ahead, hours of downloading, editing hundreds of images, and combing through my notes to write captions. It would take me a few days to prepare the images from the Korengal Valley, but I wasn't in the mental space to give them more than a cursory glance that night before falling asleep.

I eventually made my way back to Jalalabad, Bagram Airfield, and then Kabul, where I sat in the airport waiting for my flight to Turkey. I was physically shattered, emotionally fragile, and thoroughly exhilarated to have survived my time in the Korengal. Coming so close to the edge of death and pushing myself to my own physical and mental limits helped me appreciate the beauty of daily life. In my late teens I had made a promise to myself that every day I would push myself to do something I didn't want to do. I was convinced it would ultimately make me become a better person. The philosophy extended to work: I allowed myself to enjoy life only if I worked hard, if I tested my limits, if I created a lasting body of work.

I wondered where Elizabeth was in the Korengal Valley as I boarded my flight with Ariana Afghan Airlines, the rickety national airline I flew only in times of sheer desperation. I was seated in an exit row, and as I stretched out my legs, pleased not to have anyone sitting too close to me, a male Afghan flight attendant came over and stirred me from my solitude: "Madam. You cannot sit here. This is an exit row."

"So?"

"Women cannot sit by the exit door. If there is a flight emergency, a woman wouldn't be capable of opening the exit door."

I got up, and as I moved to my new seat I watched the attendant usher over a frail old man with a white beard, hunched with osteoporosis, to sit by the exit door.

WHEN I GOT HOME to Istanbul, Paul's lifelong mentor, Peter, was in town visiting with his wife. Usually when I arrived home from an assignment, I was able to switch from the life of drinking electrolyte-filled water in a refugee camp to sipping pinot noir in our apartment with a Bosporus view. They came over before dinner. I was excited to meet someone who had shaped Paul's life, but much to my surprise, I was struggling to speak.

My head was fixated on the Abas Ghar ridge, the Korengal Outpost, the villages of Aliabad and Donga, Camp Vegas, Rougle laughing, Rougle in a body bag.

"Lynsey is a really famous war photographer!" Paul exclaimed proudly. Hearing his description of me made me wince slightly. I wasn't sure when I had become a war photographer.

"Shut up, baby," I joked. "I am not famous, and I am not a war photographer."

"So tell me about your last assignment," Peter prodded.

"I was in the Korengal Valley with the 173rd Airborne, living at one of their remote bases on and off for a few months."

"Really? Was it dangerous? Have you ever almost died?"

It was a question I had received often since I started covering war. Everyone wanted to reduce my entire career down to the one or two moments when I might have lost my life.

"Yeah. Um. I guess. It was really intense. We were getting shot at almost every day and then we went on this big mission, where we got ambushed by the Taliban."

And suddenly I felt as if words were completely inadequate to describe what we had just endured. How could I describe the disconnect between the soldier's mission in Afghanistan and the Afghan's desire to be left alone? How could I describe the terror I felt when I was crouching behind the tipped-over log, with bullets skimming the top of my head; the sadness of seeing Rougle's body in a bag, of seeing these strapping American boys in their twenties reduced to tears and horror after being overrun by an enemy they never saw? How could I describe that feeling of freedom and exhilaration I had when I was living in the dirt in a place like Camp Vegas, where life's utter necessities, like water, food, sleep, and staying alive, were all that mattered? How could I describe how I was still trembling from the trauma of the ambush, and still regretting flying out ahead of Elizabeth, and chastising myself for being an inadequate journalist? How could I describe how important I thought it was to be there, with the troops in Afghanistan and in Iraq, to document my generation's War on Terror without sounding lofty and self-important?

"It was great!" I said. "Yeah, we lived on the side of a mountain and got ambushed at the end."

I could feel my chest tightening and my body getting hot. It was an unfamiliar feeling, being overcome with emotion in the middle of drinks with friends.

"Please excuse me for a second," I said. "I have to go to the restroom."

I walked back to our bedroom in the rear of the apartment, closed the door behind me, and collapsed into tears. I pulled my cell phone out of my pocket and dialed Elizabeth's number.

"Elizabeth?" I said, my voice wavering.

"I can't stop crying," she said.

"Me neither. Oh, God. And Paul has company here. I am locked in the bathroom and can't stop crying."

"You will be OK. You will be OK."

We stayed on the phone until I stopped crying, and eventually I went back to my guests, finished my glass of wine, and left for dinner along the Bosporus.

THREE MONTHS LATER I was in Khartoum, Sudan, preparing to go into Darfur, when Kathy Ryan, the director of photography at the *New York Times Magazine*, e-mailed to tell me that Elizabeth had finally submitted her story from the Korengal Valley; the piece would close in the next two weeks. Elizabeth was nine months pregnant. The editors were polishing her piece; the fact-checkers were checking the facts. My picture of Khalid, the boy with shrapnel wounds smattering his face, was being considered as a cover. It was a stark, powerful image that spoke to the ambiguity of war and the inevitability of civilian casualties.

Five days before the piece went to press, I got a frantic call from a deputy photo editor at the magazine, asking me to go through my notebooks from the Korengal and produce every shred of evidence I could about Khalid.

There was a question back in New York about how Khalid had sustained his injuries. My captions for the images of Khalid were inconsistent with what Captain Kearney, Elizabeth, and I believed to be the truth—that Khalid was most likely injured by NATO bombs the night before we flew into the Korengal Valley. But almost five months before, when I was downloading my pictures in a bunker at the KOP, I naïvely entered into the file information of the digital image a rough summary from one of the medics—" . . . medics with the 173rd treat local afghans who claim they were injured by american bombs, though their wounds were NOT consistent with the timing of us attacks on villages near their homes . . ."—intending to flesh out the information with a more factual account of the events later. I felt that the medic's remarks were an obvious attempt to protect the U.S. military from a journalist's scrutiny of civilian casualties from American bombings, but that, as a journalist, I needed to include his opinion. By the time I filed the images from September and October in the Korengal, we had been through weeks of intense experiences, including Operation Rock Avalanche, and I mistakenly submitted photos without updating the captions, instilling doubt in the mind of the editor in chief. The editors at the magazine proceeded to fact-check the issue with one of the public affairs officers with the 173rd Airborne, who very predictably said that the military couldn't verify 100 percent that Khalid had been wounded in a NATO bombing. The magazine was questioning whether to even run the photo at all.

After months in the Korengal, the image of Khalid was one of the few instances of a civilian injury caused by a NATO bombing that I witnessed with my own eyes. There was no question that these kinds of injuries were happening all around us, but we weren't able to access the villages or the victims because of security or timing. I missed the opportunity that day on the side of the mountain overlooking Yaka China, and I felt uncondi-tionally that the image of Khalid's innocent, blood-spattered face both aesthetically and narratively was crucial to our story.

But after all that we had endured in the Korengal, our testimony did not seem to matter. Elizabeth and I had watched the events unfold on the screens in the Tactical Operations Command center, had witnessed the in-surgents shooting mortars at troops on the ground, had watched the United States drop five-hundred-pound bombs on the compounds, and had been present the next morning when the boy and his family came to the Koren-gal Outpost for medical treatment. Most of us who had been in the medical tent and at the base that morning had assumed that Khalid was injured in the bombing the night before. Captain Kearney even expressed this to the editor in chief on our behalf, and the debate went on for days. But because of my incomplete caption, the editor trusted the U.S. military public affairs officer—whose main responsibility was to polish the image of the U.S. military to the greater public—over us.

To make matters worse, from the time we set off to document the story in the Korengal to the final two weeks of the story's closing, the angle of Elizabeth's article shifted from the original idea of civilian casualties in war, to Operation Rock Avalanche, to a profile of Captain Kearney. In the eyes of the editor in chief, the image of Khalid as an illustration of civilian casualties was no longer relevant. And he was so resolute that the picture would be too controversial without tangible evidence of the cause of the boy's injury that he decided to strike the image from the story altogether. He then declared he would refuse to run a slide show of images to accompany the piece online. In a time when the space allotted to photographs in magazines was shrinking, a slide show was the consolation prize; images that didn't fit into the print edition were at least viewed by the public online. I was desperate. I spent almost two months traipsing around the mountains of one of the world's most dangerous places, and as the piece went to press, my reporting was being questioned, some of my strongest images were being removed from the layout, and the editor in chief decided uncharacteristically that he would not run a slide show. From my perspective, it seemed that he was fed up with our story. Perhaps the reason was the length of time it had taken Elizabeth to write it, or that *Vanity Fair* had recently published a multipage piece focusing on the Korengal Valley, or simply that we were challenging his editorial judgment while he was being bombarded with doubt by the military public affairs office.

Elizabeth helped plead my case: She tried to persuade him to at least permit a slide show of my images to accompany her story. Almost until she gave birth, she helped compose e-mails to him, pleading with the editor to honor our reporting.

The photo department stood by my work, but ultimately the editor

in chief had final say. I sat heartbroken in my dismal room at the
Acropole Hotel in Khartoum, steeling myself for yet another war, feeling utterly defeated. Kathy, the director of photography and one of the
most important women in the business, had by then become a close
friend and mentor. By 2008 I had worked on probably five cover stories
and several smaller stories with her, and we had developed a deep professional trust in each other. There is a bond between some photographers and their editors, in part because their relationships are so
symbiotic. Photographers depend on editors to sponsor and publish
their images; editors rely on those images to create powerful visual stories. Our success depended on each other. I seldom faced issues of censorship or questions about the authenticity of my photographs, but
when these issues arose, I relied on the photo editor to go to bat for me.
With Kathy's permission and Elizabeth's edits, I wrote the following
e-mail to the editor in chief—something that many would view as
overstepping my role as a freelance photographer:

> As journalists, we risked our lives for two months, getting shot at and
> ambushed, walking through the mountains at 6,000 feet day after day in
> order to bring you first hand facts from the field. We do this only because we
> believe the New York Times will stand behind the material we get and fight
> to get it published. Not pull pictures at the last minute because of public
> relations guys with the US military saying they can't confirm a victim of
> collateral damage was in the suspected compound. Dan [Captain Kearney]
> has all along been saying the boy was probably injured nearby by the shrap-
> nel. The military PR on the other hand does not want a picture of a little boy
> covered in shrapnel wounds most probably from a bomb they were respon-
> sible for dropping printed in the NYT. I am so shocked and dismayed at how
> the word of the US military has more weight than my own, when they are so
> blatantly worried about salvaging their reputation with these emails, and I
> am presenting the facts to you to bring to the public. We were in the TOC
> when they dropped the bomb, and in the medical tent when the Afghan

elders brought the boy in the next morning and claimed he was in the compound. Simple. This is war. There is ambiguity.

. . . After all I have done to get these images of war, up close, personal,
soldiers and civilians, please stick your neck out in the most minimal way. To
hear that you don't want to "risk further scrutiny" after I risked my life for
two months is the most offensive thing I have ever heard. We represent the
New York Times. We have a responsibility to put out material we get, not
cower and question ourselves and worry about military scrutiny.

. . . We owe it to the Afghans, the soldiers, everyone we spent time with
and promised to show the TRUTH. Our readers deserve to see what's happening over there.

The magazine ended up running a small slide show of my images with
the online piece. The photograph of Khalid never saw the light of day.

CHAPTER 10

Driver Expire

The boat skimmed over the turquoise waters toward our Bahamas bungalow, tucked amid a palm grove abutting the sea. It was New Year's Eve 2007, two months after I flew out of the Korengal Valley, and Paul had taken me on vacation, a rare week of indulgence. Our eco-friendly, whitewashed room's French doors opened to a private Jacuzzi. The resort had provided us with our own golf cart with a quaint straw basket affixed to the front to accommodate our beach gear. The weather was slightly overcast and chilly, but we didn't care. We spent our days going for runs along the shore and lying in bed. At night we lingered over long, calorie-laden meals: butter-drenched lobster, bottles of white wine, crème brûlée or chocolate cake.

It was hard to reconcile the Korengal Valley with a paradise like the Bahamas, but by then I had learned to accept these strange incongruities of life. I turned off the trauma and sadness of my work in order to enjoy my happiness with Paul. Walking between worlds is one of the great privileges of the foreign correspondent. I never forgot what I had witnessed, and I talked often of my experiences, but I didn't let them overwhelm my personal life. There is a somewhat accurate cliché of the ever-haunted war correspondent who can't escape the darkness of what he has seen and drowns himself in drugs or sex or more war because he can't face the ordinary or leaves the profession because he is finally broken by it. I didn't want to be that person.

On the morning of New Year's Eve, Paul paced the room.

I asked him what was up. Did he want to tell me something? Was he cheating on me, like the others? It's fine, I'm used to it, I explained, but I needed to know where I stood. Paul laughed. He began frantically packing our golf cart for a picnic, which seemed strange, given the foreboding clouds along the horizon. I lay on my back under the covers and pleaded with him to come to bed and take a nap with me.

"Let's go for a walk on the beach," he said.

"What? Now? Can't we go later?" It was so delicious in bed on a chilly, gray day by the sea.

"No. Let's go now."

We got to the beach, and Paul hurriedly unpacked our golf cart and started walking toward the shore.

"Let's just stay right here," I said. "Why do we have to walk far?"

"Let's keep walking."

I grew anxious. Paul was never skittish. He was neurotic at work but relaxed on vacation. Now he was neurotic on vacation.

We made our way to a spot that looked like any other. He stopped and laid out the blanket. I plopped down on my stomach and propped my chin up on my palms. Paul sat down. And then kneeled, and then paused, and then told me to stand.

He already had the red Cartier box with silver trim in his hands, and he was crying. "Will you marry me?"

He was the first man I'd ever considered spending my life with, but I couldn't believe he would want to marry *me*, the woman who was

forever told she was an inadequate girlfriend by all her past lovers. I
had long convinced myself that my cameras and I would grow old together alone in some remote corner of the planet.

"Me? Are you sure you want to marry me? I am never home," I said.
We were both crying, kissing. "You don't have to marry me, you know."

"Baby, I love you," he said. "I want to spend my life with you."

We set the wedding date for July 4, 2009.

IN MOST WAYS my life and my career didn't change after my engagement. The countries I covered continued to be torn by violence and humanitarian catastrophe. And at age thirty-four, after ten years in the
business, I wanted to cover these stories as much as I did when I was
twenty-four. The only difference was that I didn't have to fight for assignments or live hand to mouth, and this relative comfort nurtured my
passion for photography. I even started shooting regularly for *National
Geographic* magazine, an honor for any photojournalist. My ambition actually seemed to grow with time. Quite often the most ambitious or
prestigious assignments were the riskiest ones. I spent much of 2008 and
2009 in Pakistan and Afghanistan, where the War on Terror still raged.

Paul was surprisingly selfless and objective about my choice of stories. He trusted my inner voice as much as I did. When I presented him
with the risks involved in an assignment, he was always levelheaded in
his feedback, asked the important questions, and only selectively questioned my journalistic judgment. That summer, when I was asked to
cover the growing presence of the Taliban in Pakistan, he replied, as
always, calmly: "Nice. How are you planning on doing that? By meeting the Taliban?"

Paul knew the answer to his own question. My old friend Dexter
Filkins was reporting the story for the *New York Times Magazine*, and
to do the story right we had to meet face-to-face with one of the world's
most fundamentalist jihadi groups, one that had repeatedly threatened

to capture and behead Westerners. Dex had arranged for safe passage to meet one Taliban commander, but there were many Taliban groups in the tribal areas. Just because one had ensured our safety didn't mean we couldn't fall into the hands of another that wanted us dead.

But as with Elizabeth, I trusted Dex. In our professional circle many saw him as a reckless foreign correspondent who would do anything for a story. But I think much of that stemmed from envy: He was a great journalist. He always wore the same white Brooks Brothers button-downs, khaki pants, and loafers, which, especially in Iraq or Afghanistan, made him look like a CIA agent. This didn't seem to worry him. In Iraq we had spent countless days working together, and evenings talking, and I found him a fun and loyal friend. I respected and admired his work. I also knew that any story he did might land on the cover of the magazine, or the front page of the newspaper, and have a better chance at actually influencing American foreign policy. More often than not, it was that combination that swayed me to do a story.

I was convinced by my case, and so was Paul.

I HADN'T BEEN to Peshawar since 2001, when I was twenty-seven and trying to rig up assignments from Green's Hotel as the United States prepared to bomb Afghanistan. This time Dex and I were staying at the relatively luxurious Pearl Continental Hotel. Through a network of photographers who had spent years working in Pakistan, I was connected with the wonderful Raza. Almost fifty years old, with stringy, graying hair combed over to the side and a weathered, smiling face, he was one of the savviest drivers I had ever worked with. Raza dressed me up as his wife and sneaked me into the Swat Valley to photograph secret girls' schools that had recently opened after the Taliban closed schools in the valley; he bullied imams into allowing me—a female infidel—to photograph prayers at mosques in Peshawar; and he snuck me into the gun market for a few quick shots before fleeing, because we feared we might be spotted and attacked.

Dex and I were to meet a Taliban commander named Haji Namdar. The day before our meeting, Haleem, one of our interpreters, relayed a message from the commander: "You cannot bring a woman with you." Dex and I were adamant that we would not separate. The long-bearded Haleem, who himself was sympathetic to the Taliban and wouldn't look me directly in the eye because I was a woman, was tormented. He wracked his brain for the entire day and finally came back with the solution: "I know! Lynsey can be Dexter's wife! And we can say that Mr. Dexter did not want to leave his wife alone in the hotel while he traveled out of Peshawar." I was always being dressed up as someone's wife.

We arrived at Haji Namdar's house in the early afternoon, in the midst of a torrential downpour. I tried to steal glances through the thin white cloth of the *hijab* that covered my face. We were inside high compound walls, and everything was tan. Haleem and Dex jumped out of the car to greet the commander. I was told to wait until permission was granted for a woman's presence.

Within minutes Haleem returned and told me I, too, could enter the house. The room was pungent with foot odor and full of heavily bearded, armed men in varying states of Friday sprawl against the walls. Their AK-47s stood up against the walls alongside their prosthetic legs or lay alongside their masters. I tried to walk without tripping over my *abaya*. Dex, in very Dexter fashion, started the interview.

"Haji Namdar," he said jovially. I was surprised he didn't add "dude" or "man." "Thank you so much for welcoming us today. Before we begin, I want to introduce you to my wife, Lynsey." I was grateful he didn't waste time, because I was clearly the elephant in the room. "And by the way, my wife has a camera," he continued. "Can she take some pictures?"

It seemed like an absurd proposal.

Haji Namdar agreed. I often found that some of the biggest extremists were open to meeting with women so long as we were not *their* women. Western female journalists didn't have to abide by either male or female traditions, and I assumed they had given up trying to figure us out long ago. I removed my hulking Nikon D3 with a 24–70mm f2.8 lens from my bag and tried to look unprofessional.

I started out with a few frames of Haji Namdar as Dex interviewed him. I wasn't sure whether the other Taliban fighters were comfortable with being photographed, but I figured if their commander agreed, they would also agree. After a few minutes I started pointing my camera around the room. My rule of thumb was that once I got permission to photograph, I shot as much as I could, because I was never sure how long that permission would last. Some men shielded their faces when I turned my camera on them; others didn't flinch. And some were proud to be photographed for the most important American newspaper in the world. They might have been illiterate fighters, but most insurgents understood the influence of the *New York Times* on the U.S. government.

I grew more brazen and took another lens from my bag. My hand got tangled up in my layers of cloth instead—my eyesight impeded by my *hijab*—and I dropped the lens. After eight years of trying to shoot from beneath myriad disguises, I was exasperated, and I opened a teeny horizontal crease in my *hijab* for my eyes. I needed to work.

About ten minutes into the interview, tea was served, causing a flurry of activity around Haji Namdar. I stayed focused on shooting. Some men whispered among themselves and then included Haleem in quiet conversation. Finally a declaration was made. I worried they had had enough of a woman's presence and were going to ask me to wait in the car.

"Madam," Haleem said, "the commander's men are worried you can't drink your tea through your veil. They would really like for you to drink your tea." The whispers continued, and if it weren't for the veil, I would have had a difficult time concealing my smile. Only among Muslims is the hospitality so great that they cannot bear the notion that someone's tea will be left untouched.

Haleem had another brilliant idea: "I know! You can stand in the corner of the room, with your back facing all of us, and lift your veil to the wall and drink your tea. Once you finish, you can replace your veil."

And so, in a room full of some of the most vicious fighters against the United States and everything it stood for, I stood in the corner and faced the wall as I drank my tea.

Some eight months later our magazine story, "Talibanistan," was part of a package of stories that won the Pulitzer Prize. I congratulated Dex; hours later, to my surprise, congratulation e-mails began pouring in for me. Apparently two photographers—myself and my childhood friend Tyler Hicks—had been included in the winning team, which was unusual for the Pulitzer. For years, my only dream was to work for the *New York Times*, and now my work for them was part of journalism's greatest award. I was honored and overwhelmed.

SEVEN WEEKS BEFORE the wedding, Dex and I met up again in Islamabad. The Pakistani government had made a large public display of their internal battle against the Taliban, and we flew in to cover, among other things, the thousands of Pakistanis displaced from the Swat Valley into camps on the outskirts of the city of Mardan, the second-largest city in the North-West Frontier Province.

On a Friday morning, Raza showed up at my guesthouse door at five thirty. He brought with him an unexpected addition, Teru, an old friend and fellow photojournalist from New York, who asked if he could ride along with us. Dexter had decided to stay in Islamabad and report that morning, and I was happy to have Teru's company. We drove to Mardan, where the camps for Pakistani civilians fleeing their Swat Valley homes were swelling by the day as the government continued its offensive against the Pakistani Taliban. Teru and I spent the morning photographing in the camps as Raza shuffled between us, providing us with rough translations for our photo captions.

We had a successful morning. We were in the heart of the story, in a region I cared deeply about, less than a year after I had photographed the Pakistani Taliban, and we were working in a safe area. The soft morning light eventually turned too harsh for photographing, and we packed up our gear and headed back toward Islamabad to file pictures. The plan was to meet Dexter back at the guesthouse that afternoon.

Around 1 p.m., Teru, Raza, and I stopped for gas along the highway and had some tea, biscuits, and nuts to tide us over until we reached the guesthouse in Islamabad. Raza filled his tank with gas and handed me the receipt, along with the receipt for his hotel room. I had insisted that he sleep in Islamabad the night before—rather than Peshawar, which was a two-hour drive away—so that he was well rested for our journey that day. We got back into the car and I resumed my natural position when on assignment: horizontal in the backseat, making up for sleep lost to days of hard work. I sent texts to Dexter and Paul saying how great the morning was, tucked my camera bag into the nook of a triangle made by the recline of the passenger seat in front of me, and dozed off.

I was in a deep sleep when I felt my body being pulled to the left. I assumed I was dreaming. My muscles tensed up; I heard a loud screech and waited for the sound of the crash, as if I were a spectator in my own dream. But then there actually was a crash, the world went blacker than in my dream, and a gentle warmth washed over me.

Since I was a little girl I often had nightmares that I died in strange ways. But I always woke up in time. This time I was unconscious. I don't remember how much time passed before I started to be cognizant of my surroundings: chaos, frenzy, noise. I couldn't actually see. I wasn't coherent enough to react or strong enough to move. It was the first time in my adult life that I couldn't move without assistance, and it came with an unfamiliar sensation of submission.

For a brief moment I opened my eyes to a minivan and a man with a mustache. The man with the mustache was carrying me. I was still horizontal.

And then I was on a concrete slab in what seemed like one of those rudimentary roadside clinics. I couldn't figure out what had happened, and I had no idea what country I was in. I looked around to see strangers in the room, many of them heavily bearded men. I couldn't move; I was injured. My back burned, and my bones sent intense waves of pain through my shoulder.

A nurse with a head scarf stood over me, to my left, holding a giant needle full of fluid. I asked her if the needle was clean. She looked at me as if I was insane. Where was I? An image of a refugee camp flashed before my eyes. More bearded men. I wondered why I wasn't wearing a head scarf. I raised my right arm, the one I could still move, and felt the top of my head for my usual *hijab*. My hair was exposed, but I knew that I should have had my head covered.

To my right I heard a man let out a series of rhythmic, gut-wrenching groans. I looked over, and it was Raza. *Oh, Raza,* I thought. *My Pakistani driver. Next to me. Moaning. To my right. Raza. Making noise.* It seemed like the most natural thing: Raza and I on adjacent concrete slabs, in a Pakistani clinic similar to ones I had spent years photographing around the world. Now Raza and I were the patients.

Oh, Raza is moaning, I thought. *That's good. He is alive.* I still had no idea what had happened, but for some reason I understood that it was a good sign that Raza was making noise. Everything hurt as the head-scarfed nurse stood over me with the needle that still hadn't been injected in me. What had I been doing that morning? Was I dreaming?

Teru appeared before me, at the foot of my slab. His faced looked as if he had just finished a boxing match, but he was standing on his own two feet. I wondered what Teru, from New York, was doing at the foot of my bed. The nurse stuck the needle in me. She never answered my question about whether it was clean. Who cared if I got HIV? I was in excruciating pain. The refugees. Mardan. We had been in Mardan all morning. It was starting to come back. There were so many people in the room, standing around, looking at Raza and me splayed out on the tables. Refugees, I recalled. The *New York Times*. I had been photographing. The skid, the crash. It was real. Teru explained: "We are in Pakistan. We were photographing at the refugee camps with Raza, and we have been in a bad car accident." A doctor started immobilizing my arm by bandaging it close to my body. My bones were broken. My back burned. My Pakistani dress, *a salwar kameez*, was melted onto the raw patch of flesh on my back where my skin had rubbed off in the friction of the accident. My hands were a raw mix of pus and blood. My ankles were sprained and swollen, and my ribs hurt. Where was my head scarf?

Teru and I were transferred to an ambulance, and Raza wasn't with us anymore. The paramedic, Khalid, sat at my feet and leaned over me, saying his name over and over again, pleading with me to repeat his name so I wouldn't pass out. "Khalid. My name is Khalid. Say my name." He was relentless, and I was grateful, vaguely aware that he was trying to keep me alive. "Khalid. Say my name: Khalid." I was horizontal, arm taped to my side, drugged up on morphine, when I realized that my camera bag wasn't with us.

"Khalid, where is our car?" I said. "Where is my camera bag? Is the car far from here? We were on our way to Islamabad."

"No," Khalid said. "The car is close to here."

I could see only within the confines of the ambulance but assumed we were traveling along the highway toward Islamabad.

"Khalid," I repeated his name as instructed, "can we stop at the car to get my camera bag? I need my cameras, my phone." I only half-expected him to agree.

He turned back toward the driver and said something in Urdu, then turned back to me: "OK. We can stop at the car."

I felt the ambulance make a detour and eventually come to a stop. I was so curious what the remains of our demolished car looked like, but my arms were taped alongside my body to hold my broken bones in place, and I couldn't muster the energy to raise myself up to look outside. The back doors to the ambulance flung open behind me, and a

Pakistani policeman stepped in and announced that he had been tasked with guarding our car so that no one could steal our belongings. In an effort to prove that he hadn't pilfered anything from our bags, the policeman then stood over me, lying flat on my back and wrapped with flimsy gauze, and held out my little change purse.

"Look," the policeman declared triumphantly as I struggled to keep my eyes open. "All your money is here!" And he riffled through my little travel wallet, showing me that he had meticulously separated out all the different currencies, arranging them in order by country.

"Thank you. You can have the money," I said. "Where are my cameras? Where is my camera bag? I wanted my cameras and my telephone."

He immediately produced my black Domke camera bag, in perfect shape. And at that point someone—either Khalid or the ambulance driver—obviously felt some sort of urgency to return us to the original mission of rushing us to the hospital, and the doors behind me closed, the police officer who had safely guarded our things disappeared, and we continued on our way toward Islamabad.

I asked Khalid to fish my orange cell phone out of my bag. He handed it to me, and as I held the phone I wasn't sure whom to call. One side of my brain told me to call Paul; the other side of my brain wondered who Paul was. My mind was cloudy. *Paul. Fiancé. Call. Paul.* I scrolled through the names in my contact list and found "Paul Baby" and wrote a text: "Baby I have been in a bad car accident. But I am ok. Please call my parents and let them know I am ok." I then dialed my friend Ivan, who had started working with CNN and was in Pakistan at the time. Ivan answered the phone, and I vaguely remember asking him to call my friend Kathy Gannon, who was still living in Pakistan from the days when she helped me secure my first Taliban visa, to find out what hospital we should go to as we made our way back to Islamabad. Somewhere in the reserves of my memory, I was able to recall that Kathy knew the country well. My eyes started closing again when my phone rang. It was Paul. "Baby, I am OK. Please call Kathy Gannon and find out what the best hospital is in Islamabad. And can you call my sister Lauren and tell her I am alive?" Lauren was my oldest sister, to whom I often turned during a crisis. In childhood she had been my protector, and she was solid and nurturing during any crisis—truly maternal. I must have sensed that Lauren would be the right person, rather than my mother, to handle the news and to disseminate it to the rest of the family without drama. I then called Dex, explaining that we had been in a car accident and asking him to meet me at the hospital. And then I passed out again.

The next time I woke up I was being wheeled down a hospital corridor on a stretcher, watching the lights on the ceiling and the upper halves of bodies scurry past me. The medics were rambling on in Urdu when I heard " . . . driver expire . . . ," and I knew they were talking about Raza. My heart broke.

"Where is Raza?" I pleaded—to no response. "Where is my driver, Raza?"

Silence.

They wheeled me to the emergency room at the Shifa International Hospital, where a sea of familiar faces met our arrival: Ivan, Dex, Pamela Constable from the *Washington Post*, Kathy Gannon. I couldn't move and was flying on morphine. Ivan had brought along a CNN security adviser who doubled as a medic to look me over with a series of quick tests to ensure that I didn't have brain damage. He put a flashlight to my eyes and asked me to follow it. He was already one step ahead of the doctors at Shifa.

I noticed Dex, in crisis mode, scurrying around the emergency room with a clipboard of papers to register me and Teru at the hospital.

"Dex, where is Raza?" I asked, knowing he would be honest with me.

"He is dead, man. Raza is dead."

The words sank in—*driver expire*—and I started to cry.

I felt that Raza's death was my fault. We weren't in a dangerous place or driving at some ungodly hour of the night. We weren't being chased by Taliban or insurgents or running on no sleep. It was one of the few times in my career when my driver and I were actually operating in a safe environment, on a full night's sleep, caffeine and food in our stomachs, driving along a perfectly paved road. But I still felt guilty.

When, a few hours later, his sons came to collect Raza's belongings, and visited the hospital room where Teru and I were being treated temporarily, I started crying uncontrollably. "I am sorry. I am so sorry." Raza had been the breadwinner for his wife and eight children.

Kathy came to my room before leaving that night. She stood at the foot of my bed and offered some advice to Dexter: "Do not leave her alone for one minute in this hospital. Monitor everything they give her. They will come at all hours of the night to administer tests, and someone must be with her." And then she explained that she had asked her private doctor in Islamabad—a trusted doctor who treated the foreign diplomatic, aid, and journalist communities—to pass by and check on me daily.

For three days Paul struggled to get a visa to Pakistan. Under normal circumstances, that could take weeks for a journalist. To make matters worse, the accident happened on a Friday afternoon. He somehow persuaded the ambassador to open the consulate over the weekend to issue him a visa. In the interim Dexter and Ivan rotated shifts in my room. The Pakistani staff was thoroughly confused by their presence— women in Pakistan didn't usually have men who weren't husbands or family members in their room—so I told everyone that Dexter and Ivan were my brothers.

There were other problems. The first night, a handful of male nurses arrived at my bedside at about one in the morning, ready to take me for an MRI or a CT scan. In lieu of a rolling stretcher they grabbed the edges of the sheet from my hospital bed and picked me up in the sheet, jamming together the shattered bones of my collarbone and chafing the open wounds on my back where I had lost layers of skin. I screamed bloody murder while Dex yelled at them to be careful, as they shifted me from the sheet to a rolling stretcher. They ushered me down the hall onto an elevator and down to a basement room, where I was placed on a table at the entrance to a monstrous, tunnel-like machine. I drifted in and out of consciousness as I waited for the mysterious scan to begin. Nothing. What seemed like hours passed, with no progress, when I turned to Dex to ask what was happening. He turned to the male nurses and said, "Dudes, what is taking so long?"

The men stood over me awkwardly, and one cocked his head as he offered up: "Madam has metal."

Dex was confused. He turned to me: "Dude, do you have metal on you?"

I still had my underwire bra on. No one had dared to remove my clothes since I had arrived at the hospital. My rust-colored *salwar kameez* was still stuck to the open wounds on my back, and my bra was still fastened around my chest.

"Dex, I have a bra on."

"Well, take it off."

"I can't take it off. I can't move my arms. You take it off."

The Pakistani nurses were completely riveted.

"I can't take your bra off. Paul will kill me."

"Dex. You are fifty years old. You have seen tits before. Take my bra off!"

The poor nurses were confused again.

"It's a simple bra with a front clasp," I explained to Dex.

He nodded, and I passed out again.

THE SCANS FROM SHIFA Hospital revealed no internal bleeding and no damage to my head. I had a smashed collarbone; loss of skin on my back, arms, and hands; two sprained ankles and possibly sprained ribs.

I felt as if I had been thrown into a washing machine on the spin cycle. Every three hours a nurse would come into my room and administer morphine directly into my veins. With each injection my body felt as if it were sinking into a warm bath and then rising up to float through the room, weightless and painless.

In a rare window of lucidity, I started looking through my e-mails and asked Dex to bring in my computer so I could download and look through my pictures from the refugee camps. I wanted to file a selection of images from my hospital bed and get them published in the paper, as if somehow this horrific day would have been justified by our work. Or maybe I was so accustomed to filing at the end of a long, exhausting day on a breaking-news story; I had once filed under fire in Fallujah from beneath the protection of a Humvee. The instinct to file the images from the camps before they got outdated was automatic.

Paul arrived in my hospital room on a Monday morning, clipboard in hand, in the midst of one of my doped-up hazes. I remember seeing him and his concerned but reassuring face and knowing everything would be OK. And I knew the nurses would be relieved to finally see my fiancé by my bedside to replace my questionable "brothers."

The day before I left the hospital, the Turkish ambassador arrived at my bedside with a posse of diplomats and offered Paul and me a place to stay in the Turkish Embassy in Islamabad once I was released. The nurses continued watching the flurry of activity in and out of my room with curiosity. Almost immediately after the ambassador left, another set of visitors arrived: Haleem, my sympathetic-to-the-Taliban interpreter from the "Talibanistan" story the year before, along with one of his cousins. I was mortified that my hair was uncovered and I was wearing a hospital gown with skin exposed in front of two deeply religious men. Each visitor had a very long beard and wore an ankle-length kurta, a loose-fitting collarless shirt. Haleem toted a bag of hand-picked oranges, and Paul invited him and his cousin to sit down.

I thanked them for coming. "How are you, Haleem?" I asked.

"Well. We are fine," he said, "though my cousin's house was hit by a drone yesterday . . ."

Life in Pakistan went on.

A FEW DAYS LATER Paul and I flew back to Istanbul, and on May 19, 2009, I had a titanium plate put in my shoulder. I was completely unprepared for the post-op misery. I only wanted to be healthy again, to be able to walk down the aisle at our wedding in six weeks.

Night after night I woke up screaming and weeping with daggerlike pains shooting through my shoulder and chest. For the first time in my life I was injured; I could not take care of myself, and I realized how long I had taken my independence for granted. The simplest tasks became impossible without the use of my left shoulder and arm: I couldn't bathe, I couldn't put on my own bra, and I couldn't fully dress myself. In the weeks leading up to our wedding, Paul spent every morning before work walking me to the shower, washing my body, toweling me off, putting on my underwear, clasping my bra, dressing me, and preparing whatever I needed for the day while he was off at work. I knew that seeing me so fragile and vulnerable was taking a toll on him emotionally, wearing him down. He was taking care of me, running a hectic news bureau, and planning our entire wedding—alone. I had never relied on someone so completely before, and I felt guilty for being so helpless. Paul's determination to nurse me back to health was humbling.

Only once did he allow his own suffering to show. He was sitting at the desk in our living room, looking at his laptop, and suddenly he started to cry. He had received an e-mail from Bill Keller, the executive editor of the *New York Times*, who wrote to say how relieved he was that I was OK. Keller's simple words broke something in Paul. I could hardly bear to see it.

I spent the end of May and the beginning of June lying on my back, sleeping, or watching the cargo ships float along the Bosporus outside my window until Paul came home from work. My attention span wasn't focused enough to help him with our wedding planning, to read a book, or to watch a movie. I tried working at my computer, but the pain was often so excruciating that I couldn't sit up. I couldn't work or go on assignment, and I couldn't earn money. It was the first time I couldn't rely on determination, physical endurance—or myself—to do anything.

Some weeks later I was well enough to have lunch with my Istanbul friends Jason and Suzy. Jason looked concerned. "When are you going to just stop all this war zone stuff?" he finally said. "Why not get pregnant?"

It was a valid question but a deeply private and anxiety-inducing one. I didn't want to discuss it over lunch with friends when I was still physically and emotionally fragile. The suggestion that my work had become too dangerous, or that somehow getting pregnant was an adequate replacement for photography, struck chords deep down in me about my work, my life, and how I chose to balance the two—especially as I approached my wedding date. The car accident in Pakistan was just one more example of me walking away from a near-death incident relatively unscathed, and each time I survived I knew my luck wouldn't last forever. Paul, like my parents and sisters, never asked me to stop working; he never asked me to tone down my life or shy away from risk. He knew better than to ask me to change, or to compromise what I believed in. But every traumatic incident inspired inner dialogue that I wasn't necessarily ready to confront, and in this case it was especially easy to chalk the accident up to chance: It was just a car accident! That could happen anywhere! I talked things through with Paul, updated my will, and moved forward.

But I got angry when my friends challenged a resolve that was already often painful to maintain. As I moved out of my twenties and into my thirties, my friends' advice evolved from "stop running around war zones" to "stop running around war zones *and get pregnant.*" It was even more infuriating. In my early twenties my response was simple: "I don't have a man. And I prefer to be doing exactly what I am doing."

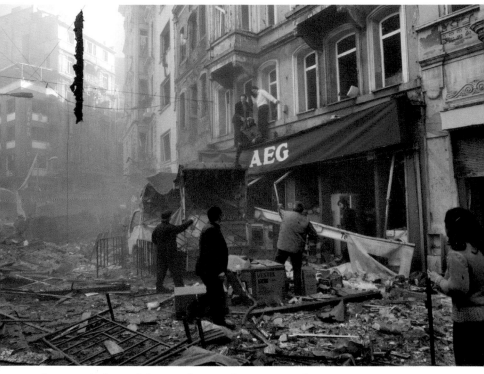

The scene in front of the British Consulate minutes after a car
bomb exploded, killing at least thirty people, including
Consul General Roger Short, November 20, 2003.

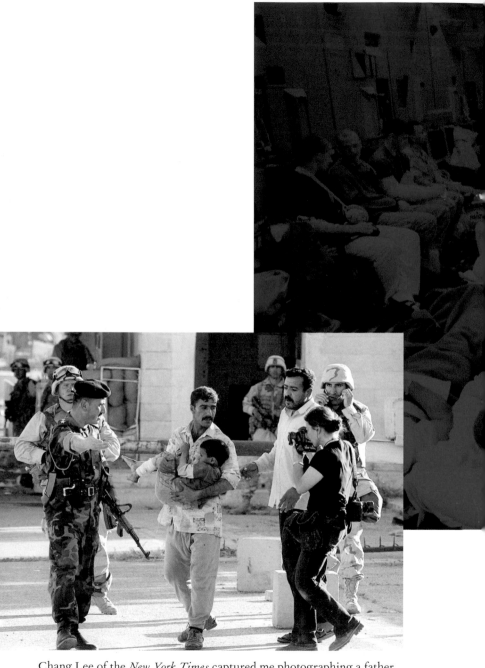

Chang Lee of the *New York Times* captured me photographing a father and his injured son as they are turned away from medical care at a joint American-*peshmerga* military base in Kirkuk in the days following the fall of Iraqi leader Saddam Hussein, April 2003.

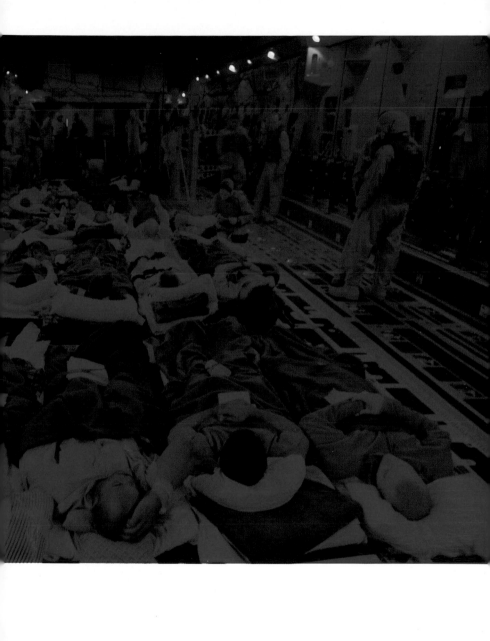

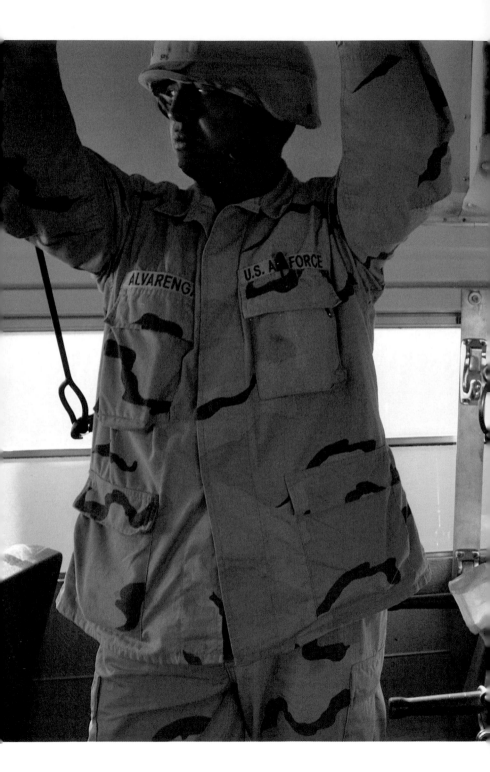

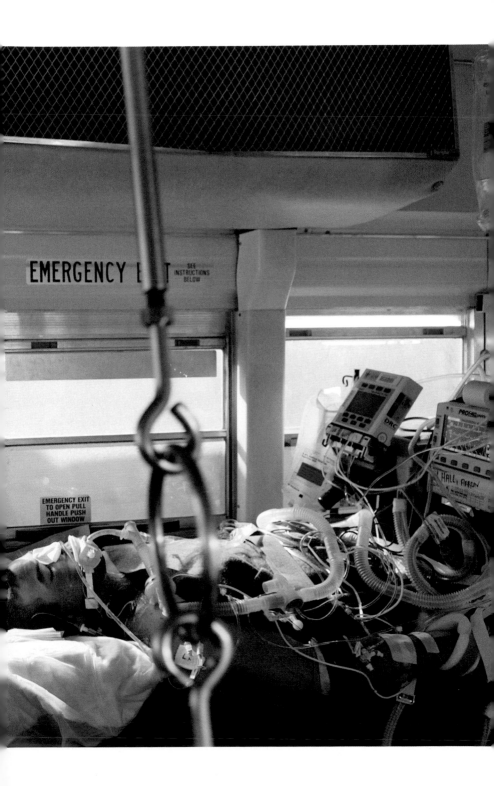

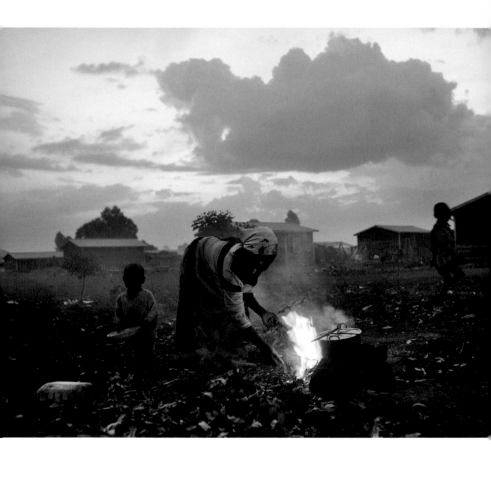

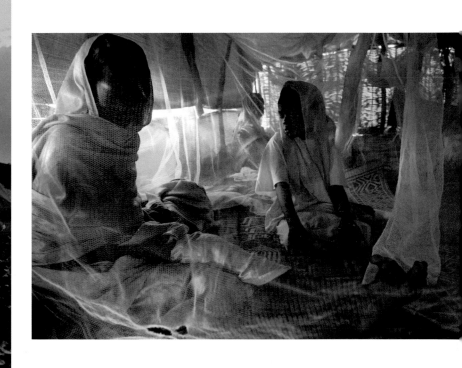

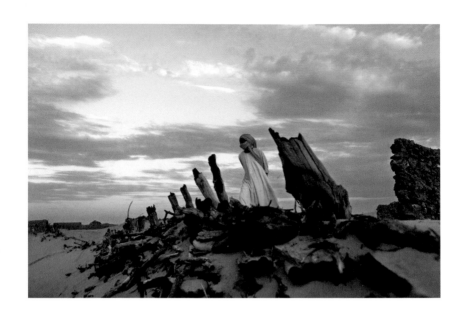

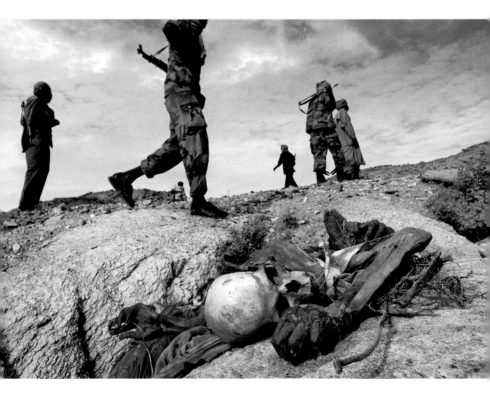

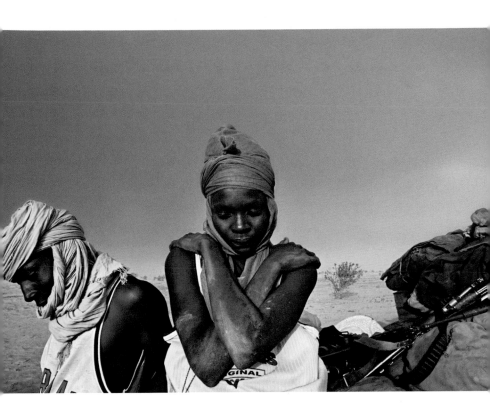

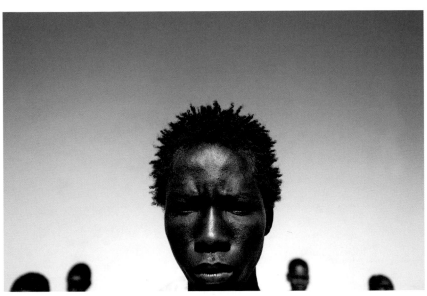

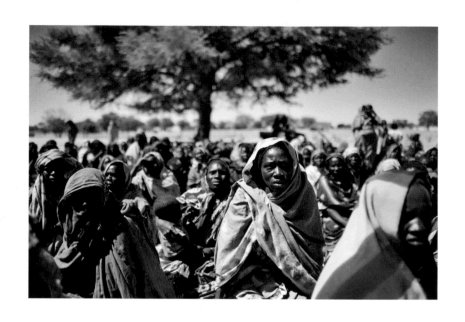

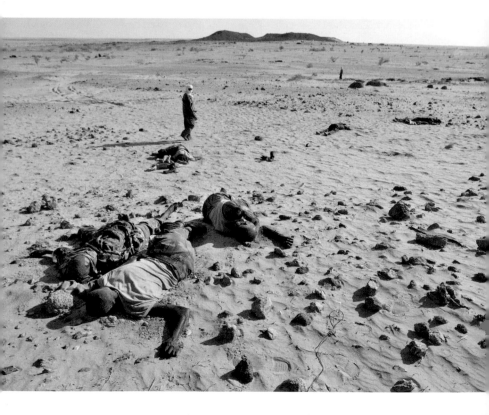

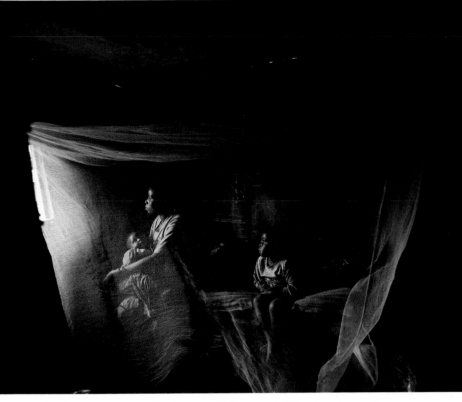

Kahindo, twenty, sits in her home with her two children born out of rape in the village of Kanyabayonga, North Kivu, in eastern Congo, April 12, 2008. Kahindo was kidnapped and held for almost three years in the bush by six *interhamwe*, who she claims were Rwandan soldiers. They each raped her repeatedly. She had one child in the forest and was pregnant with the second by the time she escaped.

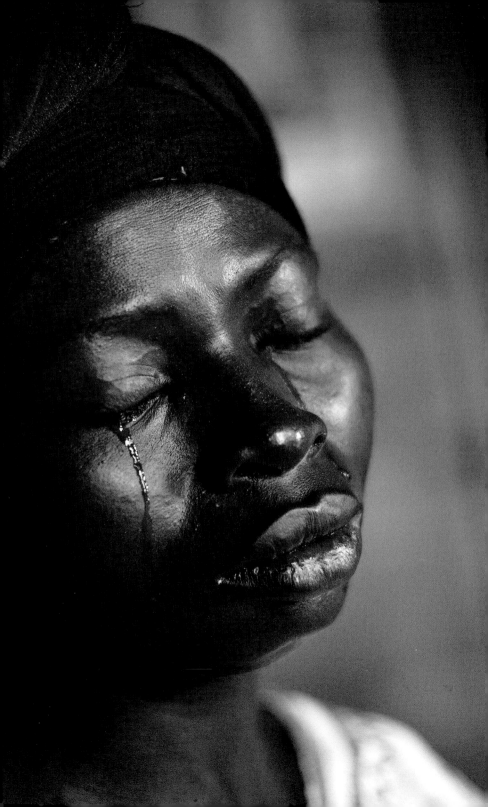

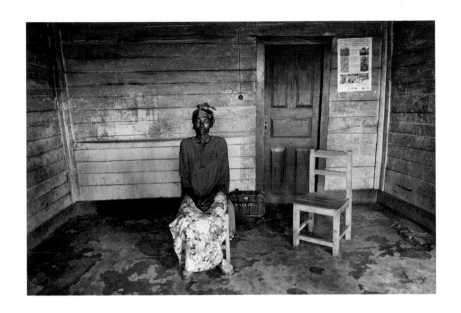

LEFT: Bibiane, twenty-eight, South Kivu.

ABOVE: Vumila, thirty-eight, Kaniola.

BELOW: Mapendo, twenty-two, Burhale.

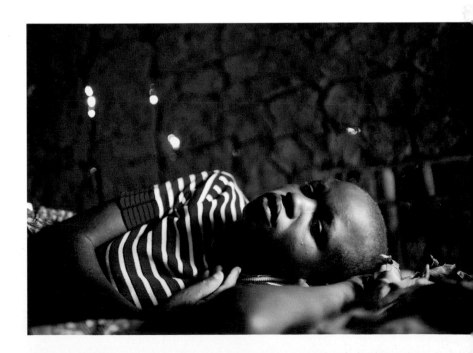

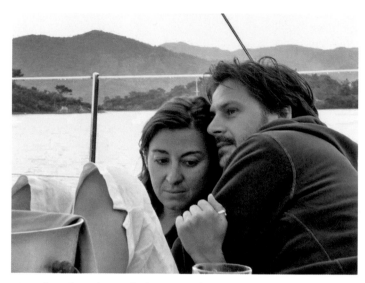

Me and Paul on the Turkish coast, July 2007.

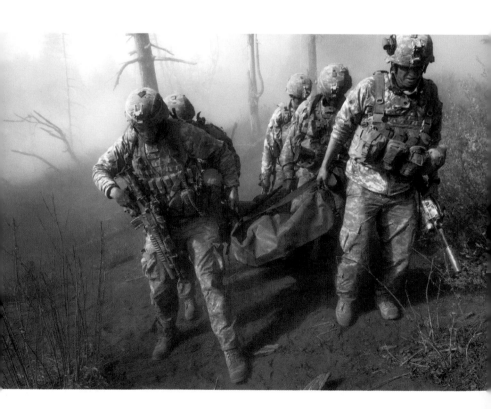

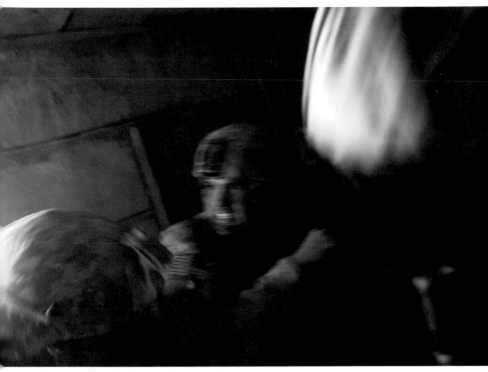

Soldiers with the 173rd Airborne, Battle Company,
react as they receive incoming mortar rounds near the
shelter at the Korengal Outpost.

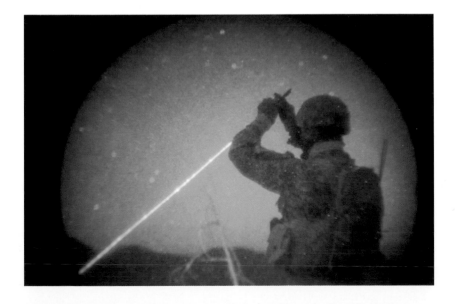

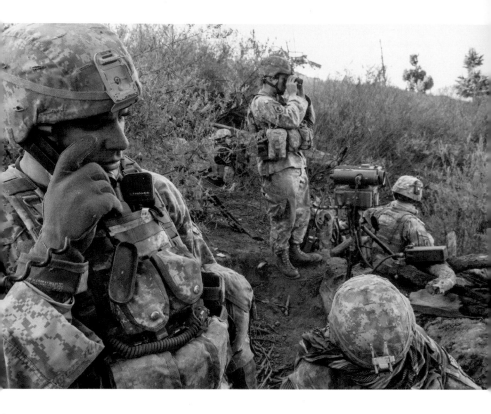

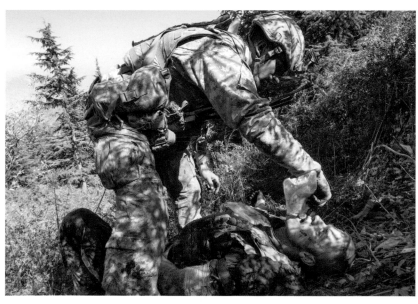

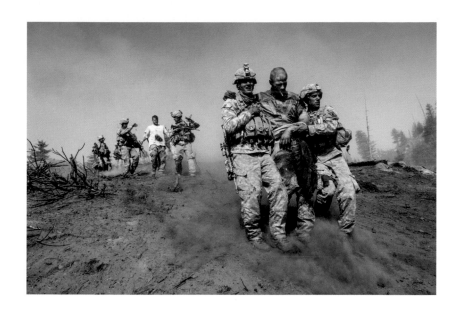

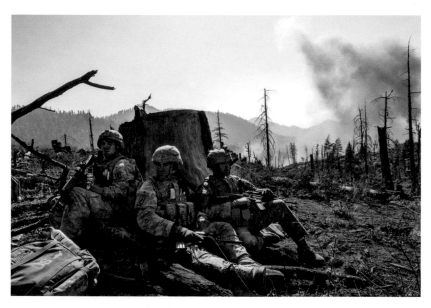

OPPOSITE AND ABOVE: Operation Rock Avalanche.
The Korengal Valley, October 18–23, 2007.

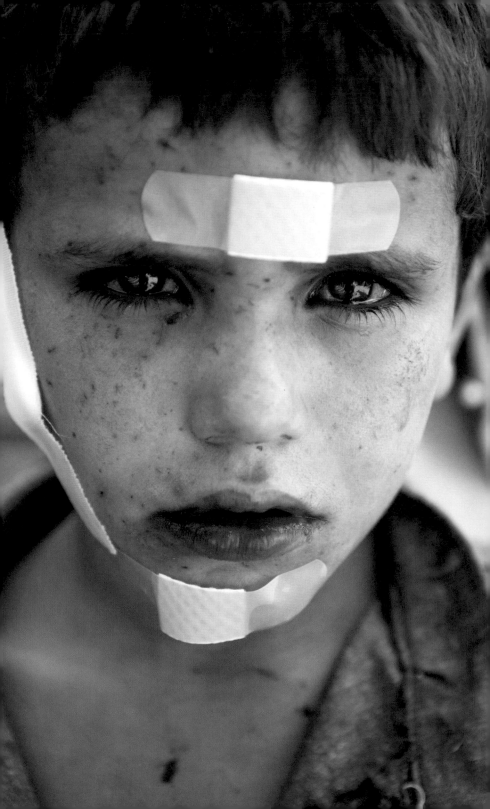

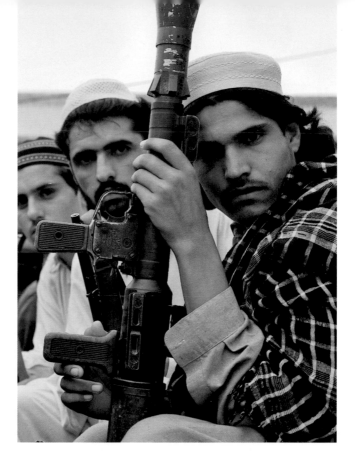

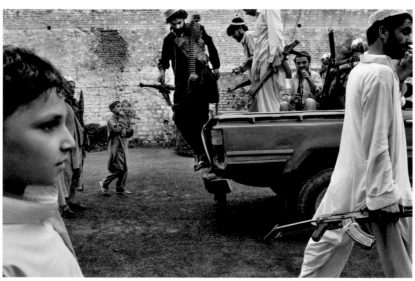

ABOVE: Talibanistan series for the *New York Times Magazine*, July 2008.

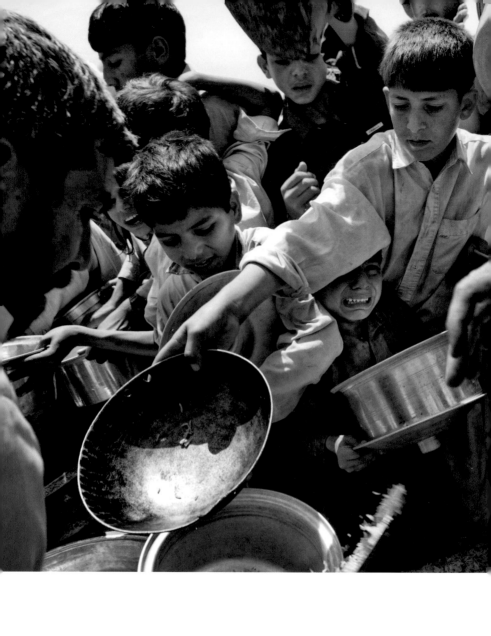

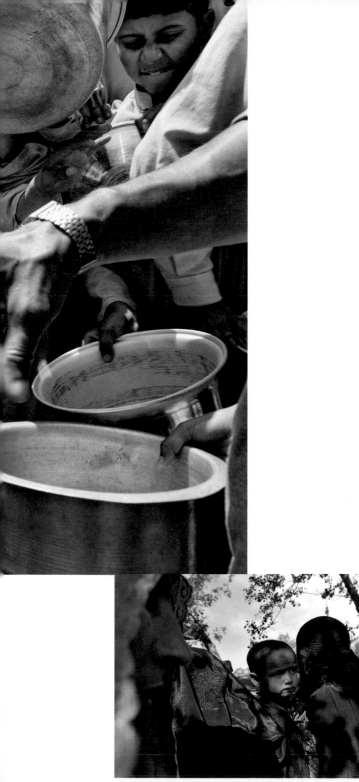

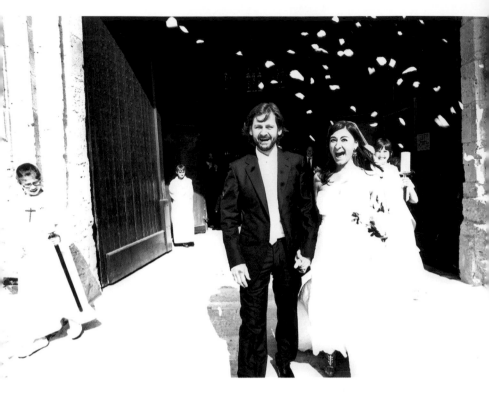

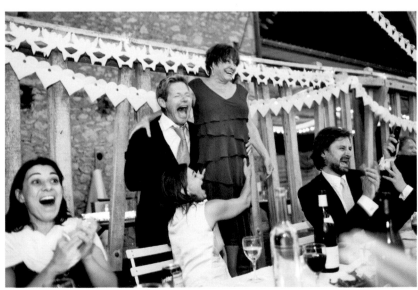

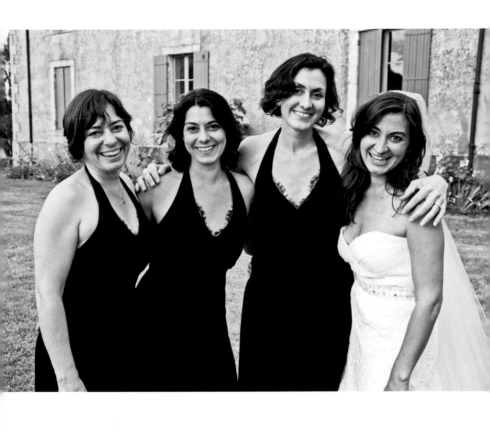

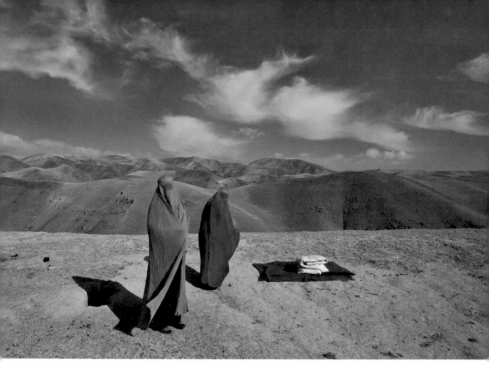

ABOVE: An Afghan woman, Noor Nisa, stands in labor on the side of the mountain in Badakhshan Province, Afghanistan, November 2009.

BELOW: The death of a U.S. Marine in southern Afghanistan, 2010.

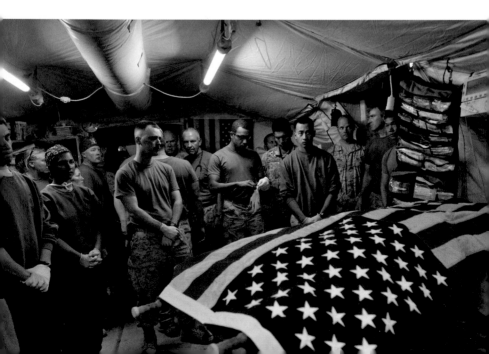

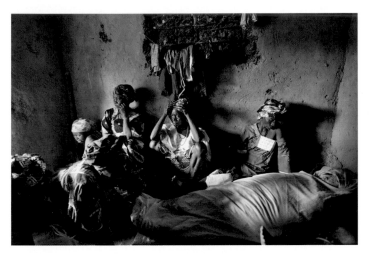

Maternal mortality in Sierra Leone, 2010.

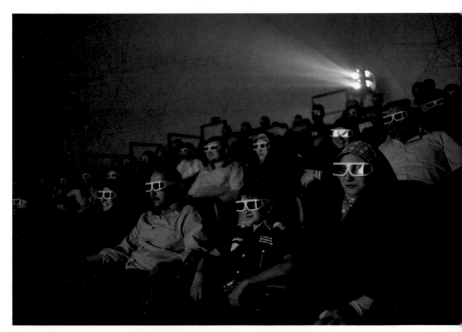

Iraqis watch a 3-D movie in Baghdad, 2010.

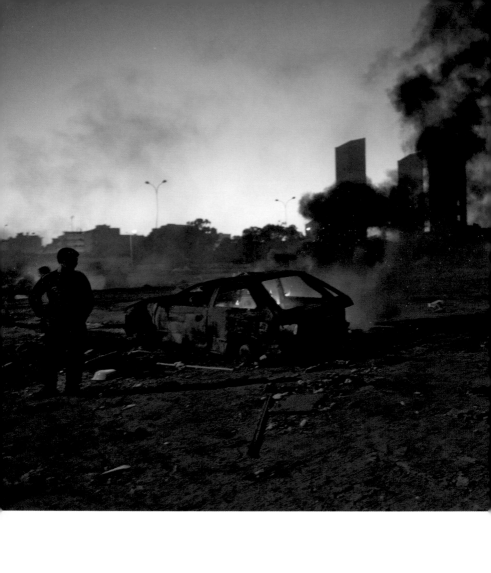

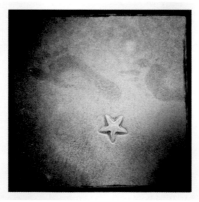

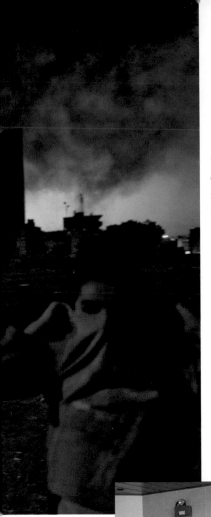

Children play around a burning car in a residential neighborhood in Benghazi, in eastern Libya, as the uprising gathers momentum, February 28, 2011.

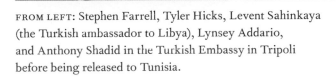

FROM LEFT: Stephen Farrell, Tyler Hicks, Levent Sahinkaya (the Turkish ambassador to Libya), Lynsey Addario, and Anthony Shadid in the Turkish Embassy in Tripoli before being released to Tunisia.

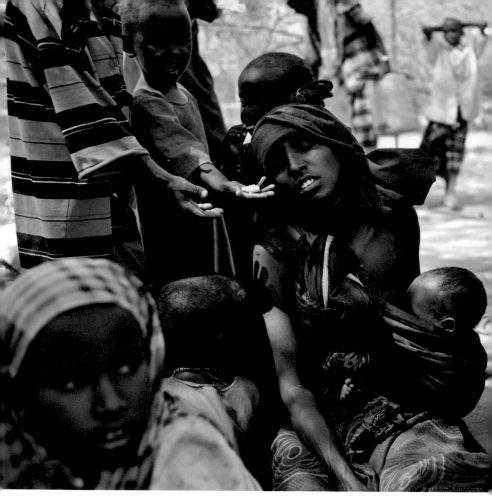

Somali children try to feed biscuits to a woman suffering from
dehydration and hunger moments after she arrived at a reception
center the morning after crossing from Somalia into Kenya to
flee a prolonged drought, August 20, 2011. Dadaab, with roughly
four hundred thousand refugees, is the largest refugee camp in
the world. The camp is grossly over capacity, and the refugees
experience an ever shrinking access to essential services such as
water, sanitation, food, and shelter, in part because they have
been sharing their rations with the new arrivals.

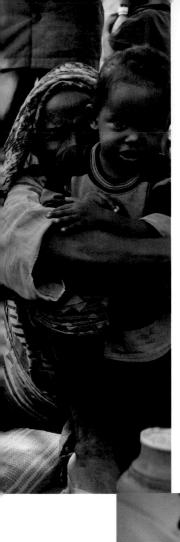

A Somali doctor checks for a heartbeat as Abbas Nishe, one and a half, struggles to fight severe malnutrition in Banadir Hospital in Mogadishu, Somalia, August 25, 2011. The hospital is overflowing with people sleeping on the floors throughout most wards.

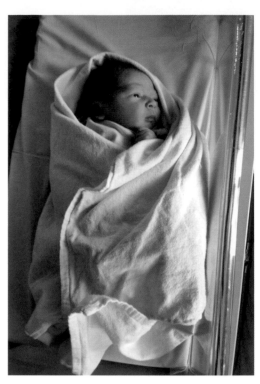

Lukas Simon de Bendern,
December 28, 2011.

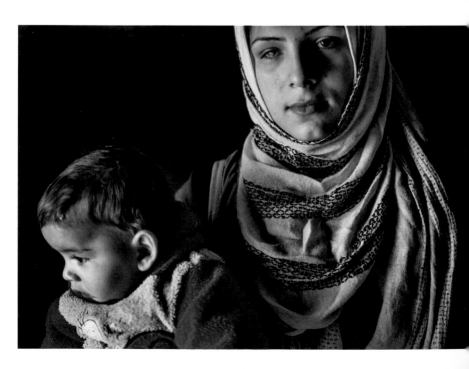

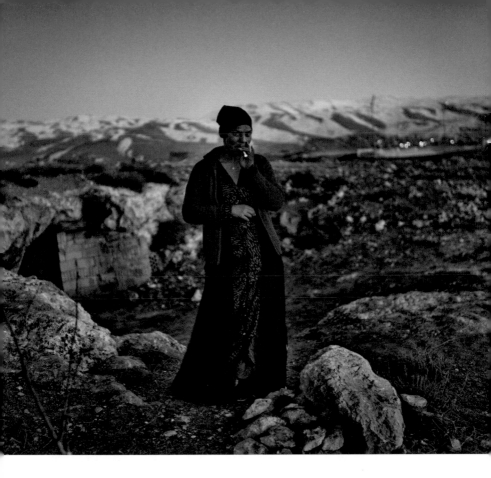
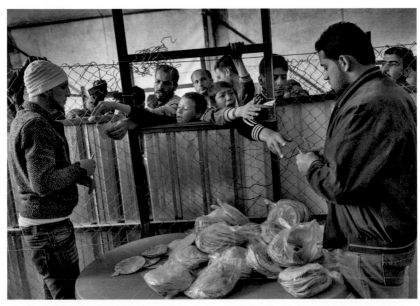

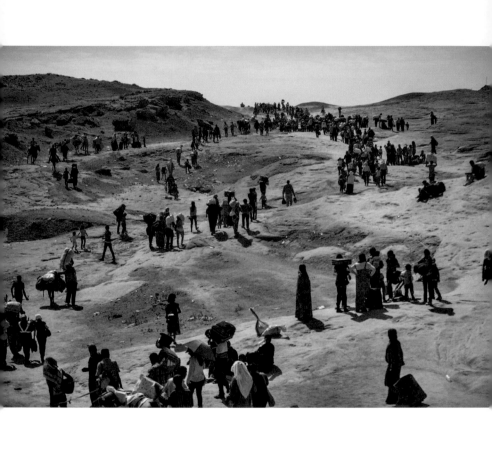

Since Paul and I had gotten engaged, however, he had talked repeatedly about his desire for a family. I knew I wanted a family *eventually*, but I was finally at the height of my career, shooting all the assignments I had dreamed of shooting, for some of the best publications in the world. The last thing I wanted was to interrupt that momentum for a baby that I wasn't yearning for at that point in my life. Unlike many of my female friends in their midthirties, I was definitely not sensing my biological clock ticking; in fact, I often wondered if I had been born without one.

And I couldn't just have a baby and go back to Afghanistan. If I took a month off, I was likely to be replaced by one of the other, say, two hundred freelancers vying to get my assignments. If I took six months off to have a baby, I believed I would be written off by my editors. I was in a man's profession. I couldn't think of a single female photojournalist who was married or had a child. If Jason didn't think I struggled with all this, he was wrong.

OUR WEDDING TOOK PLACE at Paul's father's home in southwest France: a stone castle in the midst of rolling cornfields, off a narrow country road lined with English plane trees that made of it a green tunnel, specks of sunlight bursting through the leaves. I thought of the opening passage of James Salter's *A Sport and a Pastime*, even though he was referring to life in a city, every time we sped along the road from the stone house toward medieval Lectoure, the nearest town.

> September. It seems these luminous days will never end. The city, which was almost empty during August, now is filling up again. It is being replenished. The restaurants are all reopening, the shops. People are coming back from the country, the sea, from trips on roads all jammed with cars. The station is very crowded. There are children, dogs, families

with old pieces of luggage bound by straps. I make my way among them. It's like being in a tunnel. Finally I emerge onto the brilliance of the *quai*, beneath a roof of glass panels which seems to magnify the light.

Our actual wedding day began with a massive hangover from the pink-champagne party the night before. Paul and I had planned on respecting the tradition that bride and groom shouldn't see each other the day of the wedding, but we were so hungover, we didn't wake up until around 11 a.m., just hours before we were due at the church. During the Catholic ceremony Paul almost gave the elderly priest a heart attack when he said, "I, Paul de Bendern, take you, Lisa, to be my wife." Lisa was my sister.

My family, meanwhile, had reunited happily. Paul and I loved spending time with Bruce and my father, who were still together. They had made up with my mom; we even all went on vacation together sometimes. It was a testament to my mother's warm and forgiving nature and to my father and Bruce's effort to bring us all together again. At my wedding dinner my mother stood up on a chair, her arms around Bruce, and said how excited she was that her daughter was marrying into royalty—"but I thought I'd introduce you all to a real queen!" And with that she thrust the flamboyant Bruce forward. The party roared with laughter. Nothing made me happier than watching my mother and Bruce, the original best friends, stand on a chair side by side and make a toast together as my father looked on. I wrapped my arms around her ankles and gazed up at her with admiration.

That day I looked around at all the guests—the collection of friends and family who had gathered from as far away as Peru, New York, Hong Kong, and California—then back at Paul, who was beside me, holding my hand. After all the years of hard work, unsuccessfully searching for love, the kidnapping in Fallujah, the ambush in the Korengal Valley, the car accident in Pakistan, I was so grateful to be sitting in the middle of the rolling hills of France with my family and closest friends, happy, drinking, and celebrating life.

AFTER THE WEDDING, I was finally able to go back to work. I was in a transitional phase in my photography, trying to edge out of daily news stories and focus almost entirely on more time-consuming magazine features and projects. In mid-September, three months after the wedding, I sat at my desk having an unsettling conversation with an editor from *National Geographic*. Sometimes the long lead times between the start and finish of a story for *National Geographic* made me question the impact of the work I was doing for them. Eighteen months passed between when I began a story and when I saw it in print. After years of photographing for the *Times*, I had grown used to the immediate gratification of working on stories and seeing them published within days or, at most, weeks. I had to convince myself that the stories I was photographing could have as much relevance published long after I shot the photos as those published the day after I shot them.

The editor and I had been talking about an assignment I had just begun shooting.

"Don't shoot this story like a *New York Times* story," he advised, in a slightly patronizing way. "Take your time with this story, get into it. Use the time you have to explore."

He was right: I had spent so many years working on stories on deadline that I had to retrain myself to shoot with time and patience. I understood where the editor was coming from but was annoyed with the conversation, which left me feeling that he didn't have faith in my vision as a photographer.

Minutes after I hung up the phone, it rang again. The number showed a Chicago area code and I thought it might be the fraud department of my credit card, telling me for the millionth time they had blocked my card because it showed usage overseas.

I picked up the phone, exasperated.

A man's voice: "May I speak with Lynsey Addario, please?"

"This is she."

"This is Robert Gallucci, the president of the MacArthur Foundation."

"Hi."

"This is the first of such phone calls I have to make in my new job as president of the foundation, so I will just go ahead and begin: I would like to tell you that you have been selected as a MacArthur Fellow."

I was silent. Every year I combed through the announcement of the year's MacArthur "genius awards," people from all professions who got the famous "phone call out of the blue" telling them they had won $500,000 "with no strings attached."

"Hello? Are you there? Do you know what a MacArthur fellowship is?"

"I think so," I said, wanting to be told again.

"We will give you half a million dollars, with no strings attached, over the course of the next five years, in quarterly deposits of $25,000. This is not based on work you have done in the past but to help further your work in the future."

"Are you sure you have the right person?"

"Your name is Lynsey Addario, and you were born November 13, 1973, in Norwalk, Connecticut, correct?"

"Yes, that is me." I felt my chest tighten with emotion.

Mr. Gallucci offered a brief explanation of how the next few weeks would unfold in relation to the announcement, passed on the name and contact details of the head of the fellows program, and congratulated me once again. He then asked me what I thought of the situation in Afghanistan, and I was so overwhelmed, I used some lame word like "quandary" and then wondered if he was going to take the money back, thinking, "She isn't really a genius."

Our phone call ended, and I put my BlackBerry down and stared at the phone. I was sure "Robert Gallucci" must be Ivan playing a practical joke on me. I looked at the caller ID and entered the number into Google: MacArthur Foundation. It was true.

I sat down on our couch, alone in our happy, sunlit apartment, and wept with joy. I wouldn't have to worry about money for the next five years. After years of traveling from country to country with no home, of trying to bring attention to injustice, of witnessing war, funerals, and hunger—the MacArthur Foundation had recognized how devoted I was to this work. All that time, sacrifice, and commitment had been worth it.

I had promised Mr. Gallucci that I wouldn't tell anyone other than my husband. I walked to the metro stop in Taksim Square, where I knew Paul would eventually surface from among the throngs of commuters, and hovered over the subway exit for almost an hour before he came out. When he saw me, he was confused by what could possibly have brought me to meet him at the subway for the first time since we had met.

He spoke first. "Are you pregnant?"

It may not have been the good news he wanted, but Paul was overjoyed. My success was his as well. Paul, who understood the limitations of fast-paced breaking-news journalism, had always encouraged me to work on longer-term projects, which, he argued, would allow for more artistic freedom as well as a chance to go deeper into a story. Larger independent projects also often become exhibitions, which are a way of connecting with a world outside the news and media. Only something like the MacArthur fellowship would allow me that kind of time for my work, without worrying about where my next assignment would come from. And yet I decided to continue working with the *New York Times*, *Time*, and *National Geographic* because I believed in those publications, and their readership reached a wide audience. Part of me recognized that there was little point in doing this work if no one saw it. So while the MacArthur changed certain aspects of my professional life, it didn't change everything.

TWO MONTHS LATER our lovely existence in Constantinople ended. Paul and I moved to New Delhi, where he took a job as the new India bureau chief for Reuters. I hadn't realized how attached I had grown to my life in Istanbul over seven years—having Ivan as a neighbor, colleague, and best friend; enjoying Mediterranean salads topped by grilled halloumi cheese with Suzy, Maddy, and Ansel; spending summers drifting around the Aegean on a sailboat with my dad and Bruce. I was a married woman, and for the first time in my adult life, decisions about where I would live and how long I would stay were no longer determined by which war I was covering or which correspondent I wanted to work with. These decisions were going to be determined in large part by the fact that Paul had a staff job at a large company, and Reuters had needs.

I sank into a depressed state. I had lived in India nine years before and was fine with all the noise and chaos then, but I had grown into a different person in my thirties. In an easy, home-base city like Istanbul, simple things felt like luxuries: that I could walk from one location to another without having to rely on taxis or drivers; that I could run out and meet my friends for a coffee in a hip neighborhood; that a flight to visit my family in the United States wasn't sixteen hours long. After Istanbul, Delhi seemed isolating. The only nice gyms were inside five-star hotels. I couldn't really walk anywhere; every excursion required a car. I worked almost three hundred days a year in difficult places, and I craved simplicity and ease at home. My little amenities were a fundamental part of my sanity.

Paul was also busier than usual. Our relationship usually worked well with consistent two- to three-week breaks after assignments, because we both felt that the distance kept our romance fresh. But his demanding new job kept him extrapreoccupied those first months. So I traveled incessantly. Rather than see the MacArthur as an opportunity to slow down, I saw it as encouragement to go even harder. From the end of 2009 until early 2011, I was traveling more than ever—from embeds in Afghanistan to stints in sub-Saharan Africa. With every return home, Paul argued that we didn't know how long it would take to get pregnant and that, at age thirty-seven, I might be running out of time. I was terrified of losing my independence and refused to admit that he might be right.

Instead I always responded with the same argument: I had sturdy southern Italian genes, and each of my sisters had gotten pregnant the first time she tried and had healthy pregnancies. The Addario women were made to reproduce, I argued, knowing deep down that my case could be very different from theirs. I finally brokered a deal: I would stay on my birth control pill until January 2011, and then we would let biology and our libidos decide when we got pregnant. I didn't want a child then, but I knew how important it was to Paul. And a small part of me did worry that I would run out of time.

January came and went. I stopped taking the pill, as we'd agreed, but planned back-to-back assignments that left me little time at home for conception: I hopped from South Sudan to Iraq to Afghanistan to Bahrain in less than two months. I was in Iraq for *National Geographic* in late January when David, my editor at the *Times*, called me in Baghdad and asked whether I wanted to go to Egypt, where there appeared to be a revolution under way. I was dying to go, but I couldn't leave my *National Geographic* assignment half-completed. By the time I finished my work in Iraq, the *Times* was well staffed in Egypt, and David sent me to Afghanistan. But the more I watched the news—the uprisings in Egypt, Tunisia, Bahrain, and apparently now Libya, too—the more I realized how historic this Arab Spring would be. All my colleagues from my Iraq and Afghanistan years had been reporting and photographing from Tahrir Square, and there I was, drinking tea in Kabul, watching a pirated DVD of *Up in the Air*.

I couldn't take it anymore and got on a plane. I was headed to Libya.

PART FOUR

Life and Death

LIBYA, NEW YORK, INDIA, LONDON

CHAPTER 11

You Will Die Tonight

LIBYA, MARCH 2011

Three weeks into the Libyan uprising—a revolution that quickly became a war—I was kidnapped. My colleagues—Tyler Hicks, Anthony Shadid, and Stephen Farrell—and I had been covering an antigovernment revolt started by ordinary Libyan men, and Qaddafi saw us journalists as the enemy. Along with Mohammed, the quiet, twenty-two-year-old engineering student we had hired to be our driver, we had run directly into a military checkpoint. Now we were at the mercy of Qaddafi's soldiers, our hands and feet bound, and blindfolded.

Will I see my parents again? Will I see Paul again? How could I do this to them? Will I get my cameras back? How did I get to this place?

Someone placed me in the backseat of a car. My mouth was cottony with fear, my hands were numb from the tight cloth around my wrists, and my watch was digging into my skin. A soldier opened the door and slid into the car beside me. He looked at me for a few seconds, and though I felt the weight of his gaze on me, I was too scared to look up and make eye contact. For a moment I thought perhaps he had arrived to offer me water. But instead he lifted his fist and punched me hard on the side of the face, bringing tears to my eyes. It wasn't the pain that made me weep; it was the disrespect, the fear of what was to come, and the knowledge that a grown Arab man could have so little self-respect that he could punch a completely bound and defenseless woman in the face. I had worked in the Muslim world for eleven years and had always been treated with unparalleled hospitality and kindness. People had gone out of their way to feed me, to provide me with shelter in their homes, and to protect me from danger. Now I feared what this man might do to me. For one of the first times in my life, I feared rape.

Steve was placed in the car next to me, and I was relieved. Soldiers surrounded the car, looking at us and laughing, as if we were monkeys in a cage. They said things in Arabic—things I thankfully didn't understand. Outside I saw Tyler and Anthony in another car about twenty feet away. Tyler and I had attended high school together. We'd known each other since I was thirteen years old. There was something comforting about his brave, calm, familiar presence.

I had lost all sense of time. I found the courage to look at our own car, the one Mohammed had been driving. One, or maybe it was two, of the doors of the gold four-door sedan were open, and a soldier was emptying our belongings onto the sidewalk. On the ground beside the driver's door lay a young man, facedown and motionless, wearing a striped shirt, one arm outstretched. He appeared dead. I was positive it was Mohammed, and I was sick with guilt. No matter how he finally met his fate—either in a cross fire or executed by one of Qaddafi's men—we had killed him with our relentless pursuit of the story. I began to cry, trying desperately to hold it together, and at that moment one of the soldiers put a cell phone to my ear.

"Speak in English," he said.

"Salaam aleikum," I stammered. (Peace be unto you.)

A woman's voice spoke back to me in English. "You are a dog. You are a donkey. Long live Muammar."

I was confused.

"Speak to my wife!" the soldier ordered me.

"Salaam aleikum," I repeated.

She paused, perhaps wondering why an infidel would greet her with the traditional Muslim greeting. "You are a dog. You are a donkey."

"I am a journalist," I said. "*New York Times. Ana sahafiya.* I am a journalist."

The soldier pulled the phone away from my ear and laughed into it, speaking softly and joyfully to his wife, proud of what he had accomplished that day.

We sat in those cars for hours—incoming artillery smashing and crackling and raining all around us—tied up and defenseless. The sky above us darkened. At dusk, the rebel attacks increased in intensity, bullets spraying the area around our car. Tyler managed to wriggle himself out of the electrical cord around his wrists, and a sympathetic soldier untied mine. We dived out of our car and onto the ground beside the door in search of cover. Steve and Anthony soon followed, and we huddled together on the ground like sardines.

"That's outgoing tank fire," Tyler explained after a long series of piercing explosions. "And that's incoming machine-gun fire." We recoiled every time we heard the crash of incoming explosions, certain we would get hit by shrapnel or a bullet. Soldiers surrounded us, and we pleaded with them to allow us to remain prostrate on the ground. In a rare moment of kindness a few of them came with thin mattresses, which they lined up behind the cover of a truck. They ordered us to lie down there, in the middle of the road. We curled together under a dirty blanket.

It was impossible to get a sense of who was in charge. All we had been told was that we would be delivered to "the doctor." Some soldiers later referred to him as Dr. Mutassim, one of the more vicious of

Colonel Qaddafi's sons. Each son had his own militia, which seemed to operate on its own, with its own rules.

At 4 a.m. they woke us up. Nearby we could hear the troops speaking. Anthony, who was half Lebanese and the only one among us who spoke Arabic, closed his eyes to concentrate on what they were saying. "The rebels are amassing nearby," he said. "The troops are saying they want to move us to a safer place."

"That's a promising sign," I said.

Several soldiers approached us, and one by one they tied blindfolds around our eyes and refastened our arms behind our backs. A large, muscular soldier lifted me like a pillow into his arms and loaded me into the back of the armored personnel carrier—a vehicle resembling a giant tin beetle. I tried to remain as still as possible, to draw as little attention to myself as I could, when I felt a soldier climb into the vehicle and position himself with his front pressing tightly against my back. There was a lot of movement, and soon I heard Steve's voice: "Is everybody here?"

One by one we all answered yes.

The vehicle began to move, and within seconds the soldier spooning my back started tracing his fingers across my body. I prayed he wouldn't find my money belt with my passport. I squirmed and pleaded, "Please, don't. Please. I have a husband." He covered my mouth with his salty fingers and ordered me not to speak as he continued groping me. I could taste the salt and mud from his skin on my lips as he continued grabbing at my breasts and butt, clumsily tracing my genitals over my jeans.

I knew that the armored personnel carrier, a common military vehicle used to transport troops, was full of men, and I wondered how long I would have to endure this torment before someone came to my rescue. I heard one of my colleagues groan in pain—I thought it was Anthony but later learned it was Steve getting a bayonet shoved in between his butt cheeks, not quite ripping through his pants—and I knew we were all being abused simultaneously.

"Please. You are Muslim," I said. "I have a husband. Please." He ignored my words and kept his hands on my breasts for the thirty minutes or so we drove, until miraculously another soldier pulled me into the protection of his embrace. He was trying to shield me from the groping. The salty-fingered guy pulled me back against him. The savior pulled me back. Someone had a conscience.

The vehicle finally slowed and pulled over to the side of the road. The door opened, and I was roughly pushed out. With our arms tied and eyes blindfolded, they shifted us to the back of a cramped Land Cruiser. Inside, Anthony was moaning loudly.

"My shoulders," he said aloud, his voice drenched in pain. "My arms are bound so tightly, it's killing my shoulders."

My shoulder with the titanium plate that reset my collarbone after my car accident also ached. Anthony and Steve began to speak a smattering of Arabic to a soldier, pleading with him to retie our arms in front, rather than behind our backs. One by one the soldier untied our arms, and the relief was immediate. I was eerily calm in the back of the truck: My hands now tied in front, the close proximity to my colleagues, and the hope that we would all remain together were enough to get me through the night.

I kept my eyes closed under the blindfold and tried to slow my breath, to distract myself from my fear, my thirst, my need to pee. That's when I felt another hand on my face, caressing my cheek like a lover. Slowly he ran his fingers over my cheeks, my chin, my eyebrows. I lowered my face into my lap. He raised it, tenderly, and continued with his caresses. He ran his hands over my hair and spoke to me in a low, steady voice, repeating the same phrase over and over. I kept my face down, ignoring his touch, his words. I didn't understand what he was saying.

"What is he saying, Anthony?"

Anthony took his time answering. "He's telling you that you will die tonight."

I was numb. Since the moment we'd been taken that morning, I'd resigned myself to the likelihood that I was going to die, and every minute since then had felt like a gift. I focused on the moment, on staying alive, on not getting overwhelmed by emotion.

Tyler suddenly said, "I need some fresh air. Anthony, could you please ask them if I can step outside for some fresh air?"

Tyler's request was strange to me; he had endured the previous hours without so much as a whimper, and now he was asking for fresh air. I would later learn that Saleh, the soldier who kept telling me I would die as he caressed my cheeks, had told Tyler repeatedly that he was going to "cut his pretty head off," and Tyler had been nauseated.

SOMEHOW WE ALL FELL asleep sitting up in the back of the Land Cruiser. It was light out when we awoke, stiff and sore, to the sound of soldiers banging on the door. We were thrown into the back of a pickup truck. Bound, blindfolded, and lying on the bed of the hard metal pickup, we drove west for two hundred fifty miles along the Mediterranean coast under an unforgiving sun. I imagined what we looked like, being paraded through the streets like medieval trophies of war from one hostile checkpoint to another. I was so tired of being scared, of wondering what was next. The unknown was more terrifying than anything. Tyler was our eyes: He was able to see out from beneath his blindfold and narrated the scene to us in a hushed voice as we drove along the endless road. Anthony was our ears: He translated the slurs and shouts, like "Dirty dogs!" (a grave insult in Islam). For most of the time I crouched in a fetal position to shield myself from the street and rested my head against the metal arch of the wheel, my bound hands covering my face. My collarbone and shoulder ached with every bounce of the truck, but I thought if I could dig myself deep into the flatbed, no one would notice I was there.

At each checkpoint one of us was beaten. I heard the thump of what I imagined was an AK-47 or a fist to the back of my colleagues' heads, and a whimper of contained agony. At one checkpoint I felt a soldier sidle up next to me alongside the truck, and immediately afterward he poured the weight of his body onto my cheek with his fist. Tyler, in a gesture that would get me through the next few days, managed to move his bound hands over to me and hold mine while I wept in misery.

"You are OK," he said. "I am with you. You are going to be OK. You are going to be OK."

"I just want to go home," I said aloud as hot tears dampened my blindfold. I found reassurance only in the fact that we were all still together.

It was afternoon when we arrived in Sirte, Colonel Qaddafi's hometown, which lies halfway between Benghazi and Tripoli. We were still blindfolded when they led us downstairs into an area that felt, smelled, and sounded like a prison. The man leading me put me up against a wall and told me to place my hands above my head and spread my legs. I imitated the position I had seen so many times on police TV shows. We were being searched again. Like all the other Libyan men before him, he rested his hands on my breasts for a bit too long while he checked my pockets. I had a small container of saline for my contact lenses that I was able to convince the previous soldiers to let me keep for medical reasons, but this soldier confiscated it immediately. He took the plastic watch off my wrist. The man felt me up one last time and walked me into a cell.

"Is everybody here?" Steve asked.

"Yes," we all replied.

Eventually they untied our hands and undid our blindfolds and brought us a dinner of orange rice and plain white bread rolls. Our cell was about twelve feet by ten. There was a small sliding window in the upper left corner, four filthy foam mattresses on the floor, a box of dates, a giant bottle of drinking water with some plastic cups, and a bottle for urine in the corner by the door. I was too distressed to eat and, despite my thirst, too terrified of needing to use the restroom to drink. I had a splitting headache from caffeine withdrawal, and my contact lenses were dry and irritated. My eyesight was -5.5; I was near-sighted and almost blind without them. My glasses had been stolen with our gear. If I cried a few times a day, I thought, I could keep my contacts moist.

The men took turns urinating into the bottle in the corner, and I longed for a funnel, or a penis. There was nothing to do but sleep, talk, and wait. They came to take Anthony away for questioning a few times, and we couldn't decide whether the men in the prison in Sirte had gotten word of who we were from Tripoli or whether they still had no idea we were *New York Times* journalists.

"Do you think anyone realizes we're missing?" I asked.

Anthony, Steve, and Tyler were sure. "The *New York Times* is a machine," Steve said. "They will be doing everything they can to find us."

"Really?" I asked skeptically. I couldn't imagine that anyone even realized we were missing in the chaos of the front line. I had been so immersed in my own head, in staying alive, that I hadn't once thought about the mechanisms in place for trying to rescue us.

"Four missing *New York Times* journalists is a big deal," Tyler stepped in.

"This is it for me," Steve said, unwavering. "No more war. I can't do this anymore. I can't do this to Reem [his wife]. This is the second time in two years."

"Yeah . . ." Anthony trailed off, eyes lowered onto the prison cell floor. "Poor Nada. I feel horrible for putting her through this."

Would we even have a chance to tell our significant others how much we loved them? Covering war was inflicting immeasurable pain on our loved ones, and we knew it. This was the second time I was putting Paul through this pain. Anthony and Steve both had infants at home, too. And yet as guilty as we felt at that moment, and as terrified as we were, only Steve sounded convinced by his own declaration that he wouldn't cover war anymore.

"If they bring us to Tripoli, we will probably end up in the hands of the Interior Ministry," Anthony said, referring to a ministry infamous for torture. "And probably in one of their solitary-confinement cells, or where Ghaith is." We had heard that Ghaith Abdul-Ahad, an Iraqi journalist and photographer for the *Guardian*, was being held by Qaddafi's men. He had been missing for days, and we assumed the worst.

"But we need to get to Tripoli," Anthony said, "because we will never get released if we don't get to Tripoli. We will probably survive—it will be difficult, but we might live if we get there."

"If we do, I am going to be so fat in nine months!" I exclaimed suddenly. I knew that if we made it out of Libya alive, I would finally give Paul what he'd been asking me for since we'd married: a baby. After all those years of feeling conflicted about having a child, I found myself praying for the chance to start a family with Paul. I felt confident that I could endure anything—that I would be able to survive psychological and physical torture—if it meant we would eventually be released.

Sometime in the night the clanking of our prison door woke me; I feigned sleep. A young man opened the cell door, looked at the four of us asleep, and grabbed my ankle. He started dragging me toward the door.

"No!" I screamed, frantically twisting my way back toward Anthony, who was asleep near me. The young man pulled my leg again toward the door. I squirmed back, pressing myself against Anthony, in search of protection. The man gave up and left.

Eventually I closed my eyes. I breathed slowly and took in the silence of our cell. Steve, Tyler, and Anthony were all asleep. Images of others who had spent time in prison echoed through my head: my Iraqi interpreter Sarah, who was jailed by the U.S. military in 2008 after she spent two years risking her life and interpreting for them; Maziar Bahari, a *Newsweek* colleague who was put in solitary confinement in Iran and hummed Leonard Cohen songs to stay sane. I sang "Daydreamer" by Adele over and over in my head, because I had been listening to the song as I painted my toenails the morning we were captured. I knew so many people had endured worse—captivity, torture—and their resilience helped me face my fear of what would come next, the physical pain of being bound and punched. My thoughts reverted back to Paul and my family, who had no idea where I was.

Throughout the night we listened to a man screaming in a cell nearby.

The familiar clanking sound of our prison door woke us in the morning. We heard them say Tripoli, and we knew that was our fate.

Soldiers led us outside of the prison once again blindfolded and bound, but this time with plastic zip ties that cut deep into our wrists. I asked them to loosen them. They tightened them even more, these plastic ties I had seen used by the U.S. military on so many Iraqis and Afghans. I felt my hands start to lose circulation, and when I let out a whimper, the soldier pulled the plastic cuffs even tighter, slicing them into my wrists and punishing me for my weakness. We were driven to the airport and loaded onto a military aircraft, which I recognized by the ramp, the hum of the engine, and the seats lining the walls.

"Is everybody here?" Steve's question was first answered with a gun butt in the face.

"Yes."

They sat us at least a few feet apart from one another, and with ropes and strips of cloth, tied our hands and ankles to the webbing covering the walls of the plane, like cattle. I heard one of my colleagues get smacked again, and then the whimper. Suddenly I was overwhelmed by desperation and helplessness. Tyler, Anthony, and Steve kept getting beaten with fists and rifles. Getting felt up and fingered through my jeans didn't seem nearly as bad as that physical abuse. My hands and feet tied to the webbing along the inner fuselage of the plane, my eyes blindfolded, and the mystery of what would happen next was just too much to bear. I started crying uncontrollably. I was ashamed and lowered my head so whoever else was on the plane wouldn't see me and wouldn't hit me or tie me tighter for being weak and making noise.

I cried and cried until a man came up beside me and said, "I am sorry. I am sorry." And he untied my blindfold, undid my zip ties, and released my legs and arms from the walls of the plane. I was too scared to look around. I kept my eyes down and continued crying. They were evil. These men were the epitome of evil. They understood psychological torture and deployed it.

When I finally looked up, two middle-aged men dressed in military uniforms were sitting across from me. They looked at me sympathetically. They had kindness in their eyes. Anthony, Steve, and Tyler remained tied to the walls and blindfolded, their heads slouched over toward their knees. Were they sleeping? I again felt guilty for getting easier treatment because I was a woman. When we began our descent, one man refastened my blindfold.

We landed in a frenzy. We were off-loaded from the plane, and Steve and I were put into a police wagon. Men with automatic weapons stood over us. I could see the tips of their guns through the bottom of my blindfold. They were thugs. Qaddafi's famous "Zenga Zenga" speech played on someone's mobile phone. (In the midst of the uprising Qaddafi gave a speech vowing to hunt down protesters "inch by inch, house by house, room by room, alleyway by alleyway [ʐenga ʐenga].") Hearing his speech again motivated them to beat us down. A few different men put their hands between my legs, over my jeans, and rubbed my genitals with their fingers. They were more aggressive than all the others before them, laughing when I pleaded with them to stop. I prayed they didn't find my second passport tucked into a money belt nestled in my underwear. It was all I had left of my identity at that point.

Outside I heard them beating my colleagues with their guns—that awful thumping sound. Someone let out a muffled squeal and a moan, and I strained to decipher—by the sound of the moan—which one of my friends was being brutalized. It wasn't Steve, because he was in the paddy wagon with me, being forced to yell "Down, down Ireland" by someone who had no idea that Ireland wasn't part of any foreign coalition against him. With the next round of thumps I recognized Tyler's voice. He had been silent throughout his other beatings, and I knew this was a terrible sign. He was getting beaten on the tarmac. I couldn't hear Anthony.

When their parade was over, we were transferred to a Land Cruiser again.

"Is everybody here?"

"Yes." "Yes." "Yes."

Tyler's voice was empty.

We rode for about twenty minutes in the Land Cruiser as a man who spoke very clear English explained that we would not be beaten anymore and that we were now in the hands of the Libyan government. Anthony later told us that before this announcement there had been a fight (in Arabic) over who would "get" us on the tarmac: the Interior Ministry or the Foreign Ministry. When we were put into the police wagon, we were initially to be released to the Interior Ministry. But somehow the Foreign Ministry won. I didn't care anymore where they were taking us. I was so resigned to whatever fate lay ahead, too beaten down to feel fear. I rode along in a stupor.

When the car stopped, the man who spoke English helped me out of the car—I was still blindfolded—and as he placed his hand on my shoulder and offered to lead me up to a building, I flinched.

"Please just stop touching me! Please don't touch me anymore!"

"Listen to me," the man with perfect English said. "You are now with the government of Libya. You will not be beaten anymore. You will not be mistreated. You will not be touched."

I didn't say a word. I felt the tears welling up again in my eyes.

WE WERE LED into a room with a clean, soft, off-white carpet. We had all endured misery on the trip from Sirte to Tripoli, but when our blindfolds were removed, it was as if we had to confront one another's pain. I looked first at Tyler, my stoic friend whom I admired so much. He was hunched over, crying. Perhaps they were tears of relief that we had survived so much brutality and finally were given a reprieve by a man who spoke English, offered us juice boxes, and promised not to beat us anymore. Or perhaps Tyler was just broken. Seeing him, usually so strong and poised in the face of anything, tore me apart, and I cried, too. I looked over at Anthony; his eyes were glassy. Steve was stone.

A nameless Libyan man who claimed to be with the Foreign Ministry reiterated that we would no longer be beaten or bound. We would, though, be blindfolded when interrogated, and they were going to hold us in a nearby guesthouse while they questioned us. The interpreter, who had a permanent, gentle smile from the moment we were able to see his face, leaned in close to me and in a hushed voice asked, "Are you OK? Did they touch you?"

I was surprised by his candor. "Yes, they touched me. Every soldier in Libya touched me."

"But were you raped?" he persisted.

"No. I was not raped. I was touched, punched, pushed around, but no one took my clothes off."

"Oh, good." His body language immediately relaxed. I was shocked at how relieved he was; it was so jarring to come out of this world of abuse and fear and meet someone who cared for my well-being. Perhaps he was worldlier, or perhaps he was just worried about a potential public-relations nightmare. But it was as if rape was his own red line— the beatings, gropings, psychological torture, and threats didn't matter, but rape did.

The man in charge asked us whether we had any passports or possessions, and at this point I surrendered my passport and was reassured it would be returned before we were released. They transported us to our temporary accommodations, and they told us that if we attempted to open a door or a window, we would be shot.

The apartment had two bedrooms: one with three beds for the men and one with two beds for me. We shared one large, dormitory-style bathroom with several stalls and a shower. We had a kitchen with a table just large enough for the four of us and a youngish, handsome cook, who was always pleasant.

The Libyans sat us down in a reception room of our VIP prison and, over tea, offered to get us clothing, toiletries, and food. Qaddafi propaganda blared on the TV set in the background like white noise; I was riveted by the presence of a television—any connection to the outside world. None of us wanted to ask for much, because a long shopping list might imply we were staying for a while. As I finished up my list, the smiling interpreter whispered in my ear: "Do you need any women things? Any feminine things?" I shook my head. My body had a perfect knack for shutting down all monthly rituals in the face of trauma. I found it odd that the Libyans would tie us up, beat us up, psychologically torture us for three days, and then offer to buy me tampons.

As the officials sat across from us, they filled the room with empty pleasantries. Anthony grabbed the TV remote and changed the channel from the pro-Qaddafi propaganda videos to CNN. Within seconds still images of our faces flashed on the TV screen, along with the words "the Libyan government still cannot ascertain the whereabouts of the *New York Times* journalists . . . but they have reassured *New York Times* Executive Editor Bill Keller that they will cooperate . . ." I started crying again.

The dignitaries sitting across from me begged me to stop.

"Don't you have children?" I asked. "How could you do this to our parents? Our families? Our families think we are dead. Why can't you let us make one phone call?"

The next time any of us entered the TV room, the only thing remaining of the cable box was a dangling wire.

A few hours later our Foreign Ministry interpreter returned with a crew carrying maybe a dozen bags of groceries and new wardrobes for all of us. It was a terrifying sight—did the bags and bags of groceries mean we were staying for months? There were roughly six jars of Nescafé, cookies, chips, packaged croissants, dry little Italian-style toasts. We were each handed a tote bag full of everything we had requested. The men received shiny, cool Adidas tracksuits. In my bag there was a giant tan velour sweat suit with smiling teady bears embroidered on the front, emblazoned with cursive script that read THE MAGIC GIRL!! There were also three pairs of underwear, with the words SHAKE IT UP! written across the front, as well as a toothbrush, shampoo, conditioner, and a hairbrush.

SOMEWHERE AROUND two in the morning there was commotion in the hallway outside the room and a knock at my door.

"Wake up! You get one phone call."

I paused. Without my BlackBerry I had no idea what Paul's telephone number was. I didn't want to waste my one call on my mother's phone, because I was sure the phone would be lost somewhere in the depths of her purse and she wouldn't answer. And my dad never answered his phone. The four of us met up in the guys' room and conferred with one another on whom each of us would call. Without Paul's number, I offered to be the one to call the foreign desk at the *Times*, to let them know we were OK. Tyler, Anthony, and Steve all knew the number of the foreign desk; I committed it to memory.

One by one we were blindfolded and led into the TV room without a functioning TV. I was placed in a chair near a man who I presumed was there to monitor our calls. I recited the foreign desk's phone number.

Someone answered, and I said, "Hi, this is Lynsey Addario in Libya. Could I please speak with Susan Chira?"

Susan immediately came on the line: "Lyyyyyyyyynnnnnnnnnsssseeeeeeyyyyyyy!"

I was so relieved to hear a familiar voice. I told her we were all OK and that we were now in the hands of the Libyan government. She told me they were working hard to get us released. The man next to me told me to be quick. I asked Susan to please call my husband and tell him that I was OK and that I loved him very much. She said she would. And the conversation was over. Tyler called his father. Steve and Anthony called their wives. I wished I had been able to speak with Paul.

The next day rolled into night, and no one came to visit us. We spent most of our time sitting around the kitchen table talking, telling war stories, recounting what had happened to us thus far so we wouldn't forget by the time we had access to pens and paper. Tyler talked about being imprisoned in Chechnya and held at gunpoint in South Sudan. Steve described his ordeal only two years earlier of being kidnapped by the Taliban in Afghanistan, which had ended in the death of *Times* Afghan journalist Sultan Munadi and one British commando. This was Steve's third time being detained, Tyler's second time being held at gunpoint in less than three months, and Anthony's second near-death experience after being shot in the West Bank. Steve reiterated his declaration from Sirte: "I can't do this anymore. I am done with this."

Anthony, Tyler, and I remained silent. The fact is that trauma and risk taking hadn't become scarier over the years; it had become more normal. It had become the job, especially as journalists became more of a target themselves, with an increase in abductions. The acceptance of that was a natural defense mechanism against questioning ourselves too much. Maybe the three of us didn't want to admit how sick it was that we would even contemplate continuing to cover war while we were sitting in a glorified prison cell, kidnapped in Libya. We intermittently made small talk about our families, and wondered quietly how long it would be before we saw them again.

Finally we broached the subject of what happened that March 15, three days earlier, the day we had been taken. We all had slightly different recollections of how it had gone down. Each of our brains had a selective memory to deal with trauma. We questioned whether our captivity could have been avoided, whether we stayed too long, and what the likelihood was that Mohammed, our young driver who had been pleading to leave for up to thirty minutes before we actually left, was still alive. Steve and I thought we saw his limp body on the pavement next to the driver's side of the car. We were collectively responsible for what we assumed was Mohammed's death. Like many Libyans at the time, Mohammed had seen driving Western journalists as a way to make money, and his way of supporting the revolution. During the uprising, most men his age were either fighters or helping journalists get the word out about what was happening. But was the pursuit of a story worth his life? This was a question without direct answers, in a way. Of course, none of us could say that a story was actually *worth* a life, or *worth* the pain we caused others. That was ridiculous. But I hoped we'd been clear with our families, our drivers, and our interpreters about how great a risk it was to love us or work with us.

When the mood got grim, we would all retire to our beds. One morning I tried to cheer up the men by dancing around in my new Magic Girl sweat suit, singing Olivia Newton-John's "Physical" while doing jumping jacks and flailing around my arms. Steve asked why I was singing Britney Spears. We read the books they'd left for us—*Richard III, Julius Ceasar, Othello*—and Tyler suggested that if we got bored enough, we could always put on a play.

More than twenty-four hours passed. I thought again about the amount of groceries they had bought us. Would we be here for weeks? Months? As captives, our only contact with the outside world was the man who delivered our hot meals for breakfast, lunch, and dinner, our guard, and the mysterious men from an undisclosed branch of government who came and blindfolded us in the middle of the night to allow us our one phone call. We looked hard for any tinge of emotion in their faces that might indicate what our futures held. When our main guard was rude to us, we were sure there had been some decision made higher up that we were no longer worthy prisoners, and perhaps we would be transferred to a basement somewhere for torture.

THE NEXT DAY one of our captors came to get us. We were all blindfolded, placed in cars, and driven about fifteen minutes toward what we assumed was the center of Tripoli. People screamed epithets at us, and my captor told me to put my head down in my lap for my own protection.

We arrived at an office in the Foreign Ministry building in downtown Tripoli, where our *Times* colleague David Kirkpatrick was waiting for us. It was so surreal—our being led out of cars as prisoners, broken and mentally scarred, at the same time that David waited for us in a shiny conference room, fresh out of his five-star hotel, with a mobile phone connected to the outside world. How could it be that we were captive and he was operating freely in Tripoli? The meeting began. Everyone talked about logistics, getting us out, getting passports made for those who had theirs confiscated. David explained that the Turkish Embassy was acting as proxy for the American Embassy, and then he got someone from the State Department in Washington on the phone so we could each work out our passport needs. When the phone came to me, I heard the voice of this cheery American girl who introduced herself as Yael and reassured me that they were going to get us home, and I cried at the mere sound of a fellow American. I was overcome with hope.

We weren't released right away. But eventually we were transferred to another location, in the middle of Tripoli. In a room on the ground floor, TV cameras were set up on tripods and Libyan and Turkish diplomats had gathered. I actually believed we might be released. We were told to take our seats. I had dressed in a hand-laundered green Zara tunic and Levi's jeans—the outfit I had been wearing the day of the kidnapping. While we waited for the formalities to begin, one of the Turkish diplomats there to help negotiate our release handed me his cell phone and told me to speak into it. He somehow had Paul on the line: It was the first time I had heard Paul's voice since the ordeal began, and I fell apart.

"Baby?" I whimpered between tears. "I am so sorry."

"I love you, baby." Paul was firm, loving, and reassuring. "I will see you soon. Do you have your passport?" After a few more words of tenderness, we ended the conversation.

I returned to the room just in time for our official handover to begin. A Libyan diplomat handed each of us an envelope with $3,000 in it to compensate us for the cash that had been stolen from us at the time of our detainment. I stupidly declined mine, saying my cash hadn't actually been stolen (though $35,000 worth of camera equipment and gear was gone). Then the Turkish and Libyan officials signed documents, handing our custody over from the Libyans to the Turks. I was convinced the Libyans might change their minds.

We were escorted into the crisp March air. It was the first time we had been outside without blindfolds. I hadn't seen the sky for six days, and as we walked toward the diplomatic vehicle waiting to take us one step closer to freedom, I looked up at the cornflower-blue sky, dotted with fluffy clouds, and took a deep breath. The car ferried us to the Turkish Embassy. This was the second time the Turks had helped me, and I would forever be indebted to them.

Libyan and Turkish diplomats arranged a convoy to the Tunisian border, where we would be handed over to a private security team hired by the *Times*. I called my mother and then my father and Bruce and told them I was safe and how sorry I was to have put them through so much stress. My father replied very simply, "We love you. This was not your fault. You were only doing your work."

It was difficult to get words out. We were all emotional, and I didn't want to talk long. Conversation only brought my fragility to the surface, and I preferred to keep it tucked away until we were properly released and in private, rather than at the Turkish Embassy on a phone line that I assumed half of Libya's intelligence services were listening in on. But I realized how selfless my parents were: Regardless of how much pain they suffered as a result of my professional decisions, they always supported me. They had given me a boundless inner strength.

TWO FORMER BRITISH SPECIAL Forces soldiers with wide chests and salt-and-pepper hair had been tasked with being our guardians. The plan was to escort us from the dusty Libyan border to the Radisson Blu hotel in the Tunisian seaside resort town of Djerba, then catch a flight to Tunis, and eventually out of the country. In the moments after our release, any logistical tasks—even purchasing a plane ticket and going to the airport—seemed too overwhelming to take on.

Before we reached the hotel in Djerba, we stopped at a Western-style supermarket to purchase necessities to get us through the next few days. The massive grocery store—a North African Kmart—was like an emotional oasis. There was something reassuring about owning things. I reveled in selecting my own toothbrush, shampoo, face moisturizer, body lotion, and cheap, lacy Middle Eastern lingerie. I knew Paul would bring a suitcase full of my things to Tunis. But for some reason I wanted to use my freedom to buy something. Anything.

At the relatively extravagant Radisson Blu, the *New York Times* security team arranged for a physician to look us over for signs of assault. I was weirdly ashamed that the seven days of physical torture—getting punched in the face and having my wrists and ankles bound—had left no visible marks on my body, save for little red marks where the zip ties had dug into my wrists. Without physical evidence, I felt that there was no proof of how much I had endured.

Eventually we landed in Tunis. I walked through the baggage-claim area and out the doors, to where Paul and Nicki, Tyler's girlfriend, were waiting for us. I collapsed into Paul's arms. For seven days I hadn't known if I would ever be able to hold him again. The relief, of course, was inexplicable—just like the morning in Pakistan when I looked up out of my morphine-induced haze to see Paul entering my hospital room with a clipboard after my car accident. I knew he would take care of me forever.

I looked around for my colleagues and prison mates from the past week, Anthony, Tyler, and Steve. We would be bound for life by this experience. As I hugged Paul, I heard in my mind Steve's voice, *Everybody here?*

Yes.

Yes.

Yes.

CHAPTER 12

He Was a Brother I Miss Dearly

After I got out of Libya, Paul and I went to Goa for four days to decompress. The Zen destination that Indian friends had recommended to Paul was full, but the owner graciously offered us his private home on the resort grounds by a small creek. We were overcome with exhaustion. What might have been a celebratory, passionate several days was, in fact, a somber hibernation. Neither of us cried. We didn't make love nonstop. We simply held each other, kissed tenderly, slept, walked, swam, ate, drank, and slept some more.

That handful of days was enough for Paul and me to recenter ourselves before heading to New York; by that time, after so many years of travel and distance, five days together was the equivalent of five weeks of rest. My colleagues and I had to debrief the *Times* and do press interviews. We didn't realize it while in captivity, but our kidnapping had made a lot of news, and we had been asked to appear on several news programs and talk shows. Our first stop was the *New York Times*.

Walking into the shiny *Times* building, I was ashamed at what we had put our editors through with our kidnapping. I knew that countless hours of time and energy had gone into securing our release, and I steeled myself for reproachful glances. Journalists who got kidnapped several times were not necessarily heroes in our business. Bravery was one thing, recklessness another.

I went to find Michele McNally, the paper's director of photography, with whom I had worked for almost a decade and whose job it was to decide whether or not to send correspondents to this war or that revolution. It was one of the most stressful jobs at the paper, and she cared for us as though we were her children. When she saw me, she crumbled in my arms. Everyone in the photo department and others from the foreign desk surrounded us, took pictures, and clapped and cried. Everyone celebrated us. I felt like an idiot for having caused so much grief.

And while I thought I was stable, seemingly meaningless statements or normal emotional reactions from friends or family turned me into a quivering mess. The four of us shuffled from a brief appearance on the *Today* show to an hour-long session—like therapy—with Anderson Cooper on CNN. We trudged dutifully from interview to interview because we felt, as journalists, it would have been hypocritical to turn down interviews with our peers. We spoke collectively about the guilt and sorrow we felt for possibly ushering our young driver, Mohammed, to his death. I spoke openly about being sexually assaulted but not raped; it was important to me to set the record straight, publicly, about what happened to me in captivity. We had been completely at the Libyans' mercy. But we had lived. I felt lucky. I had interviewed suffering people all over the world, and they never felt like victims. They felt like survivors. I had learned from them.

Everyone asked us the inevitable question and my answer was yes. I knew I would cover another war. The hardest part about what happened to us in Libya was what we had put our loved ones through, but that had long been the excruciating price of the profession—my loved ones suffered, and I suffered when they suffered. Journalism is a selfish profession. But I still believed in the power of its purpose, and hoped my family did, too.

A MONTH LATER I met with three editors from Aperture Books in New York City. Prints of my work had been laid out on their conference table. We discussed the possibility of collaborating on a coffee-table book, something I had always dreamed of doing with my photographs but had never felt ready for. We were flipping through prints from Darfur, Iraq, and the Korengal Valley when I found myself distracted by the red light flashing on my BlackBerry. I did what I never did during a meeting: picked up my phone.

The top e-mail on my phone was forwarded from Major Dan Kearney, who had led Battle Company and Tim Hetherington, Balazs Gardi, Elizabeth Rubin, and me through the Korengal in 2007. The subject line read:

> Tim Hetherington killed in Libya.

My heart stopped. I was sure I was reading wrong. I looked at the body of the e-mail.

> Tim was killed in Libya. Please keep him in your prayers. I know the BATTLE Family will come together to support.
>
> He was a brother I miss dearly.
>
> MAJ Kearney

How could Tim have survived more than a year in the Korengal Valley, arguably the most dangerous place on earth, only to be killed in Libya? I did not want to believe the e-mail. As usual, I needed to say the words out loud to believe them. Tears rolled down my cheeks.

"Tim Hetherington was just killed in Libya."

Everyone gasped.

I scrolled down over more e-mails, trying to get some sort of explanation as to how this could have happened. Another e-mail had this heading:

Chris Hondros killed in Libya.

It couldn't be possible. Suddenly all the anxiety, post-traumatic stress, and sadness I had escaped after being released from Libya washed over me, flooding me with emotion. I fell apart in the austere conference room. The three people I was meeting with at Aperture excused themselves, telling me to stay in the room as long as I needed to.

It was not as though I hadn't experienced the loss of friends or colleagues before: Marla Ruzicka was killed by a car bomb in Baghdad in 2005; Solid Khalid was gunned down on his way to the *New York Times* bureau in Baghdad in 2007; *Times* photographer and mentor João Silva stepped on a land mine in Afghanistan in October 2010, losing both his legs and suffering debilitating internal injuries; Raza had died shortly after we lay on adjacent concrete slabs in a roadside clinic in Pakistan after our car accident; and of course Mohammed, our young driver, had died in Libya, too. But given all the death we had witnessed in Afghanistan, Iraq, Liberia, Darfur, Congo, Lebanon, Israel, and during the Arab Spring, death and injury had rarely come to the foreign journalist community—until now. Something in me snapped.

Tim and Chris were friends of mine. They weren't close friends in the typical sense of the word, but nothing in any of our lives was typical. We shared friendships born of long, intimate talks in lonely, morbid places and epic, intoxicated dinners back in the real world. Their sudden deaths hit me profoundly, in a way that my own experience in Libya failed to affect me. For the first time I felt the weight of the years of accumulated trauma. Perhaps it was because I realized how precarious life was and how arbitrary death was. Those e-mails could have easily been about me, Tyler, Anthony, or Steve. There were scores of inexperienced young photographers running around the front lines of Libya, but it was Tim and Chris, two of the most experienced photojournalists in the world, who met their fate in Misurata, in a mortar attack. It didn't make sense. Did our lives depend on statistical probability? Was it that the longer we covered war, the more close calls we sustained, increasing the chances that something would go wrong? Our lives were a game of odds. I sat paralyzed in the Aperture conference room. I needed to collect myself and walk home, but I couldn't do it. I messaged Paul and asked him to meet me. I needed him to come pick me up at Aperture. I couldn't find my way home alone.

THE WEEK OF APRIL 20, 2011, was a reckoning. Dozens of photographers, journalists, and editors came together in a way I had never witnessed before, flying in from all corners of the globe to grieve collectively. But before I could confront the overwhelming sadness, I needed strength. I boarded an Amtrak train for Washington, DC, and took a taxi to Walter Reed Army Medical Center, where I found my friend the photographer João Silva among dozens of other wounded and maimed veterans of war. I hadn't had a chance to visit him since a land mine severed his legs from his body and forced him into months of serial surgeries, but I knew that I craved his inner strength. Even after his injury, after one of his closest colleagues and friends had taken his own life and after another had been killed beside him, João remained resolved to cover war. His unfaltering belief in what we dedicated our lives to and his sage generosity of spirit and experience—despite the fact that he had lost half his body to war—rivaled the fortitude of anyone I knew. I simply needed to be with him to face reality head-on, to sit beside him in the very place that epitomized the devastation of war. I needed to hear how he kept going.

THAT SAME EVENING, I took the train to New York and reunited with Elizabeth and many other colleagues from throughout my travels.

Groups of us met up, night after night, and traded stories about Tim and Chris, often clenched in long embraces, expressing years of pent-up sorrow from, for many of us, exactly a decade of covering war. Along with our editors, who functioned as adopted parents, we had formed an iron bond, inexplicable to those outside our circle. The colleagues I had spent the decade with—sharing meals of stewed lamb with mounds of rice woven with sweet raisins and grated carrots in Afghanistan, or stale bread in cities overrun by insurgents—had become an essential part of who I was; they were family, and the only people with whom I found consolation at such a desperate emotional time.

One night that week a group of us close friends got together for dinner on New York's Lower East Side: the photographer Samantha Appleton; Marion Durand, a photo editor at *Newsweek* and the wife of the Magnum photographer Chris Anderson, who'd stopped covering war after the birth of their son; the brilliant photo editor Jamie Wellford; Tyler and his girlfriend, Nicki; and me. Samantha, Marion, and I arrived first and ordered a bottle of wine. Tyler, Nicki, and Jamie showed up shortly thereafter, their faces blotchy and swollen. No one seemed to be able to stop crying.

I was shocked by Tyler's appearance. I saw in his face the same devastation I was experiencing: These deaths broke him in a way that Libya hadn't. Hondros was one of Tyler's oldest friends. He had ushered Tyler into the world of photojournalism when they were young men fresh out of college, living in Ohio and working for the *Troy Daily News*. Their careers developed in tandem as they covered wars in Iraq, Afghanistan, Lebanon, and Libya. They'd amassed accolades together, grew into accomplished men together. We all sat and looked at one another and cried openly, a display of emotion that was uncharacteristic of our profession. The bravado was gone.

Two days later we went to Chris's funeral in Carroll Gardens, Brooklyn, at the church where he was supposed to have married that summer. Instead of walking down the aisle with his beautiful Christina, he was carried down the aisle in a casket, his mother and his bride-to-be walking a few steps behind. Bach, Beethoven, and Mahler echoed off the cathedral walls. The simple image of one of us in a wooden box, after leading such a full life, was too much to bear. The finality was inescapable. Friends, colleagues, relatives, and people who never personally knew Hondros squeezed inside and spilled out onto the sidewalk. During the eulogies I stood with Michael Robinson Chavez, a photographer I had met in Iraq and who had become a dear friend over the years, and David Guttenfelder, another photographer and friend. We were wrecked.

Paul stayed with me in New York that week. His bosses at Reuters allowed him to take time off to console me after Libya. And I finally felt that it was the right moment to step back from all the drama and death of the past decade and make love, without worrying about the consequences.

CHAPTER 13

I Would Advise You Not to Travel

Three weeks later, in New Delhi, the little blue line appeared in the window—making a positive out of the negative sign. Already? April was the first month Paul and I had physically spent time together since I went off the pill. I counted backward, calculating that conception must have happened the week Tim and Chris were killed in Libya—the week I had let my ever-present guard down. I cursed the genetics of my reproductively inclined Italian family and crawled back in bed with Paul, placing the plastic stick with our future on the pillow next to his head. I hated him at that moment. He had been pushing and prodding me to get pregnant since the day we got married. He even announced his intentions during a live interview with CNN anchor Ali Velshi while I was missing in Libya. On the third day of our captivity, Paul told Velshi that the *New York Times* had speculated that we might have been abducted by Qaddafi's soldiers, but no one really knew if we were alive or dead. Velshi asked what Paul would say to me when we had the opportunity to speak again and Paul replied, "I'm going to say, you know, you gotta come back here because, you know, we gotta have kids." Paul knew I would have been mortified at the thought of my husband announcing on live TV that he wanted to get me pregnant, but it was an emotional moment. Usually he made no secret of his desire to start a family. He even contrived with my oldest friend, Tara, to decipher my ovulation chart in the weeks after Libya and put the dates as a reminder in his BlackBerry. He did all this with his characteristic sense of humor and never flagged in his support for my work. But he knew he had to push me.

When Paul finally woke up, I showed him the pregnancy test, and we took another just to be sure: positive again. "You got your wish," I said. "I can't believe it happened so fast. I think my life is over."

Paul knew better than to answer. He had his coffee, got dressed, and went down to the bookstore at Khan Market, near our house in New Delhi, and bought *What to Expect When You're Expecting*. He came home and presented me with this encyclopedic book of gestation. I took one look at it, with its grinning, baby-bump-flaunting woman on the cover, and was terrified. I was not at all ready to give up my life, my body, my travels. I stared at the glowing woman with a watermelon-sized stomach. Was that really going to be me in nine months? That huge? And she was so happy. Wasn't *that* woman conflicted about her career? How was I going to keep shooting? My thoughts shifted to my colleagues—mostly men. What was everyone going to think? *Kidnapped in Libya, husband made an announcement on CNN that he wanted to start a family while wife was still missing, and less than two months later she's already knocked up!* Surely it was the most predictable outcome of my entire life. I tried to imagine my life as a mother—struggled to envision a female role model in conflict photography—and I couldn't think of a single female war photographer who even had a stable relationship. There were journalists who had taken time out to have children, like Elizabeth, who had a baby and managed to keep writing; photographers were different. What would the MacArthur Foundation say? They honor me with an incredible fellowship to foster my career as an international photojournalist, and I get pregnant.

A few days later I sat in the OB/GYN waiting room at Indraprastha Apollo Hospitals in New Delhi. The ground floor was swarming with Afghans who traveled to India for medical tourism—men with long gray beards looking disoriented and out of place in such a modern hospital, trailed by women in full *hijab*. For the first time in my life, I couldn't handle sitting in a room full of Afghan beards and head scarves as I waited for my first official visit to the doctor as a pregnant woman. Bollywood videos played on a flat screen mounted on a pink wall festooned with stencils of pastel-colored mushrooms, flowers, caterpillars, and ladybugs. Screaming Indian and Afghan children tore across the waiting room floor. Their parents sat idly by, smiling proudly and exercising zero discipline, as I waited for Dr. Sohani Verma's secretary to call my name. I prayed that the two pregnancy tests were wrong as I clenched the results of blood tests she had requested in my hands. The secretary called out my name. The doctor was a stern, old-fashioned Indian woman in a sari. She looked over my chart and introduced herself.

"I'm Dr. Verma," she announced, with no enthusiasm. "Everything looks fine."

"Am I really pregnant?" I asked.

"Yes, you are."

"Oh."

"Do you have any questions?" she asked.

I had dutifully read a few chapters of *What to Expect When You're Expecting* and had perused the Internet for the obvious dos and don'ts of pregnancy: what not to eat, when the nausea would kick in, etc. "Can I still go to the gym?" I asked, half-knowing I would continue to go with or without her consent.

"Yes, light exercise. Don't let your body overheat too much, don't sweat too much. Keep your heart rate moderate." I was relieved I would be able to hold on to one of my rituals.

"I am on my way to Senegal next week."

She looked at me askance. "I would advise you not to travel. Flights have radiation that is not good for the embryo at this stage. It could be harmful."

The words were like daggers in my heart. No travel? Impossible. "Really?" I asked skeptically. "I have never heard of that before. For how long is there a risk period involved with flying?" I was convinced it must have been an Indian folktale.

"The first three months are the most sensitive. And for the duration of your pregnancy, I would limit all long-haul flights—flights over six hours—to a minimum." I tried to contain my shock. No one had ever told me to limit my travel before. "And there is malaria in Senegal. Do you have to go to Senegal now?"

Claustrophobia set in. "Yes." The words flew out of my mouth. It was a knee-jerk reaction. "I cannot cancel now." As I said the words, I realized that to someone outside my profession, to whom journalism was just a job, I probably sounded insane, being willing to possibly jeopardize my pregnancy for a ten-day *Times* assignment.

"There is a risk you can lose the pregnancy if you get malaria in Senegal. And I would advise you not to take antimalaria tablets while pregnant."

With every sentence I felt a part of myself dying. My life was being taken over by a microscopic union of Paul and me growing inside my uterus, and I had yet to feel that overwhelming joy all these women talked about when they talked about pregnancy.

"I can use bug spray," I started, and before I finished the sentence I realized that bug spray, too, might be harmful to an unborn child.

"You can use citronella," Dr. Verma said.

I left the hospital in a cloud of defeat.

I went to Senegal in mid-May, enveloped by the exhaustion and nausea of my first trimester. I left a certain amount of the risk of malaria, of the radiation of flying, and of whether I could handle a physically challenging assignment in the hands of fate. After all, it was the philosophy that had governed much of my life. I thought often about

Elizabeth and of how she had traipsed through the Korengal Valley laden with body armor for her entire second trimester, and I suddenly understood why she had forced herself to keep working throughout her pregnancy: because in a sense, our work was our life. It defined who we were, it wasn't just a job we did for a living, and I needed to hold on to that for as long as I could.

With the exception of military embeds, I took on all my regular assignments, hiding my burgeoning belly beneath loose-fitting shirts, cargo pants, and sometimes, fortunately, the necessary *hijab*. I convinced myself that if I didn't tell anyone, I wouldn't have to compromise my life. I was adamant that my editors and colleagues were not to know until I could no longer hide it—I feared editors would deny me work on account of my pregnancy. I had fought hard to reach a place where I had a consistent stream of assignments, and I wanted to make sure that I wasn't written off with the girth of my belly.

I went from Senegal to Saudi Arabia to Afghanistan, and at four months Paul and I broke the news to my parents while on vacation in Rhode Island. No one could believe that Paul had actually managed to persuade me to pause long enough to have a baby when I barely stopped moving long enough to do my laundry. At four and a half months Doctors Without Borders sent me to photograph its medical outreach for victims of the drought consuming the Horn of Africa and Kenya—from the Turkana region to the Somali refugee camps in Dadaab, Kenya. Halfway through the assignment, working in remote African villages, I could no longer button my pants. I was almost five months pregnant. The nausea and exhaustion were gone, my energy level had returned, and I was eating normally, though I was careful to avoid harmful bacteria, which in remote Africa meant eating bread, rice, bananas, and protein bars I carried from home.

As I was finishing up my two-week assignment, I sensed that I had just been skimming around the edges with my coverage of the drought. All the refugees I was photographing in Dadaab were fleeing the drought in Somalia; I needed to go to Somalia in order to photograph the real story, what had been causing them to seek refuge. It was a fundamental missing piece among the images I had photographed. While my assignment with Doctors Without Borders was finished, the story would also be syndicated through my photo agency for other publications around the world. I would have felt like an irresponsible or misleading journalist had I only half-completed my coverage of the story of the drought—that is, if I didn't go to Somalia and expose the heart of the crisis. For me, it was because few journalists went to Somalia that I felt it was important to go. But that meant traveling at five months pregnant, less than six months after being very publicly kidnapped in Libya, to Mogadishu, the kidnapping capital of the world.

In many ways Somalia was a failed state: anarchic, violent, impoverished, its land overrun by the Shabaab, a fundamentalist militia group that terrorized civilians and kidnapped people for exorbitant ransoms. The only reason they didn't enter Mogadishu was the presence of African Union peacekeepers. Somalia was one of the few places on earth that I was actually scared to visit, as I repeatedly imagined a fate like that of the American soldiers dragged through Mogadishu's streets in 1993. And I knew that if anything ever happened to me in Somalia so soon after Libya, I would surely be written off by my editors and peers as a crazy, irresponsible photographer, making it impossible to justify myself. But journalistically Somalia was a fundamental part of the story, and I didn't want to start compromising my professional instincts before I had a baby.

I started sending e-mails to colleagues who had recently been in Mogadishu: Tyler, who had been one of the first to cover the story powerfully for the *New York Times*, and John Moore, a photographer with Getty Images whom Tyler and I had traveled with in Libya. They both passed along contacts for Mohammed, the main fixer in Mogadishu. For $1,000 per day, Mohammed could arrange a room in his guesthouse, an interpreter, a driver, and a militia of anywhere from four to eight gunmen to accompany me each time I wanted to travel out of the guest-house. Tyler and John both spoke very highly of Mohammed; they explained that he went to great lengths to prepare each shooting excursion outside the sanctuary of the guesthouse and took no task lightly. They said what I knew already: that Mogadishu was unpredictable, that it looked scarier from the outside, and that the chances were that the trip would go fine—unless it didn't.

Beyond the security risk, both Tyler and John recounted something very worrisome: that they had gotten horrible stomach ailments from the food at the guesthouse, which I worried might cause harm to the baby. *Just bring Cipro*, they said, the pharmaceutical elixir of choice for many of us, which basically microwaved the body free of bacteria. But I wasn't allowed to take Cipro. I still hadn't told my colleagues I was pregnant.

I needed just two to three bacteria-free days on the ground to visit the hospitals, which were allegedly swarming with drought victims, with at least a handful of children dying each day from diarrhea, dehydration, and complications from diseases that often accompanied malnutrition. And I needed to visit the camps for the internally displaced, which were sprouting up all over Mogadishu, populated by people from other parts of the country. Nothing would happen in a few days, I reassured myself, especially if I ate only bananas, bread, and Pure Protein Bars. I had two more orders of business before I could book my flight: I had to call Paul—even though I had pretty much decided on going—and make sure he felt comfortable with my decision. For the first time I actually felt that I needed his permission to risk my life, because I would also be risking the life of our baby.

Paul and I talked through the potential risks involved, and he asked me to limit my stay in Mogadishu to as few days as possible in order to get the images I needed to complete the story. I finished my assignment for Doctors Without Borders in Kenya, and Jamie, my *Newsweek* editor, offered me some expense money to publish the work from Somalia.

In the days of decreased magazine budgets, this was the next best thing to an assignment.

Something strange happened once I arrived in Kenya: The baby—whom I had been imagining for weeks as an avocado-pit-sized embryo, based on regular updates from the BabyCenter app—started kicking. He came to life as a little person inside me as I entered Somalia, the land ridden with death. He was very active, and suddenly I was acutely aware of him all the time.

Once I got to Mogadishu, I went to the guesthouse to meet with Mohammed. He looked at me, shrouded in my flowing black *abaya* and matching head scarf, and smiled: "You look Somali! We don't have to worry about you!" Mohammed didn't think I was in great danger of being kidnapped.

I went right to work, starting with Banadir Hospital, the main hospital in the city. In Africa white people were often presumed to be aid workers, doctors, people there to help in a very immediate way with medicine or food distribution. I walked into the main foyer of the hospital and was immediately overwhelmed by the scene. Throngs of hollow-faced Somali women and children filled the wards, littered the halls, lying prostrate and listless anywhere they could find the space. Their sunken eyes pierced my white skin with hope: They thought I was a doctor who had come to save them from their fate. All I had was my camera. Somali medical reserves were tapped. The hospitals had only a few doctors, a few more nurses, and little medicine. Most people were simply given IVs of rehydrating fluids and left to recover, to wither, to die. They shared beds, rested on the floors. I had never seen a situation that bad, with little interest from the international aid community. Somalia was simply too dangerous for foreign aid workers, and so the people were left to their own resources. As dangerous as it was, I knew I had made the right journalistic decision by going to Mogadishu.

I went to the upstairs ward to look around. I always felt horrible photographing people in such states of misery, but I hoped my images, in bringing greater awareness of the desperation, might also bring food and medical aid. I worked quickly, deliberately, abiding by Mohammed's instructions to not linger very long anywhere in order to avoid the risk of kidnap. I had spent my career navigating dangerous assignments based on risk calculation, and I wanted to trust that ability, even though I was pregnant. Our kidnapping in Libya did weigh heavily upon me. I was constantly fighting against a freshly developed fear, a new reflex to finish my work that very second and get on the first plane out of Somalia. But I was holding on to my identity, my freedom, what I had been working toward my entire adult life—as well as panic that it was all about to disappear with the birth of my child.

I entered the third room to the left off a long, window-lined hall. A woman named Rukayo and her sister Lu prayed over Rukayo's son, Abbas Nishe, one and a half, who was dying from complications associated with severe malnutrition. His skeletal chest pumped up and down as he labored to breathe; his eyes rolled back into his head and then forward again as he focused on his mother. I kneeled down beside the two women, introduced myself as a journalist, and asked permission to photograph. They agreed. I began shooting as the two women put their hands on Abbas's tiny frame and then onto his mouth. Each time his eyes rolled back into his head, the women thought he was dead. To my horror, they began closing his tiny mouth with their hands, a premature death ritual evidencing a loss of hope. They were covering his eyes and closing his mouth, and as I photographed I felt my own baby kicking and twisting about in my uterus, making me acutely aware of the life inside me. It was the most incongruous, most unfair juxtaposition of life and death I had felt since I began my journey as a photographer.

SOMEWHERE BETWEEN FIVE and six months, my stomach popped. I found out I was having a boy. Back in New York for an assignment, I started breaking the news to a few select people. Kathy Ryan, with whom I had worked for a decade at the *New York Times Magazine*, was one of the first. She immediately offered to throw me a baby shower. Did I really have to have a baby shower? There was no turning back. Kathy's generosity to host a party at her place was overwhelming, but I hadn't even told anyone else I was pregnant yet.

"Kathy," I suggested, "maybe the shower invitation could be the way I tell my friends I am pregnant? Do I have to actually tell people before I invite them to my baby shower?"

That night I broke the news to Michele McNally and David Furst, my editors at the *Times*. The next morning my cell phone rang. It was David. I was hoping he had been too drunk to remember what I had told him the night before.

"Good morning," David said, rather seriously.

"Morning. What's up?" I asked.

"Listen: I want you to know something. I didn't get into this last night because there was a lot going on, and we were all out and drinking. But I want to congratulate you again on the baby, and I wanted to tell you that I am really happy for you and Paul."

"Um, thank you." I said. "Sorry the news is a bit late . . . I just didn't really feel comfortable telling anyone."

"Listen, I want to be clear: I will give you work until the day you tell me you are ready to stop shooting, and I will start giving you work again after the baby is born, the day you tell me you are ready to go back to work. I am so happy for you. This is going to be great. Don't worry about your career. It will be fine. I will personally give you as little or as much work as you want. I'm just really happy for you both."

I was shocked by his reaction. I assumed I would be looked at differently as soon as they heard I was pregnant. My editor's reaction gave me pause, made me think that perhaps the industry was changing a little. Was it possible I had finally proved myself enough?

Throughout my pregnancy, though, I remained terrified that my editors would write me off with childbirth and stop hiring me because the assignments were perceived as too rigorous or dangerous for a "mother." These were decisions I wanted to make for myself; I didn't want to surrender those choices as a woman and as a professional. Photojournalism, journalism as a whole, is brutally competitive. I knew that at the end of the day it didn't matter that I had won a MacArthur fellowship or been part of the *New York Times* Pulitzer team or won numerous other accolades along the way. After all, I was a freelance photographer, with no professional security other than the reputation I had built over the years. I had no guarantee of future assignments and a future paycheck. And I was haunted by the maxim "You're only as good as your last story." Too often I had seen that it was true. It was still possible that motherhood could bring me down the professional ladder.

TWO WEEKS LATER Furst sent me to Gaza for a prisoner exchange between the Israelis and the Palestinian militant group Hamas. The Israelis announced that they would trade 1,027 Palestinian prisoners for one Israeli soldier: Sergeant First Class Gilad Shalit, twenty-five, who had been abducted by Hamas in a cross-border raid in 2006. It seemed like a pretty straightforward assignment, even while pregnant, and I was to team up once again with my colleague Steve Farrell. I hadn't seen him since our post-Libya visit to New York.

The safest, easiest way into Gaza was through Israel. A journalist flew into Tel Aviv, drove to Jerusalem, and went to the government press office for media accreditation. She then drove a short two hours to Erez Crossing, the high-tech, airportlike terminal that served as the official border gate between Gaza and Israel. The *New York Times* bureau in Jerusalem was an institution: well connected, with an excellent office manager and correspondents who immediately knew which officials to contact to facilitate any kind of story. As I headed to Erez, I called Shlomo, the Israeli press official who handled media relations at Erez, and he assured me the cross would be smooth.

I passed through immigration uneventfully. Erez was built to accommodate the thousands of Palestinians who crossed into Israel each day to work and back again, until fighting between the two states made Gaza an open-air prison: Few Gazans were allowed out through Erez, and no Israelis were allowed in. The border was traversed almost exclusively by journalists and aid workers, a stark reminder of the economic consequences of Gaza's isolation.

I spent almost two weeks in Gaza, photographing relatives and bedrooms of prisoners due home after years away, and Hamas's parade of weapons for the cameras in their ominous black attire and balaclavas. The prisoner exchange came at the end. As the buses full of prisoners streamed across the Egyptian border into Gaza, men, women, and children—relatives and friends—threw themselves at the prisoners as they exited the buses. Tasting their first steps of freedom in years, they looked half-shocked by the crush of loved ones. Momentarily forgetting I was pregnant, I jockeyed for a position close enough to capture the initial moments of euphoria with my cameras, throwing myself into the mix of hundreds of frenzied relatives. As the weight of men around me started to push me to and fro, pressing against my body in the natural hysteria of the moment, I recalled my fragile state. But my stomach and I were so deep in the crowd, I couldn't extricate myself. What if someone pushed my stomach? What if I miscarried right then and there at the prisoner release? I panicked.

In the Muslim world, women and children were often put on a safety pedestal—and pregnant woman were slightly higher up on that pedestal. Naturally, no pregnant woman in Gaza would voluntarily be in that mix of madness, but it was too late to lament my stupidity. I had an idea: I threw my arms up in the air and screamed "Baby!" and pointed down at my very round stomach with my index fingers. "Baby!" I screamed again, pointing down.

All the men around me momentarily paused, and the man beside me looked at my face and down at my stomach and instinctively made a human gate around me, cocooning me from the crowd. It was as if the seas parted. And I continued shooting the madness, with my spontaneous bodyguards keeping watch over my unborn son.

Before heading back to Erez Crossing to make my way home, I called Shlomo in Israel and expressed a gnawing concern: I was twenty-seven weeks pregnant and concerned that the full-body scanners at Erez Crossing might harm my pregnancy. Shlomo reassured me that he would notify the soldiers in advance of my arrival. The crossing back into Israel from Gaza entailed an intensive security procedure in anticipation of suicide attacks. The entire border crossing is partitioned into cubes of bulletproof glass, with a series of heavy electronic doors that the Israelis open and close once the passerby's identity has been confirmed. There is a traditional luggage belt for luggage, which is handled by a Palestinian. All Israeli soldiers monitoring the movement of people passing from Gaza into Israel are standing out of harm's way, on a glassed-in balcony overlooking the entire security area. They communicate through an intercom system as they watch from above. You can see them, and they can see you, and you could potentially shout up to them in a raised voice, but the intercom stands in for any personal contact. Everyone must cross through the first metal detector and bulletproof gate and into an advanced full-body scanner; once a red light turns green, you eventually pass through a final gate and on to collect luggage off the belt, then through immigration on the other side of the security area. An American AP photographer based in Jerusalem had warned me of a tiny room off to the side where suspicious crossers were routed after the scan: It had a metal grate for a floor, so if one detonated himself, the body parts and the brunt of the explosion would fall down through the grates rather than outward. I had that image in the back of my mind as I pressed the first intercom button at the entrance of the security labyrinth.

"Hi, we are with the *New York Times*. I called Shlomo this morning and explained that I am twenty-seven weeks pregnant and wondered if you could do a manual body check rather than have me pass through the scanner? I am worried about my baby and the radiation."

A snarky voice wafted from the intercom on the door: "Well. You can strip down to your underwear and we do a strip search, or you can just pass through the scanner."

I turned to Steve, who was married to a Palestinian Christian and had been living in Jerusalem for several years.

"Steve, what should I do? I'm worried about passing through the scanner."

"Well, I think if you opt out of the scanner, they're going to keep you here *all day*. You might as well pass through once. It probably won't harm the baby to pass through once."

I pressed the intercom button again, looking up at the gaggle of Israeli soldiers at a distance above, and let them know that I opted for the scanner.

I was still worried about the radiation. I heard a loud metallic click, and the gate opened to a machine that looked like a time capsule. I stepped in, placing my feet on the stenciled footprints that marked where they should go, and raised my hands in a triangle above my head, as I've done so many times before in this country, unpregnant. I waited as the scanner moved around my body, and held my breath. The machine stopped, the light switched from red to green, and the magical gate opened, passing me through to another prisonlike cubicle. The light in the second cubicle turned from red to green, and as I started forward, the light turned back to red. I paused, confused. The same arrogant voice came over the intercom: "Could you please go back to the scanner? There was a problem."

"What?" I asked, feeling my blood pressure rise. "You want me to go through the scanner again?"

"Yes. Go back."

I went back to the scanner and raised my arms above my head. I held my breath as the scanner moved again around my body, careful not to move. The light turned from red to green, and I moved forward into the next cubicle, where I waited for that light to also turn green to pass me through after two full-body scans. But the light turned red again. It must have been a mistake. I looked up to the glassed-in balcony, now with a handful of soldiers looking down on me in my little glass prison. They were laughing and smiling as they debated whether to continue radiating me and my stomach.

"Whoops"—the arrogant voice returned— "you moved. Can you please pass back to the scanner?"

Are you kidding me? I asked myself. It took every inch of self-restraint to not lose my mind. "I did not move. I have been through these scanners before. I know I did not move."

"Go back to the scanner."

"I am sure my baby will be born with three heads after this," I offered.

"Go back," he said. The other soldiers were still laughing.

After the third time in the full-body scanner, they finally passed me through to the next cubicle. But instead of directing me straight toward the exit and the luggage belt, they had me go to a cavernous room with a metal-grated floor off to the right: the suicide-bomber room. A light flicked on across from me, and a female Israeli soldier who was perched behind thick bulletproof glass leaned forward and said, "Take off your pants."

"What?"

"Take off your pants, and lift up your shirt. I need to see your body."

"Is your scanner not working? The one you just made me pass through three times?"

"Please take off your clothes."

I took off my pants and lifted up my shirt to reveal my perfectly shaped basketball of a stomach and the red lacy underwear I don't know what possessed me to wear that day.

"Are all the men in the glass box watching this from above?" I asked.

"No, they are not."

I wondered if the woman staring at my pregnant, naked body was at all ashamed of their behavior.

"OK, you can get dressed again."

I was confused, appalled, and angry until I suddenly had a moment of clarity: If the Israeli soldiers were doing this to me, a *New York Times* journalist accredited by the Israeli government itself, who had called the press officer in advance to graciously ask to be manually searched, how on earth did they treat a poor, Palestinian pregnant woman? Or a nonpregnant Palestinian woman? Or a Palestinian man? The thought terrified me.

I left Erez and filed a formal complaint to the International Press Center in Jerusalem and the Israeli government through the *Times* bureau in Jerusalem. More than a month after we filed the initial complaint, the Israeli Ministry of Defense issued a statement regarding the events at Erez, and in an unprecedented step for the ministry, they issued a public apology for my treatment.

Just as in Somalia, when I had felt my baby moving inside me as I witnessed the suffering of other infants, I could suddenly understand, in a new, profound, and enraging way, how most people in the world lived. I had been seeing that reality for years. But somehow, I had to admit, my pregnancy and the vulnerabilities of motherhood had offered me yet another window on humanity, yet another channel of understanding.

CHAPTER 14

Lukas

Lukas Simon de Bendern was born perfectly healthy on December 28, 2011, at St. Mary's Hospital in London after eleven-plus hours of miserable labor. Paul had gotten a new job in London, and we had moved only three weeks before.

My first few weeks as a mother were a blur of sleeping and nursing and trying to reconcile my present life with the one that seemed to have existed in such a distant past. For three months, for the first time in memory, I didn't pack a single suitcase, didn't buy a plane ticket or look on Expedia, didn't stress about hotels or assignments or breaking news or who was killing whom or who was dying from an outbreak of measles or cholera in what remote corner of the planet. My days were simple and repetitive: I slept until I was woken up by Lukas's cries, nursed, made coffee, watched bad TV, and nursed again. I watched more made-for-TV movies during the last month of my pregnancy and while nursing than I had during my entire life prior. Every activity was punctuated by a diaper change and my gnawing fear that I would somehow break my new baby with my inexperienced touch. Before I gave birth, I knew nothing about infants. I had no idea what they needed, how to know when they were sick, how to dress them, how to duck their fragile skulls into an over-the-head onesie, and what to put on them in London's cold, damp winter air.

The daily rituals around which the lives of most of the women on the planet revolved had become my own. And I embraced them, because all of a sudden the notion of routine didn't seem unfulfilling. I had this baby whom Paul and I had created, and we felt a joy and a love that far exceeded anything we had ever known. For hours we sat on the couch and stared at Lukas, incredulous that he was born of nothing other than sperm and egg. We felt as if we were the first two people on the planet to have conceived. How could the most basic thing be so rewarding? Suddenly I understood why all the Afghan women over the years had looked at me with sadness when I admitted to not having children. And I knew, deep down, that I must cherish my initial months as a mother, because it would be one of the rare occasions I could allow myself to indulge in nothing other than loving and caring for Lukas, this tiny, helpless person we had made.

The euphoria of creation in the early months of motherhood came to a shocking halt one night in early February of 2012. I was in the coziness of my family cocoon, feeding Lukas at 4 a.m., when I heard my New York cell ringing from my purse in the living room downstairs. Only credit card companies and emergency calls rang me on my roaming cell in the middle of the night, and I asked Paul to bring me the phone. There were dozens of missed calls and familiar subject lines on my BlackBerry e-mails:

I'm so sorry.
Sad news.

Anthony Shadid, my longtime friend, had died in Syria of an asthma attack earlier that day. Tyler, who had been working with him, had shepherded his body across the border to Turkey, where Anthony's wife, Nada, and two-year-old son, Malik, waited to collect him. It was less than a year after we had all narrowly escaped death in Libya. I felt angry. What was he doing in Syria so soon after what had transpired in Libya? I knew that, had I not gotten pregnant, I, too, would probably have been there. But it was easier to wish a conventional life on Anthony than it was at that moment to accept his resolution to cover Syria—at all costs. His death put a mirror to the pain I caused others with my decisions. And how could he have died of an asthma attack, of all things, in the middle of a battle zone? Who wrote these miserable cards of fate? They were all questions I would never have the answers to—except one. I knew why he was back covering the Arab Spring. I knew why he returned to cover conflict, just as I knew why I would one day return to cover conflict. As with all of us, it was in his soul, and very little could have kept him away.

My heart ached for his family, and yet I, too, could not give up the work I held so close to me. Three months after I gave birth, I started traveling again. I took my first assignment for the *Times Magazine* in Alabama, photographing mothers addicted to methamphetamine. Being away from Lukas was worse than any heartbreak, any distance from a lover—anything I had ever known. I cried all the way to the airport, throughout the journey, and right up until the morning I loaded the memory cards into my Nikons, placed my lenses in their pouches, strung them around my waist, and set off for the rugged barn in rural Alabama to visit Timmy Kimbrough and his three children. With my first few frames, I lost myself in my work.

I didn't think it would ever get easier to leave Lukas and Paul. I struggled, like so many professional men and women, to find that perfect, impossible balance between my personal life and my career. Inevitably one suffered at the expense of the other, and when I returned from an assignment, I was confronted with the price of my absence: Lukas running into our nanny's arms rather than my own, or calling out "Da Da" when I called on Skype from a random hotel room in India or Uganda. In the first year after giving birth, I shot assignments from Mississippi to Mauritania, from Zimbabwe to Sierra Leone to India. I cushioned each assignment with quality time with Lukas, going to play group and music class, straddling two worlds that couldn't be farther apart. I convinced myself I would stay on the margins of war and tailor my work to my new life as a mother. When the violence in Gaza broke out in November 2012, I felt the familiar urgency in the pit of my stomach telling me that I needed to be there to document the civilian deaths. But I was in London. I went to the gym and looked around, positive that I was the only person in Notting Hill wishing she was in Gaza rather than in Café 202, sipping a latte with a coiffed poodle perched on her lap.

While I was happier and more complete with my new family than I had ever been before, I was still restless to get back out in the field and cover the stories I felt strongly about. But unlike early in my career, when I felt I needed to be in the midst of every top news story in order to prove myself as a photojournalist, I eventually started feeling comfortable saying no to breaking-news stories: I was more selective about assignments after the birth of my son, and I weighed the importance of every story with every day that would keep me away from my family. I met deadlines and editors' needs while weaving in time for Lukas between assignments; the balance was possible because I worked with trusted editors who were supportive of my new role as mother, and because I had a partner, Paul, who was a hands-on father and a champion of my work.

The risks I took now had higher stakes. Every night when I put Lukas to sleep, I thought about whether I would be there to watch him grow from this perfect soul, a beautiful infant, to a toddler, to a boy, to a teen, and into a man. I struggled with the question of why I put us, and my extended family, into that equation of uncertainty, but I hoped Lukas would understand my commitment to journalism one day, as his father intrinsically understood. Before I gave birth to Lukas, I hadn't truly understood that painful, consuming, I-will-do-anything-to-save-this-human-being kind of love. I had lived my life in defiance of fear, but now that I had this tiny being to care for, I thought about mortality differently: I worried constantly that something might happen to him, something I had never felt for myself. When I thought about his future, I hoped he would lead a life as full of opportunity and happiness and experiences as mine had been. My dreams for my child were the same ones that I knew compelled so many women around the world to fight for their families against the most unimaginable odds. My experience as a parent has taught me a new understanding of the subjects I photograph.

As a war correspondent and a mother, I've learned to live in two different realities. It's not always easy to make the transition from a beautiful London park filled with children to a war zone, but it's my choice. I choose to live in peace and witness war—to experience the worst in people but to remember the beauty.

Return to Iraq

By late 2012 the war in Syria raged. For journalists it was at least as dangerous as Libya had been in 2011. If newspapers sent in correspondents at all, they went in with the help and logistical support of a particular rebel commander and stayed for only a short time. I wanted to cover the war's civilian toll—far from the front line—and offered myself up to the *New York Times* to visit the camps for displaced civilians. I traveled to Lebanon, Jordan, and Turkey, and as I crossed the border from Turkey into war-ravaged Syria, I thought about Lukas and wondered if my love for him might overwhelm my ability to go to countries where my fate was so uncertain.

With a colleague, a security guard, a driver, and a fixer, I drove through the bucolic villages of northern Aleppo that lined the border between Syria and Turkey, my cameras tucked away in a bag at my feet, my hair neatly hidden under a head scarf. I watched the countryside whip past my window as we traversed small pockets of peace that existed precariously in a country torn apart by death: a few farmers toiling in the fields, young men lining up for haircuts at the barbershop. We drove to the rebel-controlled village of Tilalyan, where we were greeted by members of the town council, happy to see foreign journalists there to document their plight. I photographed boys who spent their days trying to secure flour for the bakery, teachers at a makeshift school who taught amid the air strikes. We visited a local clinic, swarming with Syrians who had been wounded in battle, others merely suffering everyday ailments that suddenly became impossible to treat as doctors disappeared or migrated to battlefronts to treat the gravely wounded. It was a story that had been routine in the past but took on a whole new meaning for me as a mother. With every scene I wondered how Lukas would fare in the same situation; I wondered how it would feel to be like these mothers, who suddenly couldn't guarantee security or access to daily meals for their children.

Eventually the story of Syrian refugees took me back to northern Iraq, to Erbil, where I had spent my first night in the country a decade earlier to cover the war between the United States and Iraq. Instead of driving across the jagged, snowcapped mountains between Iran and Iraq, I flew into a glassy, modern airport in Erbil and presented my passport at immigration to a pretty young Iraqi Kurdish woman with long, wavy hair and nails painted red.

"Have you ever been here before?" she asked, looking through a passport that was a stamped testament to so many memories in so many countries.

"Yes," I responded, smiling. "But a lot has changed. I was here ten years ago—in 2003."

"Welcome," she said. "You have a two-week visa." Iraqi Kurdistan was one of the few places in the Middle East that welcomed Americans.

I exited the airport to a familiar burst of dry, convectionlike, one-hundred-plus-degree heat and looked around for Tim, the correspondent I would be working with for the *Times*. He was there, wearing a Yankees baseball cap, and behind him stood Waleed, the driver with whom I had endured the kidnapping in Fallujah in 2004. He looked older, his gray hair and mustache now dyed black but faded into a black-red henna tint, his large frame still tall but slightly gaunt. He threw his arms around me and laughed a big laugh.

"Habibti!" (My dear!) "So happy to see you again."

I squeezed Waleed tightly, grateful to see a familiar face and a friend after many years. I wondered about the toll Iraq's sectarian violence had taken on him and his family. How many friends and family members had he lost? Over the ever-present kebab, Waleed ran down the list of fellow *Times* employees from 2003 and 2004 and rattled off where they were now: Basim, Canada; Zaineb, Canada; Ali, Michigan; Jaff, New York. The ongoing war had disassembled Iraqi society, scattering lives and friends across the Atlantic, across continents.

As we raced toward the Syrian border, my mind slipped back to 2003, to who I was then: a young woman who wanted nothing more than to travel the world and to document the stories of people and their hardships. I was insatiable in my quest to document the truth with my photographs and threw myself into the midst of any situation without regard for the consequences, believing that if my intentions were pure and I focused on my work, I would be OK. Though I still work with the same dedication, I have grown more cautious with every brush with death, with every friend lost. Somewhere along the way my mortality began to matter.

AT THE SAHELA BORDER crossing, six hours northwest of Erbil, four thousand Syrian Kurds snaked around the desert valleys along a dirt road connecting the two countries. I ran up a gravelly hill, oblivious to the Mine Action Group marker denoting an area once ridden with land mines, in search of a clearer view of the border crossing. I put my camera to my eye and through my long lens watched the colorful shuffle of thousands of refugees from a distance.

The biblical scene took my breath away. It was a different war, another war, and another population displaced by fear and death. The Iraqi Kurds were no longer fleeing by the thousands from Saddam but welcoming Syrians fleeing their own civil war. I photographed families escaping with whatever belongings they could carry on their backs, the elderly hobbling along the uneven road, glistening with sweat, as young mothers and fathers carried their children in their arms. I wondered what it would be like to have to flee with Lukas. I ran down from my perch on the hill and walked into the road, wading amid the refugees as they neared the first checkpoint manned by Iraqi Kurds. I photographed wide as they approached, their shoulders sometimes brushing mine, and every few minutes I lowered my camera from my eye and offered a big "Salaam!" to the endless stream of refugees.

Many smiled back, calling me by my title: "Sahafiya." Journalist. It is who I am. It's what I do.

ACKNOWLEDGMENTS

FOR ALMOST TWO DECADES, I have weaved in and out of lives across continents, and the material in this book would not have been possible without the help of so many. From my parents, whose impassioned encouragement to follow my heart and dreams sent me out into the world, to the editors, photographers, and journalists who have taken me under their wings along the way, I am forever grateful to all of you. A countless number of men, women, and children around the world have so bravely opened their most intimate moments to me and my camera: I can only hope that your generosity, resilience, and candor will help provide fortitude and inspiration to others the way they have to me.

I could never acknowledge the names of everyone, but here are a few:

Bebeto Matthews, for teaching me how to read light, the art of patience, the poetry of photography. Joan Rosen, for seeing my determination that day at the Associated Press in New York. And Reggie Lewis, for waking me up every morning in New York City in the wee hours with an assignment in the 1990s. An additional thank-you to Barbara Woike, Aaron Jackson, Cecilia Bohan, Beth Flynn, Jessie DeWitt, Jim Estrin, Patrick Witty, and Paul Moakley.

The *New York Times* is one of the greatest journalistic institutions in the world; it puts out some of the best reporting and photography of the highest standards, and I have been honored to enjoy a professional home at the paper as a freelance photographer over the past thirteen years. Bill Keller: You had the courage to call my parents three times to tell them you weren't sure I would make it out alive, and now, as a mother, I can't fathom how tough those calls were to make. I was able to cover the stories I believed needed to be covered in war zones only because of your steadfast commitment to those on assignment for you—whether staff or freelance. I thank assistant managing editor for photography Michele McNally for being a passionate and dedicated photo editor and surrogate mother when I am in the field—you never tire of fighting for those difficult images that are tough to look at and even tougher to find their way into print. David Furst: I will forever appreciate your enthusiasm and commitment to good photography and ensuring that it gets onto the pages of the paper.

David McCraw, William Schmidt, Bill Keller, Susan Chira, Michele McNally, C. J. Chivers, David Furst, and others who worked relentlessly to get me, Tyler Hicks, Anthony Shadid, and Stephen Farrell released in Libya: I will never know how to express my gratitude.

Kathy Ryan, for believing in my eye, and for ushering me into the world of magazine photography and feature stories. Year after year, you encourage me to be a better photographer, to think outside the box, to conceptualize stories in different ways. You are a dear friend and a brilliant, visionary editor.

Kira Pollack, Mary Ann Golon, Jamie Wellford, Alice Gabriner: I treasure our friendships and professional relationships. I have been so fortunate to work with each of you since the beginning of my career, to publish important stories together, to build enduring friendships, and to share in so much laughter.

To the team at *National Geographic*, who offer me the opportunity to work with one of the greatest photographic magazines in the world and who continue to push me to tell long-form stories with photographs: Sarah Leen, Ken Geiger, Elizabeth Krist, and Kurt Mulcher, and to David Griffin, who first brought me into the magazine. A special thank-you to those at the National Geographic Society, who include me in such prestigious company for lectures and exhibitions: Andrew Pudvah, Katherine Potter Thompson, Bob Attardi, Kathryn Keene, Jen Berman, and Melissa Courier.

The people and foundations who have generously given me grants to support long-term projects, and who have exhibited my work: the Nobel Peace Center, Open Society Foundation, Getty Images Grant for Editorial Photography, Ellen Stone Belic Institute for the Study of Women & Gender in the Arts & Media, Visa pour l'Image, Overseas Press Club, United Nations Population Fund, The Library of Congress, and Art Works Projects. A special thank-you to Aidan Sullivan, Leslie Thomas, Jean-François Leroy, Sonia Fry, Christian Delsol, and Jane Saks.

One of my life's great honors has been the MacArthur fellowship: I am so grateful to the MacArthur Foundation for recognizing my work and rewarding me with the gift of freedom to follow stories I believed in during the fellowship. This book would not have been possible without your support.

To James Salter: Thank you for your eloquence, and for allowing me to reproduce a passage from *A Sport and a Pastime*.

Donovan Robotham: I appreciate our longtime friendship and working relationship. You kept my finances organized, even when there weren't any finances to organize!

The two greatest travel agents in the world, who make themselves available at all hours for obscure destinations: Elif Oguz at Bedel Tourism in Turkey, and Ashu at Sadhana Travels in New Delhi. You have helped get me everywhere I needed to be, when I needed to be there.

The organizations that do important and fearless work around the world and support me in the field: Médecins Sans Frontières, United Nations Population Fund, the United Nations High Commissioner for Refugees, and Save the Children.

The men and women in uniform from the U.S. Army, Navy, Air Force, and Marines: You have helped keep me alive while navigating hostile terrain, and provided great company and a slice of home when we were anything but close to home. Lieutenant Colonel Bill Ostlund, Major Dan Kearney, and the men of 173rd Airborne, Battle Company: Thank you for your hospitality and your courage, and for trusting the integrity of our work. You enabled our uncensored view of life on the front lines in the Korengal Valley and our ability to witness and record the brutality of the war in Afghanistan. Sergeant Larry Rougle, may you rest in peace. Major Jason Brezler, USMC: Thank you for caring deeply about Afghanistan and its people, and for letting me accompany you on that ride in Nowzad.

A big thank-you to the kick-ass women in uniform who were working on the front lines of war well before women were allowed on the front lines: Captain Emily J. Naslund, USMC; CW3 Jesse Russell; Lieutenant, Nurse Corps, USN Amy Zaycek; Commander (CDR) Rupa J. Dainer; and Master Sergeant Julia Watson.

All the brave and dedicated interpreters and drivers: I could not have reported or photographed a single story without you. In Afghanistan: Jamila and Saida Emami, Arif Afzalzada, Abdul Waheed Wafa, and Zeba Alem. In India: Jaideep Deogharia, Abhra Bhattacharya, Pradnya Shidore, and Vinita Tatke. In Iraq: Sarah Aldhfiri and Sami al Hilali. The *New York Times* crew in Iraq, including Abu Malik, Warzar Jaff, Zainab Obeid, Qais Mizher, Husham Ahmed, Waleed al Hadithi, Khalid Hussein, Ayub Noori, and Yerevan Adham; in Lebanon, Hussein Alameh and Waled Kurdi; in Sierra Leone, Hawa Cawker; and in Sudan, Waleed Arafat Ali.

Sebnem Arsu, Lubna Hussein, Leena Saidi, Ranya Khadri, Sarah Aldhfiri—my female pillars in the region: I simply adore you. You make every assignment in Turkey, Saudi Arabia, Lebanon, Jordan, and Iraq fun, and feel like home.

To Tyler Hicks, my friend, a tireless, talented, principled photojournalist: Thank you for your companionship and encouragement during those dark days in Libya. Those small gestures pulled me through. Stephen Farrell and Anthony Shadid: Thank you for staying calm and centered, for finding humor in the bleakness, and for being strong and focused in Libya long enough to prevent our imaginations from running wild with the possibility of doom.

To all my colleagues who have provided the best company in the field and who have grown into family over the years: Ivan Watson, Samantha Appleton, Moises Saman, Tyler Hicks, João Silva, Michael Robinson Chavez, Michael Goldfarb, Spencer Platt, John Moore, Franco Pagetti, Michael Kamber, Quil Lawrence, Bryan Denton, Nichole Sobecki, Paula Bronstein, Kate Brooks, Stephanie Sinclair, Ruth Fremson, Anastasia Taylor-Lind, Carl Juste, Opheera McDoom, Newsha Tavakolian, and Thomas Erdbrink. And Monique Jaques—thank you for always being there to organize my life and images. A special thank-you to Bryan Denton, Michael Goldfarb, Kursat Bayhan, Chang W. Lee, Bruce Chapman, and Landon Nordeman for sharing your pictures with me for this book.

The photographers at VII Photo Agency: It has been a privilege working with and being affiliated with all of you. You helped me grow as both a photographer and an artist.

I am so honored to have worked with so many brilliant correspondents, some of whom have had the great misfortune of suffering repeated 5 a.m. wake-ups while I searched for the golden morning light: Lydia Polgreen, Dexter Filkins, Tim Weiner, Alissa Rubin, Rod Nordland, Carlotta Gall, Ann Barnard, Jim Yardley, Elisabeth Bumiller, Sabrina Tavernise, Anthony Shadid, Kirk Semple, Richard Oppel, Bobby Worth, Kareem Fahim, Joe Klein, Aryn Baker, Anthony Loyd, Sara Corbett, Andrea Elliott, Jon Lee Anderson, and Marion Lloyd.

Dexter Filkins and Ivan Watson: I will eternally be grateful for your company and care in Pakistan after the accident. You are the greatest stand-in brothers and loyal friends I could ever ask for.

Kathy Gannon: You have been so generous over the years with your knowledge, contacts, and hospitality in Afghanistan. Fourteen years ago you helped me secure my first visa to Afghanistan when it was under Taliban rule, and with that, you opened the door to so much of my professional career and personal journey.

To Elizabeth Rubin, for being both a courageous and fun partner in crime in some of the most oppressive places. You have been a role model for many years in your relentless pursuit of the story, and with your passion, humor, and wit.

Ruth and Larry Sherman: You helped change the course of my life with the invitation to India many years ago. Barbara Tuozzoli: Thank you for bringing me into the darkroom in those early days. Roxanne, Joseph, and Fabiana: You have provided so many years of laughter and love, and will always be extended family.

I am grateful for the enduring friendships of Tara Subkoff, Jordi Getman, Gabrielle Trebat, Desa Philadelphia, Riva Fischel, Katia Almeida, Sigalle Feig, Alyssa Norton, Cleo Murnane, Lisa Deroy, Vineta Plume, Angela Lekkas, and Candace Feit.

The Istanbul crew, my family in Constantinople: Madeleine Roberts, Ansel Mullins, Ivan Watson, Jason Sanchez, Behzad Yaghmaian, Suzy Hansen, Paxton Winters, and Karl Vick.

To Anthony Shadid, Marie Colvin, Tim Hetherington, Chris Hondros, Khalid Hassan, Marla Ruzicka, Raza Khan, Mohammed Shalgouf, and Anja Niedringhaus: May you rest in peace.

Amanda Urban: Your enthusiasm alone convinced me to write this book. You helped me take a vague idea and make it a reality. Thank you for believing in me, and for holding my hand every step of the way.

Ann Godoff: I'll forever be grateful you took on this project. You inspired me to write with your vision for the book, for recognizing my voice in those early days, and for helping me shape my unwieldy manuscript into a coherent text. Thank you to Claire Vaccaro for bringing your creative eye to the layout, to editorial assistants William Carnes and Sofia Ergas Groopman for your help and patience with all my last-minute changes, to Yamil Anglada and Sarah Hutson for ensuring that the book gets out there, to Gillian Brassil for your meticulous fact-checking, to Darren Haggar for the jacket design, and to Matt Boyd, Brittany Boughter, Kate Griggs, and Candy Gianetti for all your work on this project.

Suzy Hansen: I simply could not have done this without you. You are a true friend, a brilliant friend, a great editor, writer, and partner. You pushed me to write with your questions, you made me relive experiences I had tucked deep inside. You are compassionate, wise, and insightful, and I am eternally grateful and honored you embarked on this journey with me.

To Paul's wonderful family: Simon de Bendern, Kass Miskin, Ethel de Bendern, Emma and Neil Simmons—to name a few—thank you for opening your arms to me, and for being the coolest, most loving family next to my own. To the matriarchs, my two grandmothers, Nonnie and Nina, who—at one hundred one and ninety-seven years old, respectively—continue to inspire me every day with their strength, wisdom, and resilience. My sisters, Lauren, Lisa, and Lesley: You are my best friends and role models, and with me wherever I travel. Your husbands: Chris, Joe, and Jer—there aren't many men who could handle the four Addario women, and thank you for being such wonderful additions to our family. My mother, Camille Addario, who never ceases to amaze me with her love, infinite generosity, and ability to overcome hardship—I hope I can replicate a quarter of that one day. My father, Phillip Addario, and Bruce Chapman: You continue to teach me how to be true to myself, and how to build and maintain an enduring, loving relationship. My family gives me the strength to overcome any and all of life's adversities.

To Paul, my true love: I never imagined I could one day find the perfect partner, who fits effortlessly into the chaos of my life. You keep me grounded, and you encourage me to embrace my passion for this work without letting me sink into the world's darkness. You are selfless in your love and support, and I'm so grateful for every day we share together. You make me a better person.

And Lukas, my beautiful angel: You bring me an unfathomable amount of joy and love each day. You are the greatest gift of all, and I only hope we can provide you with the life and opportunities my parents provided me.

INDEX